T0229794

RETURN ON PROCESS (ROP)

Getting Real Performance Results from Process Improvement

RETURN ON PROCESS (ROP)

Getting Real Performance Results from Process Improvement

Michael West

CRC Press
Taylor & Francis Group
Boca Raton London New York

CRC Press is an imprint of the
Taylor & Francis Group, an **Informa** business

AN AUERBACH BOOK

Book cover design and art by Keith Westerberg and Kami St. John of Flourish Art & Design.

CRC Press
Taylor & Francis Group
6000 Broken Sound Parkway NW, Suite 300
Boca Raton, FL 33487-2742

© 2013 by Taylor & Francis Group, LLC
CRC Press is an imprint of Taylor & Francis Group, an Informa business

No claim to original U.S. Government works

Version Date: 20130102

International Standard Book Number: 978-1-4398-8639-7 (Hardback)

Library of Congress Cataloging-in-Publication Data

West, Michael.
    Return on process (ROP) : getting real performance results from process improvement / Michael West.
        pages cm
        Includes bibliographical references and index.
        ISBN 978-1-4398-8639-7 (alk. paper)
        1. Reengineering (Management) 2. Performance. I. Title.

HD58.87.W47 2013
658.4'063--dc23   2012036969

Visit the Taylor & Francis Web site at
http://www.taylorandfrancis.com

and the CRC Press Web site at
http://www.crcpress.com

This book is dedicated to all the people I have met who quietly, diligently, and patiently persevere and achieve real business performance results through their process improvement work. At all levels in many organizations, there are people who work tirelessly to implement process improvement that yields observable positive change; some of these individuals and organizations are mentioned in this book in the case studies and stories. I also dedicate this book to my wife and business partner, Jitka (the really smart one), for keeping me grounded when I get too ethereal, and for keeping me positive when I get cynical. She keeps me connected to myself and to the few things in life that are truly important.

Contents

The Author

Michael West is a lifelong practitioner and student of process improvement. He is the cofounder of Natural Systems Process Improvement (Natural SPI), a consultancy specializing in designing, developing, and deploying process systems that enable performance improvement gains. Mr. West's process insights and innovations have helped many organizations in various sectors of the economy achieve real process and performance improvement. His process consulting clients include ATK, Autodesk, AVL, BAE, BB&T, Crane Aerospace, DCS, Deloitte, Sandia National Labs, and the US Navy. Mr. West frequently presents and speaks at industry conferences and is the author of *Real Process Improvement Using the CMMI* (CRC Press, Boca Raton, Florida, 2004).

Introduction

What You'll Miss If You Don't Read This Introduction

Do most people read a book's forward, prologue, or introduction? I haven't always, but I do now because I found out what I was missing. This introduction will give you some very specific and useful instructions that will enable you to make the most use of the book. Unlike other tomes, you do not have to read this book cover to cover to learn something and benefit. In fact, you may benefit more quickly from the information if you skip around and just read the chapters or sections that contain information you need right now.

Those of you who are savvy in the ways of project management will get this analogy: When I began writing this book in earnest, I viewed it as a project. So the first thing I needed to do was to scope out the project. I needed to define—at least at a high level—what goals the book needed to accomplish or what problems it needed to solve. I also needed to figure out the approach the book would take to accomplish its goals. In other words, I needed a project charter.

This introduction is that project charter. It describes the book project's background, and how and why this work has come into existence. It tells you what you can expect to get out of reading the book, and it points you to the specific chapters or sections that give you information you need to apply in your particular environment. It also gives you an overview of some of the book's more critical design structures so that you can use the book more effectively and efficiently. It will be nice when people read this book, but it will be far more rewarding when they *use* it.

The Journey to Here

I won't repeat the introduction from my 2004 book, *Real Process Improvement Using the CMMI,* but let it suffice to say that I have been working in process improvement for a long time—perhaps too long. Along the way, as an employee in corporations and in my consulting practice, I have observed and learned many things about process improvement. When I sift and sort through all the work I've done over the years, all the conversations I've had, all the books I've read and presentations I've attended, I've been able to group sets of similar observations that appear to form patterns just by the sheer volume of the observations. One of the patterns that started to become visible to my mind's eye quite some time ago is this thought: People in organizations all over the world will proudly tell you that they work in "process improvement"; yet, when you start to dig a little into the topic and ask the right questions, you will see a lot of process but not so much improvement.

My earliest passion right out of college was journalism, which taught me when and how to ask the right questions. Throughout my professional life, when I have observed things that appeared to be inconsistent, contradictory, or just plain hinky, the first question I always ask is, "Why?" So began my quest with the "why" question when I started to notice that "process improvement" was bereft of "improvement."

I don't like unanswered questions; it's a situation that annoys me. So I started asking—informally at conferences, in meetings with clients, in blogs and social networks, etc.—what organizations were really getting from their (sometimes very large) investments in process improvement. What was the return on process (ROP)?

Then I learned something else: As much as I find unanswered questions about return on process unsettling, business leaders and execs are really perturbed by such questions when they don't have a good answer. Boy howdy…if you really want to kick the hornets' nest, attend a conference at which everyone wears suits and postures for the position of being the greatest sponsor of process improvement who ever lived. Then, ask the question, "What was the effect of your investment in process improvement on the "bottom line…on business performance?" Then, after receiving a gratuitous, superficial, and totally unsubstantiated response such as, "We improved government customer satisfaction," ask, "What were the measures that enabled you to correlate process improvement to that business performance result?" (Then watch yourself get marginalized and avoided for the remainder of the conference.[1]) Read more of this story and others in Chapter 6, "Process and Performance Myths."

Why This Book and Why Now?

Giant banks and investment firms, many with long histories of process improvement initiatives, show incredible financial "performance" for years and then, almost overnight, have a meltdown or outright collapse. Where were the good, proven management practices, the fact-based decisions, the risk management, and all the other "best practices" from their CMMI (Capability Maturity Model Integration) implementations when they were most needed? Where was process or process improvement as the enterprise sped down the river toward the falls?

One of the largest auto manufacturers in the world— one that has invested heavily in achieving CMMI maturity levels—reaches the state of bankruptcy and needs a multibillion dollar bailout from the taxpayers just to survive. What was the "performance" that made the automaker so large and dominant, and how did process improvement factor (or not) into the course of that ship crashing on financial shoals?

A major defense contractor known for airframe design and integration, which has a long history of achieving CMMI maturity levels and implementing "best practices," wins a very large Navy contract to build littoral combat ships (LCS). In 2007, the Navy issued a stop-work order and cancelled the contract with the contractor due to cost overruns; "cost performance" was good for the contractor, bad for the Department of Defense (DoD) and the taxpayer.[2] If CMMI maturity levels are supposed to be an indicator of "performance," how in this case was actual performance so egregiously different from what the DoD could have reasonably expected?

Hundreds of Lean, efficient, talented, and innovative companies could offer significant value to the government (DoD, federal, state, and municipal) and the US taxpayer, but they will never even be given a chance to bid on government "competitive" solicitations. Why? Because they're too small to afford the hundreds of thousands of dollars in overhead expenditure to achieve CMMI maturity levels or International Organization for Standardization (ISO) or AS9100 registrations and are thus disqualified from bidding. Historical contract and delivery performance are irrelevant because the government contracting office cannot "check the box" that the contractor is compliant with the government's favorite models and standards. Have the government's many years of funding of models and standards for "process improvement" really benefited the American people? If yes, where's the proof?

An American company contracts a company in China to develop software. The supplier selection is based primarily on the Chinese company having a CMMI maturity level 5 rating. Within months, the American company is not getting the performance—on-time deliverables or product quality—that it expected. The company wants to sue the Chinese supplier because the performance is not commensurate with what it expected from a CMMI maturity level 5 company.[3] Why couldn't the American company expect performance from a high-maturity organization?

One indicator of national economic performance—gross domestic product (GDP)—grows steeply and steadily until 2007 and then takes a nosedive into the abyss of a deep recession. Economic "performance" calculations using an income approach probably would not have been so rosy, but the calculations used for GDP were primarily an expenditure approach, which makes the economy look strong with millions of people spending money they don't have and incurring mounting debt they cannot repay. Does the calculation—the measure—of "performance" matter? I should think so.

Over the past 20 years, numerous companies have invested—sometimes heavily—in process improvement via use of the CMMI, Lean, Six Sigma, or standards compliance; however, they have gone out of business and no longer exist. Many more enterprises today continue investing in process improvement of some form or another, but cannot tell you how they are benefiting from that investment. The leaders of these enterprises can tell you or their shareholders the current return on investment, return on capital, or return on assets, but they cannot report the ROP.

There are already numerous books about process improvement, and there are also numerous books about business performance. But there is a dearth of literature on how process improvement yields business performance results.

Thus this book and thus now: I posit that the days of spending lots of money and time to achieve nothing more than a CMMI maturity level, an ISO registration, or some other kind of framed "certificate" to hang on the wall are over—gone and done. Leaders and practitioners are accountable for how and where they spend their energy and resources, especially in the new-normal economy. If process improvement is to remain a viable and valuable business pursuit, we need to start understanding and measuring how process improvement affects business performance and achieves real business results. We need to learn how to create, measure, and report the ROP.

Goals for This Book

This book is written to provide you with some very specific, practical knowledge about implementing process improvements in your organization that will yield observable or measurable business benefits. The actionable knowledge you should take away after reading this book includes:

■ What we mean by "real performance" and real performance "results"
■ What constitutes real "process improvement" and how to recognize activities that are not process improvement
■ How to implement improvements that yield performance results and how to measure both the improvement and the results
■ Understand why all meaningful improvements don't have to be grandiose, top-down, organization-wide sweeping changes and how real change is often small and local
■ How models and standards can guide improvement efforts when appropriately applied
■ How to build an organizational culture that supports and nurtures performance
■ Understanding of the myths that pervade process improvement, the dangers of myths, and how to separate fact from fiction

So for those of you who have a penchant for quality assurance, please use these for goals to build your checklist and then see if this book passes your audit!

What This Book Will Do for You

Specifically, what you will get from using the contents of this book is sound, proven, practical advice on how to improve your organization's software and systems development and delivery processes in ways that affect the business. You will be able to apply the concepts and put the practices into operation in your organization immediately. The results of your work will not be a surprise; you will be able to demonstrate real improvement and real performance measurably in your organization.

What This Book Will Not Do for You

There are a few things this book will not help you with. If you've already bought the book and want to do any of the following, Amazon.com will help you sell it as "used" so that you can recover some of your cost. This book will *not*

- Give you a "silver bullet," "magic wand," or any other supernatural answer to your organization's business problems
- Give you only one, right way to implement process improvement that will positively affect business performance results (It only gives you a range of things you can do that will work.)
- Give you or your organization a specific action plan for implementing improvements; every enterprise and every organization must tailor the concepts presented in this book to work effectively in the organization (But remember that every good plan at some point degenerates to real work. It is not enough to have a brilliant strategy and a foolproof plan; success in any endeavor always requires a good execution.)
- Perpetuate the myths and falsehoods about process improvement that have done more harm than good

■ Give you or your leadership the vision, the courage, or the conviction to change and improve things for the long-term benefit of the organization

Who Can Benefit from This Book (and Who Won't!)

People in almost every role or function in any systems or service delivery or support organization in the world can benefit from one or more of the fresh ideas and practices explained in this book. Executives and senior managers, program and project managers, engineers, designers, architects, testers, and especially people with process focus responsibility such as engineering process group (EPG) members or process improvement managers or leads will all benefit from various chapters and sections.

If you want to improve the way your organization works, if you want people to work more effectively and efficiently, and if you want your organization to stop wasting time, money, and energy on activities that don't add value to anything, then this book is for you.

If, however, you are content to continue spending time and resources on process improvement and making unsubstantiated claims about its effects or results, then this book is definitely not for you.

Assumptions about You, the Reader

In writing this book, I have made certain assumptions about readers' knowledge and experience. Out of necessity—and because I did not want to repeat entire bodies of knowledge—I assume that the reader has a basic awareness-level understanding of these topics:

■ Some of the more ubiquitous models, methods, standards, and works of knowledge currently in use for process improvement such as the CMMI, Lean, Six Sigma, Agile methods, ITIL (Information Technology Infrastructure Library), and standards such as ISO 9000, AS 9100, or TL 9000

■ Business performance measures and measurement concepts or techniques such as balanced score card (BSC)

I also assume that you are capable of invoking some level of critical thinking. As with every book about process improvement, you should not blindly accept the ideas and practices contained in these pages. Thinking critically and independently is hard work, requires you to have courage, and is essential to your success in using this book.

How to Use This Book

Whether you're reading this text online or in hard-copy form, you should feel free to consume the information any way you like. As much as possible, I've tried to make each chapter or section a self-contained unit of information so that you can get from it the essence of the knowledge it's trying to convey somewhat independently of other chapters and sections. However, the chapters are arranged such that each successive chapter builds on the ideas presented in the prior chapters, and the full benefit of this book can only be realized by reading it in its entirety.

This book is, by no means, the most comprehensive tome on model-based process improvement and there are other texts, many of them referenced herein, that you should also read.

Which Parts You Should Read

In any organization, there are a variety of functional roles that should be involved in process and performance improvement. These roles and their high-level responsibilities are defined in the following subsections. The purpose of providing this high-level role information at this point in the book is to enable you to identify your role in process and performance improvement as you read the rest of the book.

Most of the information contained in this book is of greatest value to process improvement leaders or managers. However, some sections are more relevant and useful to people in one of the following defined roles than to others. In such sections, you'll find the passage is preceded by a picture that indicates the role to which that passage is targeted. This makes it easy for anyone in the organization to scan the book and find the information he or she needs most. Of course, I would be very happy if everyone read everything, but I'd rather help you get what you need when you need it.

The Neo-executive/Leader (Exec)

Icons, for both male and female executives such as the one leading this section, indicate that the message in that section is written specifically for organizational executives and senior leaders. When you read the call-outs for this role throughout the book, you'll understand why I've coined the term "neo-executive." This is not the function or the person you have come to know as an executive; she is an upgrade. The neo-executive leader may have gotten to where he or she is by providing simple answers to his or her bosses, but he or she realizes that simple world no longer exists. Nowadays, she knows that the world, life, and work and all their challenges are extremely complex, and there are no simple easy answers. He knows he has sometimes to dive deep into the data and involve the perspectives of many others to solve problems.

She knows that, these days, one brain is no match for the "wicked problems" faced by modern organizations.

In effective process and performance improvement, the neo-executive/leader

- Develops and communicates the change or improvement vision and objectives
- Communicates (often) why the improvement and its target results are important to the enterprise and to individuals within the enterprise
- Establishes and maintains the improvement initiative as a priority among other enterprise changes, initiatives, and priorities
- Helps define the performance indicators or measures he or she wants reported, and the reporting methods, vehicles, and frequency
- Establishes motivation or incentive structures/vehicles for rewarding improvement protagonists
- Makes strategic decisions about the improvement efforts when asked to do so, and bases those decisions on facts and measures to the greatest extent practical
- Continuously learns

After many years of working in large and small organizations followed by many years of serving organizations as a consultant, I have observed a gap in the executive team in most organizations. There is a CEO at the top who leads the organization and inspires its workers. There is a CIO or CTO who leads the efforts to establish, maintain, and improve the organization's technology platforms and systems, and there is a human resources executive to ensure that the organization has the right people with the right skills needed to achieve the organization's objectives. So there is an executive for the workers and there is an executive for the technology, but where is the executive for the processes? Where is the chief process officer (CPO)?

If the process system is the third pillar—people and technology being the other two pillars—in the balanced and integrated system of systems that we call an "organization," why do organizations so often relegate that third pillar to a lower level manager? If we want accountability and responsibility for the integration of people, processes, and technology, why do organizations only have leaders for two of the three systems?

My argument is that if executives, or principals, or investors really want success in all dimensions of their business, they'll establish the CPO as an executive position—something to think about.

The Manager (Mgr)

There are sections written specifically for managers, and they are indicated by female and male manager figures such as the picture starting this paragraph. "Manager" in the context of this book is a term to mean anyone in the role to be executor of the vision and mission, who manages changes to people, processes, and technology to achieve the vision and mission. There are many management functions in product and service delivery organizations, including line managers, product managers, program and project managers, service and support managers, research and development managers, etc. The manager

- Internalizes the improvement vision and mission from the neo-executive/leader and translates it into tactical plans and action
- Helps define the indicators and measures by which process and performance improvement and the results will be measured

- Integrates process and performance improvement plans and activities with other responsibilities and deliverables and maintains an observable priority on the improvement work
- Works collaboratively with his or her peer managers to integrate process improvements with technology and infrastructure, and with worker skills
- Communicates improvements and changes to his or her reports
- Allocates resources to improvement activities based on priorities, progress, results to date, and anticipated return on process
- Makes decisions about the improvement efforts, when required, and bases those decisions on facts and measures to the greatest extent practical
- Continuously learns

The Engineer (Eng)

Female and male engineer icons indicate special sections for people who are practitioners of performance and process improvement. You don't necessarily need to have an engineering degree or "engineer" in your job title; I am using this role generically to apply to all the workers who are not managers or executives. You are the doers; the people who serve in roles that either make or break process and performance improvement initiatives. You are process leads/coaches, engineers, developers, project managers, service and support specialists, quality assurance specialists, operations managers, etc. As a practitioner, you

- Commit your knowledge, skills, expertise, and effort to organizational process and performance improvement, and support your peers in doing the same
- Challenge irrational decisions and actions in a professional, respectful way
- Challenge the status quo or "the way we've always done things" in a professional, respectful way
- Remind your boss when he or she sometimes loses sight of the priority of the improvement initiative
- Apply your expertise to help your bosses and those who report to you understand how to implement improvements in an efficient and effective way
- Manage your own time and effort based on the priorities and strategies of the process and performance improvement work
- Collect, analyze, use, and report the defined process and performance improvement measures
- Make sure the evaluation or measurement of your performance as an employee incorporates your contributions to the process and performance improvement work
- Don't condemn your boss when he or she temporarily caves under pressure from above or loses his or her mind; you help your boss recover
- Continuously learn

Special Sections

Throughout the book, you'll find special sections that are designed to help you understand, retain, and then use the information being imparted. Some special sections will also help you have some fun learning the information, while others will hopefully cause your mind just to wander off down its own path so that you can make new discoveries and explore breakthrough ideas of your own. These special sections are described next.

What Do You Think? What Do You Believe?

At the beginning of most chapters, there is a short quiz. I can't watch you use this book, so I don't know if you'll take the quiz or not, or if you'll answer the questions honestly or cheat. However, I think if you just try one, you'll want to take them all because you'll have fun.

The purpose of having a quiz at the beginning of each chapter is to help you find out how much you already know about the topic of discussion in that chapter. These quizzes also help you discover preconceptions, prejudices, and myths about the topic that you may have been carrying around and using as if they were truth or facts.

The answers to the quiz questions are not handed to you, but they're not hard to find either. Even a cursory reading of the chapter will render the correct answers.

Case Study, Story, or Example

First, a confession: When I began collecting information for this book, I sought case studies—demonstrated, documented incidences of correlation or causation between process improvement and business performance improvement. I posted requests for case studies on numerous public discussion threads on social and professional networks. I assumed—naively so, in retrospect—that organizational leaders who had proven themselves by driving business performance through process improvement would jump at the opportunity to promote their successes in a book (like I said, naïve).

I received very little response to my request, and those case studies that I have been able to substantiate are represented in this book. I did get a lot of excuses as to why I wasn't getting much response to the search for case studies, such as

■ "That information is proprietary because it is a 'competitive advantage.'" What a bunch of hooey! Nothing demonstrates market eminence like publicizing your success, and there is nothing "proprietary" or secret about process improvement or business performance results.

■ "Our measure of improvement was achieving a CMMI maturity level." Really? Are you certain? If you believe that, you need to keep reading. However, if you need to hold on to that myth, perhaps you should abandon this book.

One would think that the Software Engineering Institute (SEI), which published the CMMI and licensed all CMMI services (The CMMI Institute is now the steward of the CMMI product suite), would have collected and published a plethora of case studies supporting the relationship between CMMI use and business performance; one would be wrong to think that. As of the writing of this book, there were seven such "case studies" published on the SEI website.[4] In "Making Claims of Performance Results from Process Improvement" in Chapter 3, "Getting the Return on Process," I examine these "case studies" as a way of illustrating how you can apply critical thinking to discriminate between real process improvement and claims of process improvement.

So, my confession is that this book is not as replete with supporting cases studies and success stories as I would have liked. I can only conclude that they don't exist in the volume that one would reasonably expect. Perhaps you will implement some of the concepts described herein and build a case study for the next version of this book. I hope so.

Putting It into Practice

The concepts presented in Chapters 1 through 3 in this book progressively build on each other, from defining organizational performance to process performance to determining the ROP to improving process improvement itself. Thus, near the ends of Chapters 1 through 3, you'll find a section titled, "Putting It into Practice." These sections will transform the concepts and practices presented in the chapter into a coherent narrative that illustrates the process and performance improvements in a hypothetical (composite) but realistic organization.

Do's and Don'ts

There are some of you who love checklists, so checklists it is! At the end of most chapters, you'll find the most critical, pertinent lessons from that chapter summarized in a list of things you should do and things you should not do. Yes, of course you can skip the chapter and go straight to the check-list, but the checklist alone will not give you the full benefit of the concepts and actionable information found in the chapter. So be careful not to cheat yourself.

Reflect and Plan: What Did You Learn? What Will You Do?

At the beginnings of most chapters, there is a short quiz (see "What Do You Think? What Do You Believe?") to help you test your own understanding and ideology about the infor-mation you will acquire in that chapter. Then, at the ends of these chapters, a section provides you with a list of questions that guide you through the process of applying the newly acquired information in your organization.

You can even use the questions in these sections to build a checklist, which you can then use to verify that you and your organization are using the information you've learned about real process and performance improvement.

What Do You Want to Do Now?

OK, now if you've been patient enough to read through this introduction, you're going to leap ahead of those who skip it and jump right into the chapters because Table I.1 serves as

Table I.1   What Do You Want to Do Right Now?

I Want To...	Then Read...
Understand what real business performance is, and how to achieve it	Chapter 1, "Real Performance Improvement"
Know how to figure out what to improve in my organization, and how and where to make those improvements	In Chapter 1, read "Learn What to Improve and Why"
Be able to know what "best practices" really are, and where they fit into improvement initiatives	In Chapter 1, read "The Place for Best Practices in Performance Improvement"
Understand what real process improvement is, and how to achieve it	Chapter 2, "Real Process Improvement"
Define performance objectives and measures	In Chapter 1, read "Establishing Performance Objectives" and "Establishing Performance Measures"
Learn how to align process improvement work with the organization's strategy and business performance objectives	In Chapter 2, read "Establishing Process Performance Objectives"
Understand the difference between defined process and the performed process	In Chapter 2, read "Understanding Defined Process versus Performed Process"
Improve process performance	In Chapter 2, read "Improving the Performed Process"
Improve the defined process	In Chapter 2, read "Improving the Defined Process"
Make sure people in the organization perform the defined processes	In Chapter 2, read "Synchronizing the Defined and Performed Processes"

Table I.1 (*Continued*) What Do You Want to Do Right Now?

I Want To...	*Then Read...*
Know how to measure the effects or results of process improvement on performance	Chapter 3, "Getting the Return on Process (ROP)"
Learn how to measure improvements in process performance	In Chapter 3, read "Measuring the Performed Process Changes"
Measure improvements in the defined process	In Chapter 3, read "Measuring the Defined Process Changes"
Understand the relationship between CMMI maturity levels and business performance	In Chapter 2, read "The CMMI and Process Improvement" and in Chapter 3, read "Return on CMMI Use"
Find out all the ways to improve process and performance other than using models, standards, best practices	Chapter 4, "Small Changes, Big Performance Improvement"
Learn ways for me and others in my organization who are responsible for process improvement to improve the way we work	Chapter 5, "Improving Process Improvement"
Find out if things I currently believe about process improvement are not correct or true	Chapter 6, "Process and Performance Myths"
Better understand my role and responsibilities in process and performance improvement	Scan the book for the icon—executive (Exec), manager (Mgr), or practitioner (Eng)—that best aligns with your role in process improvement, and read those sections. (Also see "Which Parts You Should Read" in this introduction.)

a road map for getting you directly to the information you want or need right now.

Scan the left-most column of this table for topics that represent something you want to do or know. Then, follow that row across to the center column, which tells you what you need to learn and where in the book you need to look to find that information.

Endnotes

1. From personal notes and observations taken at the 10th Annual National Defense Industrial Association CMMI Technology and User Group conference held in Denver, Colorado. The presentation and session were titled, "Benefits of CMMI" and the presentation was by Hal Wilson from Northrop Grumman on Tuesday, November 16, 2010. After patiently listening to the presentation and reviewing the slides, I asked some questions that poked a little at the veracity of the conclusions made in the material. I was given courteous but brief responses that did not answer my questions. My follow-up questions were dismissed "in the interest of time" and to answer sycophantic questions from other members of the audience. Mr. Wilson, for whom I have great respect, appeared uncharacteristically squirmy, kind of the way Colin Powell appeared when presenting the argument for weapons of mass destruction to the United Nations.
2. See http://www.homelandsecuritynewswire.com/navy-cancels-lockheeds-lcs-3-contract.
3. This happened. In 2002, when I was living in Southern California, a Los Angeles company contacted me and asked if I would provide expert testimony in its litigation against their foreign supplier. I provided the plaintiff with initial input on some of the performance dimensions they should have reasonably expected from a CMMI maturity level 5 company. I don't know whether the case ever went to court—probably not since it is almost impossible for an American company to win a claim against foreign entities.
4. As of March 10, 2012, the CMMI case studies offered by the SEI could be found at http://www.sei.cmu.edu/cmmi/why/success/.

Chapter 1

Real Performance Improvement

Between theory and practice lies performance.

—Me

What Do You Think? What Do You Believe?

Take a minute and answer the questions in the quiz in Figure 1.1. Then, once you've finished reading this chapter, review the guide at the end ("Reflect and Plan: What Did You Learn? What Will You Do?") to apply the information in this chapter to your own process and performance improvement efforts.

What Is Real Performance?

According to Wiktionary, one definition for "performance" is the act of performing; carrying into execution or action; execution; achievement; accomplishment; representation by action; as, the performance of an undertaking of a duty.

1. Organizational performance means:
   a. The organization makes more money.
   b. The organization sells more products.
   c. The organization achieves a CMMI (Capability Maturity Model Integration) maturity level.
   d. People in the organization have been through HPO (high performance organization) training.
   e. None of the above.
   f. All of the above.
2. Process improvement is always the best way to improve performance.
   a. True
   b. False
3. Organizational performance can't be measured.
   a. True
   b. False
4. Organizational performance is the responsibility of executives and senior leaders.
   a. True
   b. False
5. When establishing business performance objectives, it is important to
   a. Involve everyone.
   b. Leave it to senior leadership.
   c. Set a target date for implementing Six Sigma.
   d. Understand the business your organization is in.
   e. Set unrealistic goals to challenge workers.
   f. Set easy goals to keep shareholders' expectations reasonable.
6. Usually, a change to processes will also involve changes to ____ and ____.
7. Measurements should tell you ____.

Figure 1.1   What do you think and what do you believe about real performance improvement?

However, in terms of organizational performance in organizations, this definition is too loaded with undefined[1] qualifiers such as "achievement" or "accomplishment."

The Wiktionary definition for "performance" that is most applicable to the central theme of this book, and that is most useful in defining organizational performance, is the definition given for "performance" in the context of computer science: *the amount of useful work accomplished by a computer system compared to the time and resources used. "Better performance" means more work accomplished in shorter time and/or using less resources.* It's an appropriate analogy to compare a computer system with an organization; both are systems. The computer system is really a system of systems: hardware systems, firmware systems, software systems (codified human thought), internal interfaces, and interfaces to other systems. The modern organization is also a system of systems: people (social) systems, technology systems, and process systems, with internal interfaces between people, technology, and processes, and interfaces to other organizations. Figure 1.2 shows a modern organization as a system of these three subsystems.

Using this analogy as our mental model, it's not a big leap to form the premise that better performance in an organization means more work accomplished in shorter time and/or using less resources. ("Work," by most definitions, yields results. That's why I don't like to use the word "activity," which may not yield results.)

If we accept this premise as logical and sound, there are many ways for an organization to improve its performance in most business vectors, but all of those paths to improvement can be related to one of three general categories: (1) improve the workers, (2) improve process, or (3) improve technology. Table 1.1 identifies how these three types of changes can, in general, improve organizational performance, and how each

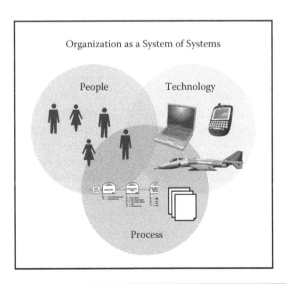

Figure 1.2 An organization as a system of systems.

Table 1.1 Three Ways to Improve Performance

Improvement Dimension	Possible Performance Improvement	Relationship to Other Ways to Improve
Improve people	Improving the knowledge, skills, and expertise of workers can enable them to perform tasks more effectively and efficiently. Systemic capture, analysis, and dissemination of organizational learning and knowledge assets lowers knowledge and skill acquisition and replacement costs.	Process: Defined processes should accommodate user spectrum of novice performers and expert performers. Technology: Technology may need to be improved to not "dumb down" task performance for workers.
Improve technology	Introducing new technology or improving existing technology can automate information transactions and task performance, which can yield faster delivery of higher quality products and services.	People: Ironically, the reason many technology insertions/changes not only do not yield performance improvement but also often diminish performance is because workers are not trained to use the technology effectively and efficiently. Improvement in technology almost always requires changes to worker knowledge and skills. Process: Defined and performed processes need to accommodate the use of the new or changed technology.

Table 1.1 (*Continued*)   Three Ways to Improve Performance

Improvement Dimension	Possible Performance Improvement	Relationship to Other Ways to Improve
Improve process	An organization can improve performed processes, defined processes, or both. (See Chapter 2.) Improving process can enable workers to perform tasks more effectively and efficiently to deliver higher quality products and services in shorter time frames and with less effort.	People: When processes are defined or reengineered, workers need to be educated in the use of the new or changed processes in order to perform them effectively. Technology: Process performance (per the defined processes) often incorporates the use of technology. Thus, improvements to processes often require concomitant changes to tools and systems that support process performance.

of those three types of performance improvement initiatives affect or relate to the other two.

The obvious focus of this book is the third form of improvement in Table 1.1: process improvement. Much has already been written about improving performance through technology, and much of that literature revolves around large, enterprise-level technology changes such as the implementation of project portfolio management, enterprise resource planning (ERP) systems, customer relationship management (CRM) systems, supply chain management systems, work collaboration systems, etc. Sometimes, the return on investment in technology (ROT) in terms of performance improvement is measured, but often it is not simply because such changes are viewed as the cost of remaining viable (staying in business) by remaining compatible with customers, and at least keeping pace with the competition.

Case Study: Fast, Simple Technology Improvement

Not all technology changes to achieve performance improvement need to be large scale, and often personal, local changes
can yield a dramatic performance result. One of my favorite
stories in this category is that of my hair stylist. Gina used
to work as a stylist and shop manager for one of the nation's
largest retail hair care companies. But that company's technology infrastructure had been evolved to such a scale that it
could realistically have only two focuses:

- The customer-facing focus was toward the entire
  customer base, but not really toward enabling an
  individual customer or potential customer to conduct
  personal interaction with the company. For example,
  a customer can book a hair appointment online, but
  only at select stores. (I could not book online in Park
  City, Utah.) Once booked, the customer would have
  to record the appointment in his or her own calendar
  (PDA, appointment book, etc.) because the company's
  system wouldn't send reminders. Additionally, although
  the large company's system did allow a stylist to
  describe a customer's preferences (profile) in a customer
  card, there was no particular incentive provided to
  the stylists to do so. The chain sought customer loyalty to the chain, but not to particular stylists. Yet from
  a customer perspective, most loyalty in the personal
  services sector is built with an individual, not with a
  corporation. So every single visit—even to the same
  stylist—required the customer to retell his or her hair
  preferences, problems (e.g., my cowlicks), and history.
  If you think of a haircut as the application of a product
  in a customer environment (my head), the customer had
  to describe his or her "configuration" to the stylist. It's
  time consuming, wasteful, and a little annoying to both
  the customer and the stylist.

■ The internal-facing focus of the company's technology
was to enable store transactions (customer pricing and
payment for services and products) and, presumably,
internal accounting. From what I could tell, the internal
systems didn't provide real-time inventory management,
so the stylists were really not able to provide current
product advice to customers. Inventory in the system was
only updated when the stores conducted mandatory—
and manual—inventory audits, and then the system was
updated weeks later, making the inventory obsolete the
minute it was updated. And the internal systems did not
enable the employees to attract new customers or better serve existing customers. For example, there was no
way for a local store to establish and maintain a customer database, or to communicate directly with the
customer. (I had to give my local store my phone number
every visit.)

At some point, Gina realized that the large company was
more of a barrier to her serving her customers than it was an
enabler, and she decided to go solo. She rented a space in a
smaller salon nearby. She also rented the postmodern retail
space—website space on Vagaro—that allows her customers
to define profiles and make appointments. She bought an
Apple iPad with a credit card reading device and subscribed to
Square for online, real-time customer payment transactions and
receipt e-mailing. So now she has an online customer database,
which she synchs with her contacts in her iPhone and iPad,
and can contact customers anytime from anywhere. When she
worked at the giant hair salon company, her personal attention
to the customer in the chair was frequently interrupted to
answer the store's phone because customers couldn't communicate with the store any other way. This caused appointment
overruns and diminished the salon experience for both the
customer in the chair and for Gina. Now, with Gina's encour-
agement, most of her customers book or change appointments

online and communicate with her via text or email, which she can respond to at a time of her choice, giving her the ability to focus on the customer in the chair.

What were the business performance results from these relatively minor technology changes? She previously could barely service five customers per day, but has since easily increased that to seven per day, increasing her service capacity by 40 percent without increasing her time spent at the salon. She previously had to reserve 2 hours for a basic cut and color service, which she now has reduced to 90 minutes simply as a result of the reduced service interruptions. This gave her 2 hours back, which she can fill with three haircuts or one cut/color and a haircut. Additionally, because her customers are now getting more personalized and focused attention while they're in the chair, they are getting a really good experience, so they refer their friends to Gina and her client base continues to grow.

Remember, one of our definitions for performance improvement was doing more work with the same resources, which is exactly what Gina's technology changes have accomplished. What I find attractive about the small, personal, and local improvement stories such as Gina's is that her improvement was super-fast (all changes implemented within a week) and very low cost. She didn't have to socialize the change with dozens of stakeholders, she didn't have to facilitate dozens of meetings in which people could grope for hundreds of politically correct ways to say, "I'm afraid of this change so therefore I don't want it," and she didn't have to submit her change to review boards or executive committees for approval. She was the neo-executive leader with the vision to change, she was the manager who drove the change, and she was the practitioner who now implements and institutionalizes the change. She was both the change agent and the change itself.

As you review and think about Table 1.1, the idea of an organization as a system of systems becomes more obvious, and you might even consider the idea that all improvement initiatives should be treated as if they are integral to an improvement "system" or strategy. In an integrated system, in which each subsystem is dependent upon the other subsystems to work properly, it is probable that if you introduce change to one part of the system, there will be derivative or collateral change to other parts of the system, whether or not you think about or plan the collateral changes, and whether or not you observe or measure them when they take effect.

As the neo-executive leader, it is your job to establish the strategies that will contribute to the long-term growth and viability of your enterprise. It is also your responsibility to collaborate with other leaders to determine the changes that must be made to take the organization into a desirable future. If you delegate such decisions and strategic work, you are abdicating your responsibilities, and someone other than you should be serving in your role. In this capacity, you must always be vigilant and aware that your reports, vendors, and consultants will try to sell you on a "solution" that aligns with their limited views of your business. The tool vendor will try to convince you that his company's tool is the ultimate solution. Your process group will try to convince you that process improvement or the CMMI (capability maturity model integration) or ISO/AS/TL compliance is the answer. The Six Sigma folks will say that Lean and Six Sigma are just the right hammer for your nail. They are all partially right and partially wrong…and they are not malicious…they just love what they know

(as we all do) and are pushing the ideas that serve
their interests and careers. Not only is it your job
to be the decider, but it is also your job to be the
includer. You need to listen patiently to everyone,
question their assumptions (and yours), and remind
yourself over and over that the "silver bullet"
exists only as a cliché that smart people mock.
As you form strategies for change and improvement, you need always to ask yourself: What
might be the unintended consequences or derivative changes? How will a change in personnel—
whether it be acquiring new skills or sending
the knowledge work to another country—impact
our technological infrastructure and processes?
Think systemically, balance your thoughts, question your assumptions and "truths," and make sure
your conclusions are supported by both facts and
emotional intelligence.

Sometimes, the collateral changes can be positive—
secondary, unanticipated improvements—but often they can
also be negative, offsetting the positive effects on performance
yielded by the intended change. When we don't think about
and plan improvements or changes systemically, taking into
consideration the possible collateral or derivative changes, we
are doing what Dr. Lloyd S. Nelson illustrated in his "funnel"
experiment (made popular by Dr. W. Edwards Deming)...
tampering![2]

In my 2004 book, *Real Process Improvement Using the
CMMI*, I spent a portion of a chapter (and later an article
in *Crosstalk*) focusing on applying systems thinking to process improvement. In explaining how to take a systems view
of process improvement, I extrapolated and applied concepts from Peter Senge's system archetypes. In particular,
I addressed the "fixes that backfire" syndrome that I have
frequently observed in process improvement efforts.

Fixes that backfire can be one of the consequences—collateral changes—that result from tampering, but here I want to make more general observations about the consequences of not viewing organizational performance improvement in a systemic way.

Case Study in Not Thinking Systemically

I once consulted with a company operating in the subtier telecom market space. This organization unfortunately serves as a poster child for what can go wrong when leadership fails truly to understand and deal with its problems systemically.

When Company X approached me for consulting services, they were still operating on venture capital, and they were growing rapidly primarily through acquisitions. Much of the success of their products in the market was due to their very rapid time-to-market with new product features and functionality. However, they were persistently plagued with two problems (or problem symptoms as it turns out): (1) Product releases were frequently over schedule and over budget, and (2) the defect density in released products was growing... exploding actually!

What's ironic from a systems thinking perspective is that each of these problems fed the other: (1) Attempts to work faster and recover schedule (including uncompensated work on weekends and nights) resulted in more defect-ridden product, and (2) a rapidly growing defect population created a higher demand for testing and field support resources, which sucked away resources needed for product development, which pushed development schedules even further to the right beyond plans.

When Company X hired my company to provide CMMI-based process improvement consulting, the thought was that implementing some of the CMMI practices or process areas could address the two major problems. I had my doubts and expressed them to management, but then (surreptitiously) dutifully looked for ways to provide real help. I conducted a CMMI-based appraisal to identify systemic problems and probable causes and developed and delivered a very detailed improvement recommendation report to address those problem causes. I was then informed by my contact that the company no longer needed my services...they were just going to achieve a TL 9000 certification. They would do this by writing some new procedures that mimic or satisfy the TL 9000 standards; that would solve everything.

Not so much, but it certainly will solve the problem of finding that last nail needed for the coffin!

In many more words, here's what I suggested they do: For the chronic problem of releases being over schedule and budget, I suggested they analyze the work that really gets done in a release so that they could define the work that gets performed but does not get estimated or planned (counted, measured) in project or release plans. By doing so, they would have more accurate bases for estimating effort, cost, and schedule for the releases. I suggested that the outcome of this discovery and definition of all the work that is performed in a release be used to build a comprehensive work breakdown structure (WBS) template that would subsequently serve as the starting point for release estimating and planning. There were a few brave souls in the organization who supported the idea, including—ironically—statements from the marketing people who said they could more easily sell customers on a longer release cycle than sell them on products of questionable quality.

Alas, "hope as a strategy" and the worship of heroics trumped realistic improvement as they painfully and often do. There were people in the organization with great influence over others who saw reality-based planning as a threat to the hero worshipping of working harder, even at the cost to family, health, and happiness. Yet others put blind faith in compliance with a standard—TL 9000 (the ISO standard for telecommunications)—as the answer to the problems.

Learn What to Improve and Why

> If I had an hour to save the world, I would spend
> 59 minutes defining the problem...and one minute
> finding solutions.
>
> **—Albert Einstein**

Key to the success of any performance improvement initiative is understanding what to improve and why; yet it's both astonishing and disappointing how many improvement initiatives are launched without anyone asking and answering these two most primal questions. Asking these two questions—what to improve and why—is the foundational premise to achieving (and knowing when you've achieved) return on process (ROP). If they are not asked and at least provisionally answered, your organization is very likely to embark on improvement initiatives that result in one of three ROPs: (1) unknown, (2) zero, or (3) negative.

It's really this simple: If you don't know what to improve, you may focus your resources on changes that don't need to be made. (See "Do Less to Do More" in Chapter 4, "Small Changes, Big Performance Improvement.") If you don't know why you're improving something, you cannot understand how much of your resources to apply to the improvement effort, and thus you cannot calculate an expected ROP. Let's explore these two questions more thoroughly.

Determine What to Improve

There are essentially two ways to determine what to improve in an organization:

1. The improvement is perceived to address or resolve a current business problem or mitigate a business risk (future problem if realized).

2. The improvement is perceived to change the organization's performance in some way to achieve business strategies or objectives.

These two sources of improvement impetus are universal in that their understanding is valuable to leaders regardless of the sector economy in which the business operates, or whether the organization is for profit or nonprofit.

If your focus is the same as the topic of this book—process improvement—then alignment of the improvement or innovation with the strategy is tantamount. In the words of Thomas Davenport: "In fact, process innovation is impossible—or at least only accidental—unless the lens of process analysis is focused on a particularly strategic part of the business, with the particular strategic objectives in mind."[3]

Table 1.2 defines a short list of problems and risks affecting many modern and postmodern organizations, and identifies initial, speculative areas to improve.

In terms of aligning what to improve with organizational strategies or objectives, remember that an objective or goal is often just a positive thinker's way of reorienting a risk or problem. You can invert any of the problems in the first column in Table 1.2 and make it a strategy or performance objective. For example, the problem "diminishing revenue" restated as a performance objective is "maximize shareholder value" or "achieve market dominance." Some people are motivated by solving problems, while other people are motivated by working toward a goal. If my strategy is "to maximize shareholder value," then I am unconsciously or consciously recognizing the current problem that my shareholders are not getting as much value as I think they should (the second problem/risk in Table 1.2).

As you can see in Table 1.2, there is no attempt at this stage to conduct a robust root cause analysis (RCA); rather, there is only an attempt to identify the areas of business performance that can affect a business performance problem

Table 1.2 Typical Business Problems and Risks as Candidates for Improvement

Current Problem or Risk	Candidate Improvement Areas
Diminishing revenue	Competitiveness
	Market/customer base
	Marketing, branding, or eminence
	Value proposition
	Product market life
	Innovation
Diminishing profit or shareholder value	Revenue
	Market space/customer base
	Operating or product realization efficiency
	Capability for innovation
Diminishing capacity	Leadership
	Workforce skills, morale, or incentives
	Cost of labor
	Cost of capital
	Operating efficiency or efficacy
	Throughput
	Technology
	Process efficiency or efficacy
	Regulatory compliance
Diminishing support	Policy/mission
	Market space or positioning
	Efficacy
	Value proposition

or risk. The purpose of defining such a table for your business is simply to build a reasonably comprehensive list of the areas in which improvement would probably have a positive effect on the business problem or risk, and to achieve consensus support for that list from relevant stakeholders.

Change occurs every day all around us...our customers change, politics change, regulatory and compliance requirements change, our workforce changes, technologies change, and business processes change. The only three rational responses to constant change that an organization can make are

1. Anticipate the change and initiate proactive or preemptive changes
2. Respond or react (after the fact) to changes
3. Ignore external change and its effects, do nothing, and accept the consequences

The leader who knows and accepts this axiom of constant change can do one of two things:

1. Anticipate the change and proactively or preemptively make changes to his or her organization and its performance
2. Respond or react to external changes by making changes to his or her organization and its performance

There are sound philosophical and logical arguments for both the proactive/preemptive approach and the reactive/responsive approach. Early adopters of change who succumb to the seduction of "life by bumper sticker" are prone to say, "Change or die," and will illustrate the slogan with dioramas of wooly mammoths or dinosaurs. But the more cautionary late adopters of change will point out that vicarious learning is a much less expensive form of learning, and we can learn from others (the early adopters) what wins and what fails in the face of a change without putting too much of our own skin in the game. That which doesn't kill you makes you stronger... but it might maim you for life.

The key to moving forward in an intelligent manner is to do the right amount of analysis. (See "The Right Amount of Analysis" in Chapter 4.)

Determine Why to Improve Something…and How Much to Improve

Once you and your stakeholders have determined what to improve, the next step is to determine why. Knowing why to improve something is an early step in setting up your ROP calculation, because the answer to "why" will lead you to understanding how much something needs to be improved which, in turn, will lead you to understand how much to invest in the improvement. Knowing why to improve something will also validate your choice of what to improve because it will tell you if you've chosen to address a real problem or merely the symptom of a problem.

Getting an answer to why something should be improved can be as complex or as simple as you make it. For example, let's say you have used problem/risk areas (see Table 1.2) to narrow down the list of areas to improve. You could then establish teams to conduct RCA on each area and report the results as a way of validating what to improve and why. But this can often take weeks or months, cost a lot of resources, and the results may be no more empirical than simpler, faster, and cheaper methods.

Too often, once people determine what to improve and why, they just set off executing the improvement; they don't take the time to determine how much improvement should be made. Knowing how much improvement to make is critically important to understanding the ROP once the improvement is implemented and institutionalized, because how much (money, resources, time) you put into the improvement constitutes the investment (the "P" in process improvement) part of the ROP calculation. One thing that contributes to the organization's failure to think about how much improvement is really needed is a sense of urgency just to get moving with the process improvement so that the problem or issue can be addressed. This impulse to take improvement action quickly can easily lead to an excessive investment in the improvement, thus diminishing the return, the ROP.

Case Study in Understanding What to Improve and Why

Here's an extrapolation of a situation that highlights the importance of spending some time to figure out the what, why, and how much of a process improvement before "just doing it." A defense contractor is getting negative feedback from its government customer on the quality of delivered documents (plans, status reports, analyses, etc.). The government customer says that there are too many defects in the delivered documents. The contractor doesn't analyze (or even ask) what the customer means by "defects" and reacts to improve the situation by implementing a peer review process on all documents. The peer review process calls for all versions of all documents to be peer reviewed by cross-functional teams, to include system engineers, developers, project managers, marketing, integrators, and testers. The reviewers are diligent in trapping and removing the "defects" based on their trained view of work products. The system engineers find defects related to requirements, the developers find errors in software specifications, and marketing personnel find misrepresentations of product functionality but, overall, the peer reviews do not result in many defects being removed from the work products. Given the high average cost of people in these roles, the organization spends a fortune on peer reviews.

Still, the customer complains about the quality of delivered documents. Finally, the contractor asks the customer what it means by "defect," and the customer explains that the documents have too many typos, misspelled words, and grammar and punctuation problems.

From that point forward, the contractor implements another improvement that requires all documents to be reviewed and edited by a technical writer before being delivered to the customer. The fully burdened rate for the single tech writer is a fraction of the cost of peer reviews involving people from all the departments.

Think about this scenario and the ratios of the organization's investment in two different process improvement efforts, and their respective ROPs. Even when you calculate the cost of the analysis, providing the situation isn't overanalyzed, it's easy to see how knowing what to improve, why to improve it, and by how much can significantly affect the ROP.

The Place for "Best Practices" in Performance Improvement

For the sake of exploration, let's assume that you haven't yet read the section "The CMMI and Process Improvement" in Chapter 2, "Real Process Improvement," and that you accept bodies of work such as the CMMI, ITIL (Information Technology Infrastructure Library), and the PMBOK (Project Management Body of Knowledge) as collections of best practices. If this is your thinking, then you should also remember and apply one of the primal rules of business: There is a right place, a right time, and an appropriate application for all knowledge, tools, and skills.

In the book *Best Practices Are Stupid,* author and consultant Stephen Shapiro gives us a simple and insightful way to think about our business called the innovation targeting matrix (ITM). My extrapolation of Mr. Shapiro's ITM is shown in Table 1.3. The ITM helps leaders focus on where to emphasize innovation in the organization, and essentially explains why it is only in an organization's differentiators—those capabilities that set you apart from your competition—that you should innovate. Shapiro further makes the case that it is only in the core and support capabilities where best practices are useful. A logical take-away from this line of thought is that the adoption of best practices is *not* innovating.

Table 1.3 The ITM and Place for Best Practices

Capability Segment	Improvement Focus	The Place for Best Practices
Differentiation: Capabilities that set your organization apart from all others in your market space	Innovate	
Core: Capabilities critical to your business but that are not your source of competitive advantage; includes areas of work such as product development, service delivery, customer support, sales/marketing, and business development	Automate Simplify Outsource	Improve technology Improve process Improve people (also reference Table 1.1)
Support: Capabilities necessary for running your business but that are not your core business; this includes areas such as IT, HR, finance, legal, security, facilities, and operations	Eliminate Minimize Outsource	Improve process Improve process Improve people (also reference Table 1.1)

Establishing Performance Objectives

In my consulting work, I sometimes have the opportunity to work directly with executives and senior leaders. I am usually invited to have these conversations under the auspices of helping them figure out how to achieve a CMMI maturity level or to give them some assurance that they're going to pass their next ISO 9001 or AS9100 audit. Often, I don't tell them anything they don't already know, but it helps them feel better about their decisions when they receive affirmation from "the outside expert."

In these conversations, one of the first questions I ask is along the lines of, "What are the organization's business performance objectives?" Ironically, the one question an executive or senior leader should be able to respond to with confidence is the one question that seems to catch him or her off guard. It's not nice to make adult professionals squirm too long—especially when they have power over your consulting revenue—so I then make it a little easier for them. I follow up with the hard question deconstructed:

■ What is your role in executing the organization's strategy?
■ What I mean is: In which areas of the business do you think your organization can do a better job?
■ Which types of work in your organization do your employees or your customers complain about?
■ Where do you feel an improvement would yield the most benefit?
■ What about your work or the work performed by your reports is rewarded—with promotions, raises, bonuses, etc.—the most?

Notice that these questions are open ended and do not presume a specific response or range of responses. Also notice that these questions don't evoke an answer such as, "We need to achieve CMMI level 3." For those of you who are working in the world of the CMMI for development (CMMI-DEV), the responses to these questions are the information you need for Specific Practice 1.1 in the Measurement and Analysis Process Area.

Establishing performance objectives is easy; establishing meaningful performance objectives that can be understood and achieved and have the achievement be observed or measured is more difficult. I've participated in numerous objective-setting workshops, facilitated by the requisite Six Sigma black belt, in which a bunch of people sat around and brainstormed objectives or goals without any rules, guidelines, or criteria. I guess the prevailing theory is that the best results will come from unstructured "creative" thinking, but I've observed the opposite. What I have observed is that the results of most such brainstorming sessions make the participants feel good about themselves when they leave the room, but then those results—a mixed bag of sentiment, most of which can't serve as performance objectives—sit idle and ignored, forgotten as soon as the next entertaining workshop comes around.[4]

Mr. or Ms. Executive, it is your job to define your organization's performance objectives; accept it. You can no more delegate this responsibility than you can delegate the direction of your enterprise or delegate your own career. People who report to you will come to you and ask you to participate in goal-setting or performance objective workshops. Do not disappoint them; few things are more important than your involvement in this work.

Framing the Challenge

Some of the best advice I've received in defining what to improve comes from Stephen Shapiro in his book *Best Practices are Stupid.*[5] In his guidance on framing challenges, Shapiro advises to adhere to the "Goldilocks principle," which means to frame the challenge not too big or not too small, but just right.

Shapiro writes that the challenge or business problem has to be framed or scoped "just right" if it is to have any chance of being addressed. If you define a fluffy, abstract problem space (too big), you'll get a fluffy, abstract "solution" that is not practical or actionable and will not yield real improvement.

My favorite "too big" challenges in performance and process improvement are

- "We need to improve our processes."
- "We need to achieve market dominance."
- "We need to be leading edge."
- "We are innovators."

Such statements, although intended to be visionary, are so abstract as to be almost meaningless, and they make the leader issuing such statements sound like he's reading bumper stickers, making him more of a chief slogan officer than a real leader.

If you define the problem too specifically (too small), you'll get a "solution" that is overly specific and too focused and probably won't even address the real problem. Examples of my favorite "too small" challenges in performance and process improvement are

- "Rewrite our procedures so they are ISO compliant."
- "Improve earned value on every project in the next quarter."
- "Implement e-learning."

Such objectives, although achievable, are so small as to be almost trivial and leave everyone in the organization thinking, "OK, sure...but why?"

Defining the Performance Objective Language

Here it is again: Definition is everything. It happens every day in business organizations all over the world...a group of people will come together in a meeting, physically or virtually, to decide something. Even though some of the people in the group have known each and worked together for a long time, they still struggle to come to agreement on topics. They are frustrated because they don't know why it's so hard to get a decision or agreement on seemingly simple topics such as defining the organization's or team's performance objectives.

One of the reasons—and I can only treat this topic superficially here because it's really its own book—is that we don't speak the same language. Oh sure, we might all be speaking English or some dialect thereof. But the words we carry in our heads and use don't always have the same definition that you'll find in Wiktionary[6] and, most assuredly, don't have the same meaning for others with whom we are communicating. The cartoon in Figure 1.3 illustrates how easily we miscommunicate every day because we assume standard meanings for the words and phrases we use.

So, how do you get a group of people to define performance objectives and emerge with all participants having a common understanding of those objectives? You first work to get consensus on the meaning of words and phrases that will be used in organizational performance and performance measurement programs. The words most commonly used that need a defined meaning for your organization include:

■ Goal
■ Objective

Figure 1.3   When we think everyone understands us.

- Target
- Plan
- Measure
- Measurement
- Indicator
- Metric
- Information
- Data
- Customer
- Organization
- Project
- Stakeholder
- Relevant stakeholder
- Dashboard
- Scorecard

Start by realizing you don't need to invent definitions from scratch; there are plenty of sources of definitions for these terms available on the web (Wiktionary and Wikipedia) and in the literature, and you're wasting time reinventing definitions. (Also see "Assume It Already Exists" in Chapter 4.) Once you've written starter definitions, get the stakeholders with whom you are defining performance objectives to modify the definitions to meet your environment, culture, and application of the terms.

One of the most important terms upon which to obtain consensus understanding and definition is "objective." (Many organizations use "goal" and "objective" as synonymous with each other; it doesn't really matter, just pick one and make sure everyone understands what it means.) When I have facilitated the effective performance measurement (EPM) with clients, I normally send an e-mail to the participants in advance of the workshop, asking them to provide me individually with a definition for the word "goal." I then bring these different definitions to the workshop and reveal them to all participants as an interesting way of getting everyone energized toward the task of defining terms and definitions. Here are three definitions for "goal" that you can use. The third definition is one I have used successfully in many different organizations:

- A result one is attempting to achieve (Wiktionary)
- A desired state of affairs of a person or of a system (Wikipedia)
- A defined statement describing a desired state or result, the achievement of which can be measured or observed

Next, after developing consensus definitions for the terms you will be using for defining performance objectives and measures, define the relationships between one term and the other terms. For example, Figure 1.4 defines the relationship between "objective" and other performance terms. You might even find that defining the relationships between terms helps you define those terms more accurately and concisely. (Also see "Definition Is Everything" in Chapter 4.)

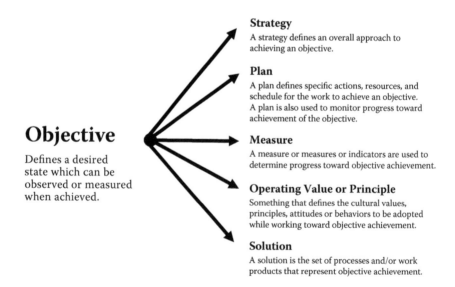

Figure 1.4   Defining the relationships between performance terms.

Getting to the Real Performance Objective

The pursuit of the false goal in software and systems development and IT is spending time and resources to achieve a goal that wasn't the right thing to pursue from the beginning. Would we pursue goals unworthy of the pursuit, unworthy of our time, our focus, and our money? You might say, "That's unacceptable," and yet that such pursuits are not only accepted, they are authorized and funded every day. Say your organization spends a million dollars (and many organizations have spent magnitudes more than that) to achieve a CMMI maturity level because leadership believes it will result in greater business capture. What if by the time the organization achieves the maturity level rating, the CMMI is no longer in fashion or maturity level ratings no longer have the perceived value they once enjoyed? What if you achieve a CMMI maturity level and then cannot really articulate the resulting business performance improvement?[7]

Similar scenarios could be framed for any business pursuit— the pursuit of quality, for example. Product and information organizations have a long and expensive history of pursuing quality, but it's easy to make the case that many of these pursuits have been wasteful because leaders did not ask or answer enough "why" questions. If you ask, "Why higher quality?" and the answer is, "Because it will save lives," now you're closer to a meaningful pursuit. If you ask, "Why higher quality?" and the answer is demonstrable increased market share, revenue, or profit, now you're closer to a meaningful pursuit. But if you ask, "Why higher quality?" and the only answer you get is, "Because we want higher quality," then it is unlikely that the goal is worthy of pursuit because no one will know the value of doing so. It will also be very difficult to rally people behind an effort to achieve the goal and almost impossible to sustain excitement and energy toward the goal.

Probably my favorite false performance objective for process improvement is the achievement of consistency. I've lost count of the number of times I've heard managers or people in process improvement say something along the lines of, "We want everyone to do things the same way." If you spend enough money, you can eventually get people to perform their work consistently, sometimes consistently poorly! In certain settings, it is possible to define relationships between people performing their work consistently and business performance improvements such as cost saving, but many leaders just don't dig that deep. When consistency is pursued for its own sake and for no deeper purpose, it is a false goal and a waste of resource. Performance objectives are sneaky: They are often other things disguised as goals. Sometimes, solutions or solution approaches disguise themselves as goals. Some example solution approaches that disguise themselves as objectives include:

- "We will improve our processes."
- "We will implement the CMMI."
- "We will be an Agile company."
- "We will simplify and optimize all aspects of doing business with our company."

The preceding statements are solution approaches rather than performance objectives because they don't explicitly or implicitly address the "why." How would implementing the CMMI address a business performance problem or risk?

Sometimes, measures or indicators disguise themselves as objectives. Examples of measures or indicators disguised as objectives include:

- "We will achieve CMMI maturity level 2."
- "We will pass 98 percent of the quality assurance (QA) audits without deficiencies."

Again, for the preceding statements, the unanswered question is, "Why?" There must be some higher performance objective for wanting to pass 98 percent of the QA audits...some higher quality or safety goal. It is that higher level goal that should be addressed in the performance objective statement.

The third form of things disguised as performance objectives is slogans, attitudes, or values. These are statements usually designed to fit on a bumper sticker, coffee mug, or badge lanyard. Even very positive and inspiring slogans are often mistaken for objectives. Examples include:

- "The customer comes first."
- "We support the warfighter."
- "Set the performance bar 'high.'"
- "Quality is job one."

The reasons why such statements are not performance objectives are multiple. First, they are written in the present— as if to imply a current state, not a desired state. Second, they state the obvious: Would the customer not come first, would we not support the warfighter, or would we set the performance bar low? Finally, such statements describe behaviors or cultural attitudes, not performance objectives. Such behaviors and attitudes might need to be prevalent to achieve performance objectives; they are not themselves the objective.

There are a number of ways to get to the real performance objective, but one method I have found to be as effective as it is simple is a method I call "Whyagnostics." In Whyagnostics, you keep asking, "Why?" until you get to a goal or objective statement that matches your definition for the same and expresses a desired state in organizational performance that can be related to business results. Figure 1.5 shows a dialog between an organization's process improvement lead and an executive. In this scenario, the executive initially stated the objective was to "standardize the processes." The savvy and intuitive process improvement lead realized that there must be some greater goal and used Whyagnostics to get to the real performance objective.

Executive:	I want us to standardize our processes so we have consistency.
PI lead:	Why?
Executive:	So that people will perform work the same way.
PI lead:	Why?
Executive:	Because then we'll reduce waste and rework associated with "reinventing" things.
PI lead:	Why?
Executive:	As an organization, we can produce more deliverables with the same resources if people reuse work products.
PI lead:	So, the performance objective is to improve productivity—more deliverables with the same resources...is that correct? (The wise PI lead understands this objective means $$$.)
Executive:	Yes, isn't that what I said?

Figure 1.5 Example of using Whyagnostics to discover the real performance objective.

As a word of caution to practitioners: Don't pursue Whyagnostics to the point of being annoying or being viewed as impertinent. If your boss starts answering your line of inquiry with responses like "because I said so" or "you heard me; that's what I want," I strongly suggest you stop asking why.

Using Criteria to Evaluate Performance Objective Statements

If you wanted to find out how to define "good" performance objectives—statements that will lead to success in a process and performance improvement initiative—what would you do? What if you could look at dozens of objective statements from lots of different organizations, find out which objectives were achieved, and then analyze the achieved objective statements for common attributes or characteristics?

Your organization is not the first in the history of business to define its performance objectives; others have gone before you and you can learn from their experiences. If you were to do such an analysis of historical objective statements that were achieved, you might find that they share many of the criteria defined in Table 1.4. Consider this list of goal articulation criteria (GAC) a starter set—a list that your organization can choose from and add to in defining your organization's performance objectives.

It's difficult to overstate the importance of using the first criterion in Table 1.4—strategic alignment. Probably one of the most successful examples I have seen in which process improvement objectives were integrated and strategically aligned with business objectives is outlined in a software engineering process group (SEPG) Europe conference presentation by Mark Frazer of Welch Allyn.[8] In this presentation, Frazer described how, at Welch Allyn, he was able to engender executive support and enthusiasm for process improvement by

- Establishing a solid connection and relationship between a process improvement and a strategic business objective
- Defining the proposed process improvement within the context of the organization's strategic plan
- Planning the process improvement to fit within the organization's strategic planning and budget cycle
- Saying the right things and using the right language with executives and senior leaders
- Integrating the process improvement in the organization's strategic road map

Against dark and noisy background of pervasive and persistent whining at process conferences about the "lack of

Table 1.4 Goal Articulation Criteria (GAC)

Goal Articulation Criteria (GAC)	*Description and Criteria Test Questions*
Strategic alignment	**The goal aligns with and supports the organization's strategies and other goals and objectives.** Is the goal orthogonal or diametrically opposed to the organization's strategic direction? Does achievement of the goal align with strategic plans? Will pursuing the goal have adverse effects upon or inhibit the achievement of other goals or strategies? Could achievement of this goal have the unintended consequence of diminishing the results of the achievement of other goals?
Capability alignment	**Work toward the goal's achievement aligns with the organization's current core competencies and capabilities.** Can we achieve the goal with our current competence and capabilities? Will achievement of this goal require special knowledge, skill, or expertise we don't possess? Will achievement of this goal require infrastructure, tools, technology, or another capability we don't possess?
Reasonability	**The goal is realistic and reasonably achievable.** Is achievement of the goal realistic and reasonable within the targeted time frame? Is the goal a "stretch goal" and, if so, why?

Table 1.4 (*Continued*) Goal Articulation Criteria (GAC)

Goal Articulation Criteria (GAC)	Description and Criteria Test Questions
Comprehensible	**The stakeholders who establish the goal and the stakeholders who will be responsible for executing actions to achieve the goal understand the goal's meaning and intent.** Do the words used to compose the goal statement have a common meaning to all stakeholders, or do they need further definition and clarity? Is the goal statement internally consistent, or do components of the goal seem to contradict other components?
Observability or measurability	**Achievement of the goal can be observed or measured.** How will we know when we have achieved the performance improvement the goal's achievement is intended to deliver? What will we see or measure? How will we be able to understand progress toward goal achievement?
Attraction and relatability	**Individuals in the organization have a personal stake or interest in goal achievement.** What about the goal is attractive to personnel who will be working toward its achievement? Can the benefits of achieving the goal be understood or implied from the goal statement? Will the goal statement implicitly or explicitly answer the question, "What's in it for me?" How can people see their roles in working toward the goal's achievement?

(Continued)

Table 1.4 (*Continued*)   Goal Articulation Criteria (GAC)

Goal Articulation Criteria (GAC)	*Description and Criteria Test Questions*
Definable and actionable	**The goal can be deconstructed into plans, actions, tasks, projects, or jobs with definable start and end dates, resources, and definable deliverables.**
Communicability	**The goal can be easily articulated by everyone in the organization.** Is the goal statement concise (yet precise) enough to be easily remembered and articulated by stakeholders? How can you test if it is clear and understood by people in the organization?
Scope, applicability, and focus	**The goal statement implicitly or explicitly indicates its scope, applicability, and focus.** How will people know if the goal or its achievement applies to them or their work? Does the goal statement define what will be achieved, but leave the detailed "how" to lower level plans? Is it easy to understand the scope or the boundaries of the goal?
Ordination/ subordination	**The goal can be prioritized with other objectives or improvement initiatives.** How will people who contribute to the goal's achievement know or understand its priority in relationship to other work?
Fact or perception	**Is the goal statement factually based, or is it based in perception?** Perceptions may be based in facts or truths, but those facts should be verified before embarking on a performance improvement initiative based solely on perceptions.

sponsorship" or the "lack of senior management buy-in" for process improvement, it's hard to argue with Frazer's shining example of success. Where this thought-path should take you is the logical conclusion that "CMMI goals" or even "process improvement goals" aren't really goals at all…they are the means to achieving real goals or objectives.

As stated, the list of GAC in Table 1.4 is merely a starter set of criteria, and you and others in your organization should think about and add other criteria that you deem important. In Natural Systems Process Improvement (Natural SPI)'s effective performance measurement (EPM) workshop, we use this list of GAC to score goal or objective statements using a numerical scale, usually 1 to 4, with the following scale definitions:

1. The goal statement satisfies the criteria very little or not at all.
2. The goal statement somewhat satisfies the criteria.
3. The goal statement mostly satisfies the criteria.
4. The goal statement completely satisfies the criteria.

When I facilitate goal setting workshops, I use a simple Excel-based tool to enable multiple participants to apply their own evaluation values (1 through 4) to each goal statement and for each criterion. The tool I use then runs a macro to pull in the data from the multiple individual participants' spreadsheets into a master roll-up spreadsheet, thus employing a wideband Delphi-like approach to aggregating multiple inputs. In the master roll-up workbook, the value for each criterion for each goal statement is the most frequent value applied by the participants. So if I have eight participants and their individual values for a particular criterion for one of the goal statements are 1, 2, 2, 3, 3, 4, 4, 4, then the master roll-up workbook will display a "4" for that criterion for that goal statement. Figure 1.6 shows a partial picture of a GAC worksheet.

Goal Articulation Criteria	Achieve 15% Revenue Growth Over FY09 with Indirects/direct Labor of 10%	Implement an EVMS Process	Maintain Voluntary Turnover to 10% or Less	Achieve 80% Reuse of Processes and Work Products	Deliver Products Within 5% of the Estimated Schedule	Reduce Support Costs by 20	Implement
The goal supports the organization's strategy and vision	Yes	Yes	Yes	Yes	Yes	Yes	Yes
The goal is aligned with the organization's core business and core competency	Yes	Yes	Yes	Yes	Yes	Yes	Yes
The goal is achievable and neither unrealistic nor mediocre	Yes	Yes	Yes	Yes	Yes	Yes	Yes
There is a consensus understanding among the goals take holders of the meaning of the words used to define the goal	Yes	Yes	Yes	Yes	Yes	Yes	Yes
Achievement of the goal is measurable and/or observable	Yes	Yes	Yes	Yes	Yes	Yes	Yes
Individuals in the organization have a personal stake in goal achievement	Yes	Yes	Yes	Yes	Yes	Yes	Yes
The goal is specific enough to be deconstructed in to plans for actions, tasks, projects, or jobs with defined start and end dates, and resources	Yes	Yes	Yes	Yes	Yes	Yes	Yes
The goal can be communicated, and can be easily articulated by everyone in the organization	Yes	Yes	Yes	Yes	Yes	Yes	Yes
The goal identifies what must be accomplished and perhaps why, but not how	Yes	Yes	Yes	Yes	Yes	Yes	Yes
This goal can be prioritized with other goals	Yes	Yes	Yes	Yes	Yes	Yes	Yes

Figure 1.6 Sample GAC worksheet.

Of course, you can also give each GAC criterion a weight to indicate its relative importance or ranking with the other criteria. The objective of using defined criteria for defining objectives is to develop concise yet precise statements that will have a better chance of being understood and successfully implemented. And remember this axiom: Don't define goals for which the achievement cannot be measured or observed or, define or collect measures that don't relate to any goals.

Performance objectives, once established, communicated, and funded, will influence workers' behaviors, so it's important that they influence the right behaviors...those behaviors that will result in intended consequences, not unintended consequences. The risk of establishing objectives that have not been carefully considered and examined against criteria is that you may get what you asked for, but not what you wanted. If, for example, you define an objective that reads: "Grow the business by 15 percent annually," you might not get what you intend if people don't know which dimension— size (number of employees), revenue, profit or margin, shareholder value, product or service lines—that you want to grow. You might grow in number of employees as you watch your profit go down.

Establishing Performance Measures

There is ample literature on how to define measures and establish enterprise performance measurement programs, and this book doesn't need to repeat that literature. However, this section will give you some ideas that are key to successfully defining and measuring process performance and ROP.

Through my own reading and learning and, more importantly, through application in my own consulting experiences, I have gathered some practical measurement practices that, when applied within the appropriate context, will enable ROP...or at least keep you out of a world of hurt. These practices, with some discussion for each, are

- ■ "Success" is never one measure or indicator.
- ■ What gets measured gets attention. Or, what you measure is what you get.
- ■ Take a contextual, wide perspective view of performance measures.
- ■ The act of measuring or observing can affect what is being measured.

The Measure of Success

In the premodern or modern world (we are now in the postmodern world), an organization's measure of success was the results of a few simple accounting equations such as return on equity or profit. "Success" could more or less be determined by the year-end balance sheet or stock price. But that world was relatively simple compared to today, and perspectives of success could be correspondingly simple. In today's business ecology, the paths to success are almost as infinitely branched and complex as the challenges and problems that organizations face on a daily basis. Believing that one or two performance measures will indicate the success of your organization is a recipe for failure.

If you are at or near the top of your organization, you have learned to streamline and simplify the many streams of information coming to you on a daily basis. You've had to do this to survive; there is just too much information in an organization for one person to digest and use. But you may have simplified too much and to your own demise as a leader. Perhaps a long time ago, you understood the math beneath those red-yellow-green stoplight charts but, once all your reports realized those were the only charts you wanted to see, the colors came to mean whatever the presenter wanted them to mean—or wanted you to see—and thus became meaningless. Now, you don't really know what you're looking at, but as long as it's all green, you are comfortable that you're doing a good job as a leader.

There is always someone somewhere trying to replace you. He is not smarter than you, but he is more adaptable than you. He doesn't simply accept the "conventional wisdom," and he asks lots of questions to test his and everyone else's assumptions.

Unless you're ready to retire, you need to reinvent yourself. You need to reach down and find in yourself the passion for learning that you once had in the days before people promoted you for knowing "everything." To take a simplistic view of today's hypercomplex world is to be, well, a simpleton. The younger,

> faster, connected, and ambitious protégé who lives
> in the modern complex world—the one who asks,
> "What does 'green' mean?"—is waiting in the wings.

What Gets Measured and Unintended Consequences

What gets measured is what you get.[9] By extension of this sage advice from researchers Kaplan and Norton, if leadership's only performance measure is earnings per share, that might be what is achieved. However, probably no one will then understand why, as the earnings per share increase, the company is losing customers, employees, and brand reputation.

As usual, statements that fit on a bumper sticker beg specificity and clarity, especially when they contain a kernel of wisdom. For the sake of practicality, I need to complement "What gets measured is what you get" with some specificity. "What gets measured is what you get" implies that what you measure is the **only** thing that you get. In reality, you may get change other than what you measure, but you won't know about it, and it may be change you did not want. Table 1.5 illustrates this concept of getting what you measure, such as changes in behaviors, practices, and possible outcomes. The table also identifies other possible changes and results, but also possibly getting other phenomena that go unobserved because they are not measured.

Context-Based Performance Measures

Whether consequences are intended or not, or measured or not, another reason why there is no such thing as a single measure of success is because "success" indicated by any single measure is relative to the performance indicated by other measures. A single performance measure only has useful meaning to a business when it is perceived within the context of other performance measures.

Table 1.5   Getting What You Measure (and Getting What You Don't Measure)

If All You Measure is…	Then What You will Probably Get is…	And You Might Also Get But May Not Be Aware of…
Return on equity (earnings per share)	• Increased earnings per share • Increased capitalization	• Capital and power consolidation • Target painting for acquisition or take-over • Loss of organizational identity
Market share	• Increased number of customers • Increased customer diversity • Increased brand recognition • Increased revenue	• Increased customer support costs • Defection of loyal customers • Bad "Borg" public perception
Regulatory or standards compliance	• ISO/AS registrations • CMMI maturity levels • Increased government or DoD bid opportunity • Greater process and practice standardization	• Loss of innovation and creativity • Talent defection • Increased product realization, service delivery, or operating costs
Productivity	• More output for less work • Reduced delivery schedule	• Lower product or service quality
Cost	• Lower service delivery, product realization, or operating cost • Increased margin	• Lower quality • Diminished customer perception • Brand devaluation

Example of Context-Based Performance Measures

Let's say that you are an engineering manager in the product development division of an organization. In a meeting with the division president, she tells you that the executive committee is stressing over the latest information that indicates a competitor is pulling ahead of your company in terms of content-rich releases for their mobile application that competes with yours, and that they want your group to move features planned for next quarter's product releases into this quarter's releases. You got where you are in the organization by finding ways to perform "miracles" and getting things done, so you meet with your functional leads and decide which features to pull into the current release. You and your leads don't have time to do a lot of analysis because marketing needs to know right away which features to start promoting for the release. You come up with the list of features that are committed for the current release and the next and then give that list to your division president and Marketing. The executive committee is ecstatic!

A week after the release moves into testing, you get some ominous defect reports from the test manager in terms of a growing defect count, but neither he nor you can let the schedule slip, so he offers to supplement his group with some contract testers in the Czech Republic.

The release gets out the door a week late, but you're forgiven because Marketing has gotten the customer base very excited about the new features. Three months later, your department gets another release out, 2 weeks late but with 20 percent more features than originally planned.

At the next quarterly review with the executive committee, you and the other department managers who make up the division staff present your quarterly performance measures.

You present your big accomplishment for the quarter—the fact that in two product releases your development team was able to deliver 40 percent more features than the content that was originally planned for those releases. This measure alone gets applause from everyone in the room. Right after you present, Sales stands up and reports that sales of the mobile application increased by 10 percent in the quarter, probably due to Marketing's ability to do promotions on the big changes in the two releases your team delivered—again, applause. Other department managers will be presenting their quarterly measures, but you have another meeting to go to so you excuse yourself and leave the meeting. On your way out, you notice the newly hired VP of Operations scribbling on her notepad, but you don't think much of it.

At a subsequent executive committee meeting, the VP of Operations presents the picture shown in Figure 1.7.

As it turns out, some executives know that performance should not be understood by just looking at one performance measure and that each performance dimension should not be viewed separately from the others. In this example, the VP of Operations collected and evaluated a year's worth of cost, schedule, quality, and content measures and then used their historical relationship as a baseline for overall performance prior to you being asked to dramatically increase the content in a couple of releases. Though no causal relationships have been established—no root cause analysis has been conducted on the affected performance dimensions—there are correlation relationships for which reasonable assumptions can be made. In their meeting with you, they validate these correlations and assumptions with your own observations from the last two content-rich releases:

■ The push to increase release content without correlating schedule relief caused developers to be under pressure to design and develop faster. This probably incurred the "haste makes waste" principle and increased the volume of defects in the product that was turned over to testing.

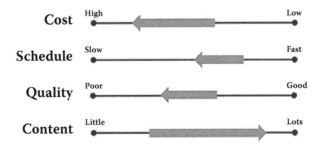

Figure 1.7   Example contextual performance measures.

■ The growing defect population in the product when it transitioned to testing required more testing resources (remember the Czechs?) to stay on schedule for the release. This not only increased cost, but also lengthened the testing schedule because of the incremental calendar time consumed to transfer work accurately to the Czech testing team and verify, record, and report on their results and progress.

■ Even with the testing capacity augmented, there was still a higher than average number of defect escapes to the released product, again speculatively due to pressure on more content without an accommodating release schedule.

Stories similar to this example play out noticed and unnoticed many times throughout the business world every day, and they should point toward the importance of adopting a holistic and systemic view of performance and performance measures. In the example, there certainly was performance improvement in the release of product content, but was there overall, holistic improvement in product delivery? Questionable, isn't it?

Herein is one of the true values of collecting and analyzing a statistically viable population of performance measures, a data population that is both deep and broad: You can use that measurement data to build a truly useful dashboard, one that not only provides you with real-time indicators of operational performance dimensions and their interrelationships, but also serves as a crystal ball that can be used for what-if scenarios to predict results.

To wit, if I crank up quality, what happens to cost and schedule? If I crank up schedule, what happens to cost and quality? If I emphasize revenue, what happens to employee morale? If I focus more on distribution, what is the effect on my carbon or greenhouse gas tax? If I improve the efficiency of my supply chain, what happens to the cost of supplies in the chain? Why do I have to speculate or guess…I have years of measures with which math can yield answers. Don't my stakeholders deserve to know? Don't I deserve to know

I can hear the cynics and critics: "Oh, hindsight is so easy, isn't it?" But after 5, 10, or 20 years of experiencing the same correlations and the same hindsights over and over, don't you think it's time to get a clue, pick up on the patterns, and convert hindsight into foresight and vision? How many years are you going to play the victim card and say, "I never saw that coming"? Really?

The Effect of Watching or Measuring

All the proof you can want of "what you measure is what you get" is witnessed in the interesting (and sometimes unsettling) effect that observing a business phenomenon has on the phenomenon itself. The minute people know the behavior or the process you're measuring is the minute it changes. As with all power, this dynamic can be used for good or bad.

If people change behaviors, practices, and performance only because they are being watched, then those behaviors are ephemeral—likely to be exhibited only for the duration they are observed. On the other hand, if the observing and measuring reveal positive changes and people can see that they were for good, then there's a chance the behaviors and practices will stick around.

Case Study

Years ago, I had a client in the online education and testing business. The VP of Engineering expressed to me multiple problems in his Product Engineering Department, but he also was of the opinion—which later changed—that implementing the CMMI would resolve most of the problems. Through various forms of investigation, such as document review and interviews with individuals, I discovered that one of the biggest problems they had was constant and rapid change in the priority and risk of the numerous projects in the project portfolio.* Engineering managers, with influence from marketing and customer support, frequently and daily changed the priorities and risks for the projects. Some days, priorities were changed for as many as half the projects in the portfolio. This volatility in the project priorities caused significant context switching among the business analysis, requirements analysts, designers, developers, and testers; this, of course, is waste.

Although everyone had an intuitive sense of how bad the portfolio volatility was, there were no measures of the magnitude of the problem. The change in priorities, the addition of new projects, and the cancellation of existing projects was mostly communicated verbally.

My team was contracted to help management gain some visibility into the magnitude of the problem. We created an Excel† workbook in which we recorded for each project the current status, current priority (–1, 0, or 1), and the current risk (high, medium, or low). The workbook was stored in a central location, and there was a process by which all managers had to check out the workbook and update the status

---

* At any given time, there were 150 to 200 projects in the project portfolio.
† I would never recommend using Excel for project portfolio management, especially in organizations with many concurrent projects. Excel is not robust for this purpose, but it was all we had at the time, and we needed to capture some measures quickly.

and priority columns whenever they changed. A macro and pivot table in the workbook could be executed to generate a report that provided summary numbers, such as numbers and types of status changes, numbers and types of priority changes, and numbers and types of risk level changes. We tracked the project portfolio volatility over 7 months and were able to deliver analysis similar to the chart shown in Figure 1.8.

Just the act of measuring and revealing the analysis of project portfolio volatility accomplished these improvements:

1. It quantified the magnitude of the problem, which helped managers extrapolate an estimate of the amount of waste caused by context switching among the workers.
2. Over time, it changed the behaviors of some managers in that they became more judicious in changing project priorities because they understood the negative downstream effects of changing project priorities in an impulsive or reactive mode.

A case of the Heisenberg principle? Perhaps, but this case study does indicate that there can be a correlation between measuring process performance and changes in that process performance.

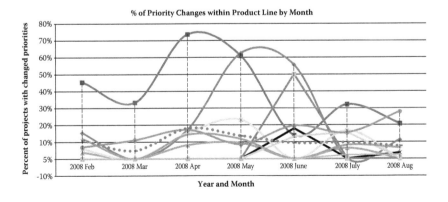

Figure 1.8 Sample analysis of project portfolio volatility.

Defining the Performance Measurement Language

If there is an effort to define performance measures, you will very likely get "volunteered" to participate. That's because this is real work and you're a worker. As with most definition activities, there is no need to reinvent definitions for performance measures. There are volumes of existing literature on this topic, and the starting point for you and your colleagues should always be to borrow from existing sources and then modify to meet the needs of your organization.

Somewhere along the way, it became cool for people to use the word "metrics" for all things associated with measures and measurement activity. Remember that words have meaning, and loss of meaning leads to ineffective communication, which is waste. Table 1.6 defines some terms and definitions commonly used in measurement programs that you will find useful.

Types of Measures

When establishing a measurement program, a useful rule is to measure what you improve and improve what you measure. When people don't think about the different types and uses of measure, they can unintentionally collect and use the wrong measures; this, in turn, will lead them to make incorrect conclusions about the effects of a process improvement effort. For example, if you improve a process but then look at product

Table 1.6   Key Measurement Terms and Definitions

Measurement Term	Definition and Examples
Measure or measurement	The quantity, size, weight, distance, or capacity of something compared to a designated standard; also, as a verb, the act of measuring.
Metric	A means of deriving a quantitative measurement or approximation for otherwise qualitative phenomena; "metric" is most accurately used in the context of referring to a measure or set of measures or indicators used to define a performance target, benchmark, or boundaries.
Base measure	The property or characteristic of an entity, object, or attribute and the method for quantifying it; a base measure is functionally independent of other measures. Examples: • Four defects were found in requirement #26-1. • Project Z missed a milestone last week by 2 days. • Module XYZ is 1325 SLOC in size. • John was 8 minutes late to the meeting. • Testing reported 36 bugs in Release 4.01. • Sally spent 11 hours over 3 days getting information from two vendors.
Derived measure	A measure that is defined as a function of two or more base measures; derived measures give context to base measures. Examples: • Our defect density is 4.3 defects/thousand function points (KFP). • Project Z's average milestone slip was 1.7 days. • Our overhead is 12 hours/week/person. • John has been at least 5 minutes late to 6 out of 10 meetings. • Requirements change by an average of 42 percent each release. • The response time ratio between vendor X and supplier Y is 2:5.

(Continued)

Table 1.6 (*Continued*) Key Measurement Terms and Definitions

Measurement Term	Definition and Examples
Indicator	The combination of one or more base measures and/or derived measures with associated decision criteria; an indicator is *information* versus a measure, which is *data*. Examples: • Earned value • Schedule performance index • As we added more engineers to the staff, schedule slips became more frequent and greater in magnitude. • After we introduced the template, the engineers stopped complaining about reporting status. • Average cycle time for processing purchase requests decreased by 20 percent after we implemented the new process.
Analysis	As a verb, "analysis" is the act of analyzing a set of measures and indicators to derive information that can be used to inform decisions and actions. As a noun, "analysis" or "analyses" are the result of analyzing measures and measurement data.
Score card	A method and/or system for representing measures, measurement information, indicators, and/or analysis in the context of performance objective achievement. A product that provides real-time graphical representation of measurement data, indicators, and analysis is often called "dashboard." "Balanced score card (BSC)" is widely inappropriately used because people often use this phrase to describe score cards that do not follow the structure and rules for a BSC as defined by Kaplan and Norton.[a]

Table 1.6 (*Continued*)   Key Measurement Terms and Definitions

Measurement Term	Definition and Examples
Measurement verification	The process of inspecting data to verify its accuracy and fidelity of transmission. Verification answers questions such as: • Are data current? • Are data from different sources correlated? • Do data match its specifications?
Measurement normalization	The process of converting data into a common unit of measure and/or aggregation level so that it can be compared or combined with other data.

[a] Kaplan, Robert S. and Norton, David P., *The Balanced Scorecard: Translating Strategy into Action*, Harvard Business School Press, Cambridge, 1996.

performance measures, you might see (or imagine that you see) a relationship that is not supported by math or facts. Table 1.7 identifies three performance dimensions and lists member measures and indicators typically associated with each dimension.

Let me be more specific about this topic: I'm not suggesting that a process improvement cannot affect project or product performance; it can and it should. What I am saying is that it is the process performance that results from the improvement that will have an effect on another dimension. For example, if I improve the peer review process, I want to measure the efficacy of peer reviews ("efficacy" meaning the improved peer review process traps and removes defects at points in the life cycle to achieve maximum cost reduction in defect removal). I then want to examine the relationship between peer review efficacy and product quality, and the cost of product quality.

Defining Your Performance Measures

The next step in achieving real performance improvement is to define the measures that the organization will use

Table 1.7 Classifying Performance Measures with Their Associated Performance Dimension

Project Performance	Product Performance	Process Performance
Cost	Quality	Efficiency
Schedule	Functionality	Efficacy
Earned value	Maintainability	Billable: overhead ratio (or direct: indirect)
Cycle time	Safety	Productivity
Scope management	Security	Tailorability/ scalability
	Cost/unit product cost	Adoptability
	Shelf-life	Adaptability
	Market life	Extensibility
		Queuing/wait or lag time
		Redundancy

to determine the achievement of performance objectives. There are many ways to define an organization's process and performance measures, but you want to start by separating the construct and content of a measurement definition from the vehicle in which the definition is contained. This means: Don't get caught up in whether your measurement definitions are going to be in a Word document, an Excel worksheet, a SharePoint list, or a database because the most important thing is first to identify the information elements that you need to define to construct a single measurement definition. The construction of the measurement definitions should then be used to decide the best way to represent that information and make it accessible and usable to a community.

You'll be lucky if you get the attention of your executives and senior managers to define the performance objectives. Don't push your luck by dragging them into measure definition work; you and your fellow practitioners in process improvement will have to take on that task. When defining performance measures, it's important to be able to answer these questions:

- *Does the measure—or a derived measure or indicator to which it contributes—help us understand if we're achieving a performance objective?* Remember the axiom: Don't establish objectives that you don't intend to measure and don't collect measures that don't help you understand achievement of objectives.
- *Given our current processes, technology, and skills, can we collect the measure?* If you don't have the capability to collect a measure, there is no value in defining it.
- *Will anyone use the measure—or its derivatives— to inform decisions or take actions?* If there is not a customer or consumer of a measure, there is no value in collecting it.

I have seen numerous measurement dictionaries and databases and have compiled a list of information elements that organizations have found essential to include in the definition of a measure. Table 1.8 defines a list of information elements that should be defined for each measure.

Table 1.8 Performance Measurement Construct

Measure Definition Information Element	Description
Measure ID	A unique identifier for the measure definition (Unique identifiers for information records such as requirements, tasks, definitions, charge codes, etc. are a standard good practice in modern information management.)
Measure name	A short descriptor for the measurement; example: Requirements volatility (RV)
Performance objective (s) supported	The performance objectives for which the measure will be collected, analyzed, and used to determine objective achievement Examples: • Improve resource planning to level fluctuations in staff size and reduce bench by 5 percent. • Improve estimate to actual project variances in cost and schedule by 5 percent.
Measure type(s)	See Table 1.7. Example: project
Description	A thorough, detailed description of the measure; example: Requirements volatility describes the amount and rate of change to program/project requirements.
Calculation(s)	A description of the formulas or algorithms used to calculate the measure. Examples: • RV = number of changes to requirements at a point in time • Rate of RV = number of changes to requirements over a period of time

Objectives/uses	Descriptions of the intended use for the measure
	Examples:
	• Requirements volatility can negatively impact a program/project's cost, quality, and schedule performance. The location in the program/project life cycle in which a requirement changes can determine the magnitude of the impact of the change on program/project performance.
	• Generally speaking, programs/projects should strive to minimize requirements volatility at the initiation of the design phase.
Required measure level	A description of the level in the organization at which the measure is collected and at which its analysis is first used to make decisions, take action, or manage work
	Example: program/project
Source(s)	A description of the process, product, or tool/system from which the measure can be collected or extracted
	Example:
	• Programs/projects that use a software tool, such as TcSE or DOORS, to manage requirements can obtain requirements volatility reports on demand. Programs/projects not using a software tool to manage requirements will need to plan and define the source of requirements volatility information.
Collected by	Identification of the role (individual or team) that has primary responsibility for collecting the measure
	Example: PM, IPT lead, or REA (per measurement plan)

(Continued)

Table 1.8 (Continued)   Performance Measurement Construct

Measure Definition Information Element	*Description*
Collection method/ system	A description of how the measure is collected. Example: • Business analysts (BAs), who are involved in program/project requirements from initiation to product delivery, will track and collect requirements volatility measures. Using the organization standard definition for a "requirement," BAs will count the number of program/project requirements at the intervals identified in "collection timing" below. Requirement counts will be collected from any of the following sources: TcSE, DOORS, requirements specifications, lists of requirements (LORs), or requirements traceability matrices (RTMs). The selected sources will be used consistently throughout the program/project.
Collection timing	A description of the periodicity or event-driven timing for collecting, reporting, and using the measure Example: Program/project requirements will be counted at the following project events: • Approval of statement of work (SOW) • Requirements baseline • Code start • Systems test start • Product release

Analysis technique(s)	A description—and examples—of the analysis techniques used to analyze and represent the measure Examples: • With multiple requirements volatility measures taken at different points in the program/project life cycle, a trend analysis will be conducted to determine if the volatility is increasing or decreasing. This information is useful to determine risks to the program/project's performance and implement risk mitigation. • Cross correlation between requirements volatility and program/project cost and schedule performance can be used to determine the effects of requirements volatility. This information can be used to take corrective action and set stakeholder expectations.
Reported to	Identification of the role—individuals or teams—to whom the measure or measurement information is reported Example: project management office (PMO)
Reported how	Definition of how the measure or measurement information is reported Example: program management reviews
Implementation guidance	Descriptions of practices, techniques, or methods for implementing the measure definition. Examples: • In order to measure requirements volatility effectively and accurately, it is critical to have a firm definition of a "requirement" because it is impossible to understand the change to an unknown or undefined entity. • Additionally, accurately measuring changes to requirements assumes that a requirements baseline is established at some point in the program/project.

As you might have guessed from reading Table 1.8, measure definitions lend themselves to being defined and represented in a relational database or some form of table-driven information management system (e.g., a SharePoint list). It is easy to see how a single measure definition could constitute a record in a database or list, with the items in the "Measure Definition Information Element" column constituting the fields within a record and then the information for each measure definition in the "Description" column populating the fields in the record.

Be stingy with the resources and time spent on defining the first set of performance measures. It doesn't require everyone in the organization and the results don't have to be perfect. (See "Use 20 to Do 80" in Chapter 4.) The initial measure definitions only need to be good enough to get started collecting, analyzing, and using the measures. As measures are collected, you will find out what you need to change in the definitions (add new measures, change the definitions, or delete measures) based on experience.

Focusing the Improvement: People, Process, and/or Technology

Remember that there are essentially only three areas in which an organization can focus improvement regardless of the business in which the organization exists: people, process, and technology. (See Table 1.1.) Also remember that it's very difficult to change just one of these three dimensions without affecting one or both of the other two dimensions.

For example, let's say that I have a performance objective that reads: *Peer reviews will detect and remove 25 percent more defects in requirements development and project planning.* With this objective, we can intuit that we will probably analyze and improve our peer review process. But what if, as part of that process improvement, we also implement an organization-level database in which to record peer review results? Haven't we also changed our technology? And as part of deploying the new peer review process and the defect database, we need to train people in the process and use of the database. Haven't we affected the knowledge and skills of the workers? So later, as we measure our success against the objective, we need to have some understanding, even if a qualitative one, of the effects of the changes in the three dimensions.

You don't have to be able to say, "Well, 55 percent of the performance improvement came from the process change, and 27 percent of the performance improvement came the technology...," but you should be prepared to have information that supports a rough order of magnitude allocation in attributing the performance improvement to the dimensions. Through the process of elimination (or marginalization) of the effects of two dimensions, you can reasonably deduce that the performance improvement is attributable to the remaining dimension.

As a manager, how resources—people and money—are allocated is often left up to you to decide. It's very important in an improvement initiative to figure out up front if the money is going to go into people, tools, or process, or the right combination of those three. It's even more important to know how much to invest. There will be times when you don't have enough budget to make an initiative successful; in this case you should find the courage not to fund it at all and put the resources

toward something else. The only thing worse than
a failed improvement initiative is one that is simply
starved to death over a long period of time…that is
a lose–lose proposition.

Let's use our previously mentioned performance objective:
*Peer reviews will detect and remove 25 percent more defects
in requirements development and project planning.* To build
on the example scenario, definitions already exist for "defect"
for most types of work products that get peer reviewed, and
MS Excel checklists already exist for most types of review.
However, if a project or the organization wanted to aggregate
the outputs from all peer reviews conducted, someone would
have to transfer the data from all the completed checklists
into a database or spreadsheet. As part of the improvement,
the improvement team decides to have IT create a SharePoint
list in which data from all peer reviews is captured; people
conducting peer reviews can enter in real time the outputs via
web-based html forms. Additionally, although product development workers are already required to take training in the
current peer review process, they will need to acquire training
in the new and improved peer review process, process assets,
and technology. Via a simple gap analysis, the peer review
process improvement team identifies a number of process-
related things that don't exist to support achieving the performance objective:

■ Standards or criteria for identifying defects in product
requirements
■ Standards or criteria for identifying defects in project
plans
■ Accommodation of requirements and planning peer
reviews in the peer review process description
■ Accommodation of the real-time peer review output capture via the html web forms

■ Definition of organization-level peer review output, measurements, measurement analysis, and measurement reporting processes

Building on the construct of Table 1.1, we can qualify the expected investment and performance return from the improvements in all three dimensions in Table 1.9.

Note that Table 1.9 is not so much a calculation of ROP as it is a business case for process improvement. As you read downward through the third column in Table 1.9, you will notice that the investment in the people improvement is mostly a standard cost already built into the process improvement, and the investment in the technology improvement is quickly and easily recoverable through the initial process improvement gains. So in this way, we can determine that the improvement should focus on process and that the anticipated return will primarily be an ROP calculation (versus the return on technology—ROT [no innuendo intended] or the return on humans—ROH).

The take-away from this section is the question to ask and be able to answer when the organization claims ROP: How much of the performance improvement is attributable to the changes made to process versus the changes to technology or to the work force? Is the answer supported by facts or measures?

Planning and Managing the Performance and Process Improvement Project

In my 2004 book, *Real Process Improvement Using the CMMI*, I wrote a chapter titled, "Managing the Process Improvement Project." In that chapter, I tried emphatically to tell process groups to "eat your own dog food," "practice what you preach," and other such sentiments that have become clichés. A few readers heeded the advice, but most did not. So, I'll try again...

Table 1.9   Example of Qualifying the Effects of Improvement in All Three Dimensions

Improvement Dimension	Investment	Performance Return Qualifiers
Improve people	Investment in people will primarily involve the development and delivery of training for the new processes, process assets, and technology	There is no need to build training materials (e.g., slideware); the improved processes, process assets, and technology can be demonstrated as-is without PowerPoint. All product development personnel are already required to receive annual process training and are allocated sufficient effort to do so; no incremental training budget is required.
Improve technology	IT charges the organization 120 hours to set up the initial SharePoint list, peer review output forms, access rights, and reports. It then is allocated 16 hours/ month to support changes.	Prior to the technology improvement, the improvement team estimated that the cost of manually transferring peer review outputs and measures and manual analysis of the measures would cost about 40 hours/month. So the technology investment is subsumed by the process improvement within the first 8 months.

Table 1.9 (*Continued*)   Example of Qualifying the Effects of Improvement in All Three Dimensions

Improvement Dimension	Investment	Performance Return Qualifiers
Improve process	Process improvement appears to be the largest portion of the improvement investment. Significant literature research and benchmarking need to be conducted to define peer review criteria for requirements-related and planning-related work products. Additionally, processes and process assets need to be developed for analyzing the aggregated peer review defect measures and quantifying the value of early life cycle defect detection and capture.	Given the negligible investment and return in terms of improving the people, and given the short recovery (8 months) from the minor technological investment, it appears that most measured performance improvement will be attributable to the process improvement, i.e., the ROP.

If you believe that a 110-story skyscraper can be built within 2 percent of budget and schedule, then there is no viable argument against using proven project management techniques to plan and manage your performance and process improvement and measurement programs. This section describes how to apply the most basic project management practices to your performance and measurement project.

This section can't do justice to the full body of knowledge for planning, executing, and managing performance and process improvement projects; that is enough content for an entire book. However, this section will provide you with innovative ways to apply project management practices to a performance and process improvement project.

> Perhaps you've been put in charge of the process group (e.g., an engineering process group [EPG]) because you're interested in process improvement, or you were on the last appraisal team, or you're a really good writer, or some other really bad reason for being put in charge. If you're not a knowledge-able and experienced project manager, do your-self and the organization a big favor and recruit a professional project manager to help you plan and manage the process improvement project.

The Most Important and Most Overlooked Measure: The Performance Baseline

Even before planning the ROP project, consider taking the time to do something that, if not performed, will preclude any and all possibility of determining the ROP: Get a performance baseline measure.

If you've been doing more than just reading this book—if you've been internalizing the information and performing it in your organization—you have enough data to collect a baseline performance measure. Will your baseline performance measure be precise to the third place right of the decimal? No, but it doesn't have to be. If you're designing a nuclear weapon component, precision counts, but in most applications, a business performance improvement doesn't require that much precision. Don't let perfection be the enemy of the good.

Table 1.10 defines what you need—which you've already been provided in this book—to establish a baseline performance measure.

Process performance can be measured a number of ways (see Table 1.9), and those measures can be used to derive the measures that executives and shareholders care about: units of value (the euphemism), which can be translated to units of money (the realism). There is a caution to defining a performance baseline measure when you are creating and introducing a new process—something the organization has not previously performed—and that is that there are two ways to assign a value:

1. Assign the current (baseline) performance a value of zero because, essentially, there is no baseline.
2. Conduct benchmarking[10] to determine the performance of other similar organizations in similar market sectors.

Table 1.10   Data and Information Needed to Establish a Baseline Performance Measure

Data/Info Item	Description	Where to Find in This Chapter
Performance to be improved	The definition of the performance improvement objective	"Learning What to Improve and Why"
What to improve	Definition of what to improve: process, technology, or people (presumably process for an ROP project)	"Focusing the Improvement: People, Process, and or Technology"
What to measure	The measures to be collected to characterize the current performance quantitatively—the baseline	"Defining Your Performance Measures"

Process Improvement Life Cycle

As much as I try, I can't lend much credibility in terms of practicality to a process improvement life cycle model that has been pushed for years: the Initiate Diagnose Establish Act Leverage (IDEAL)[11] life cycle model for process improvement. As it turns out, IDEAL is idealistic, but it's not what most organizations actually do. Having been involved in more than 30 process improvement projects, I have found that most organizations go through the following process improvement life cycle phases, even if they do so without consciously labeling their phases as such:

- **Inception.** In inception, the goals or requirements and the measures for the improvement project are defined. The goals for an improvement project need to specify the business performance change that is expected as a result of implementing the improvement, and the measures need to specify how the achievement of the objectives will be determined. (See "Establishing Performance Objectives" and "Establishing Performance Measures" in this chapter.)
- **Planning.** In planning, the improvement project team is formed and develops plans for the development phase of the improvement. The improvement project plans should include the scope of the improvement, effort and cost estimates, schedule, dependencies and constraints, configuration and data management, stakeholder involvement, and risk management.
- **Development.** In the development phase, the improvement project team develops the "solution." It encompasses the creation of or changes to defined processes and process assets, tools or systems, technology, and/or worker knowledge and skills.
- **Transition.** In transition, the improvement team tests or pilots the improvement solution to gain early insight and understanding of how the changes will work when fully

implemented in the intended environment. Transition activities often include limited-scope pilots, reviews or walk-throughs, or simulations of the improvement.

■ **Implementation.** In implementation, the improvement project, in collaboration with the organization, implements or applies the solution that was developed and delivered by the improvement project. Implementation includes training affected personnel in the use of the improved processes and/or tools. The implementation phase also includes monitoring the application of the improvement in the work environment and making adjustments or corrections as necessary.

■ **Institutionalization.** The institutionalization phase is nebulous and difficult to define. In institutionalization, which can take a short amount of time or a very long time depending on the culture and the magnitude of the change, the improvement or change gradually becomes the standard or normal way in which work is performed in the organization.

I'll grant you that the acronym "IPDTII" isn't nearly as catchy or memorable as "IDEAL," but it is the life cycle that organizations actually go through when they "projectize" the improvement work and "productize" an improvement.

"Projectize" the Work

The first, critical step to managing performance and measurement work is to "projectize" the work. Like most projects, a performance and measurement project will have these attributes:

■ Defined project performance goals or targets (e.g., earned value)
■ A beginning and an end
■ Defined deliverables

- A project team, with defined roles and responsibilities
- Defined stakeholders with defined involvement
- Defined tasks, defined schedule, and a budget
- Risk management plan
- Configuration or data management plan
- Defined communication or monitoring, control, and reporting plan

Initiate the Project (Inception)

This entire chapter is devoted to defining how to initiate a process improvement project that will yield a positive ROP. The bulk of the work in inception is defining the business performance objectives, the process performance objectives (see "Establishing Process Performance Objectives" in Chapter 2), and both the performance and process measures that will be used throughout the process improvement project to determine the achievement of those objectives.

In project initiation, we can define requirements for our project by asking and answering the following questions:

- What are the project's deliverables and who are the customers of those deliverables?
- Who are the users and what are the use cases for the project's deliverables?
- Can we envision and define operational concepts or scenarios for the performance objectives and measures in today's and tomorrow's business environment?
- Do the requirements meet our criteria for acceptable requirements?
- How will we ensure (through traceability?) that we implement and satisfy the project requirements?

Plan the Project

Once we've defined the project in inception—let's call it "2013 ROP Project"—we can plan it using all the proven project planning techniques available to us through the literature (such as the PMBOK) and through our experiences. Planning the process improvement involves defining plans for all the following aspects of the project:

- Work breakdown structure (WBS; i.e., lists of tasks and deliverables)
- Estimates of the attributes of the work and work products
- Effort and cost estimates
- Resource estimates
- Schedule
- Stakeholder involvement
- Configuration and document or data management
- Decision management
- Risk management

Develop the Solution

In the development phase, the project team designs and develops the solution that they believe will have the greatest effect on the achievement of the performance objective. In an ROP project, the solution will be a change (improvement) to one or more processes and will likely be manifested via one of the following vectors:

- A change to how a process is currently performed, irrespective of whether it is defined or how it is defined
- The creation of a new process that is not currently defined and may not currently be performed
- A change to a process that is currently defined
- The creation of new process assets or changes to existing process assets

Transition the Solution

In the transition phase, the project team performs activities intended to introduce the solution into the organization within the context of its intended use and, in doing so, limits any negative impacts such as interruptions of service or delays in the delivery of previously committed products. Transition includes performing activities such as the following:

- Conducting peer reviews or walk-throughs of the solution (e.g., changes to process or process assets) to verify that the solution will satisfy the requirements
- Conducting simulations or pilots in which the solution is tested in a scenario, situation, or environment in which the effects of other variables (technology and workforce expertise) can be controlled or limited

Putting It into Practice

Ascendance Consulting Corporation, commonly known simply as "ACC," is a diverse, global company that provides IT services, software engineering and development services, and business management consulting to organizations in the government and commercial sectors of the economy. ACC has built a good reputation on the professionalism of its employees and for its innovative practices in product and service delivery. In the Federal Division, ACC must maintain a CMMI maturity level rating in order to continue bidding on government contracts. The company's commercial sector units also maintain CMMI maturity levels because they perceive it to be a market differentiator, but they also must implement continuous improvement initiatives in ongoing efforts to reduce operating costs while maintaining a high quality of service and deliverables to clients.

Recently, the Federal Division has lost several contract bids to a competitor that is able to offer lower labor costs and, like ACC, maintains a CMMI-DEV maturity level 3 rating. Division leadership is under pressure from the CEO to make sure its annual operating plan includes increasing the division's competitiveness. The CEO also wants a plan for moving the division from CMMI maturity level 3 to maturity level 5 because he perceives that might be a deciding factor in a contract award.

Putting It into Practice: Defining Performance Objectives

The Federal Division president is frustrated. She understands the emphasis on competitiveness. However, the new demands from the CEO didn't come with any incremental budget for her division. She knows that with the kind of investment in technology that the competition has made, she could reduce the cost of performing contracts, but there is no new money for infrastructure or technology. What's worse is that the budget for continuous improvement efforts has been reduced, making the climb to higher CMMI maturity levels seemingly impossible. Finally, with the media focus on creating jobs in the United States, she can't just replace her highly skilled work force with cheaper labor from another country (like the competition did).

The Federal Division president gathered her senior functional and account managers for a 3-day off-site meeting. She wanted some strategic discussions around some very large questions that she's smart enough to know can't be answered by one person:

1. Is there really a business driver for higher maturity levels? Are there foreseeable business opportunities (e.g., government solicitations) requiring bidders to have higher CMMI maturity levels? Is the division really losing bids or opportunities to competitors because the competitors have higher CMMI maturity levels, or is there some other cause?
2. Will the market value (soft value based on perceptions of prestige and rarity) of a high CMMI maturity level (4 or 5) diminish by the time the division achieves the high maturity level?
3. What is the cost-benefit analysis for moving to higher CMMI maturity levels? Let's say that the 5-year

benefits—internal savings through efficiency gains, risk reduction, etc., plus new business opportunities— resulting from operating at CMMI maturity level 5 is estimated to be $30 million. Then, if the cost of the changes and improvements needed to achieve maturity level 5 is estimated to be $5 million, this would be a good return on the investment in improvement. If, however, the estimated 5-year benefit is $5 million and the estimated improvement cost is $8 million, leadership might want to reconsider the pursuit of higher maturity levels.

4. The division president is trained in systems thinking. When she applies systems thinking to the decision to pursue higher CMMI maturity levels, she is aware of unintended consequences and "fixes that backfire." Achieving CMMI maturity level 5 might reduce process overhead (process work that cannot be charged to a client), but it could also increase overhead, making the division even less competitive or reducing margins on contracts.

5. Higher CMMI maturity level practices, if implemented appropriately, are intended to help the organization improve performance. How can the division leadership be assured that this will be the result of the pursuit? In the division's current business sector, what performance needs to be improved, and why? What level of performance is good enough?

The off-site was conducted in Park City, Utah, and the outputs exceeded the Federal Division president's expectations. It seems that there was a correlation between the attractiveness of the off-site venue and the results.

The managers in attendance correctly decided that they don't have enough information to answer the large questions posed by the division president definitively, but that they could move forward and manage potential unintended consequences as risks. They wanted to implement improvements that will increase organizational performance in terms of cost, quality, and schedule, and they wanted those improvements also to move the division toward CMMI-DEV maturity level 5.

Brainstorming sessions in the off-site workshop yielded numerous candidate performance objectives, which the participants then evaluated using goal articulation criteria (Figure 1.9; initial candidate performance objectives evaluated using GAC show the initial list of candidate performance objectives).

The second candidate performance objective—improve communication—and the last candidate objective—improve employee morale—were dropped because of their low scores against the goal articulation criteria.

The remaining performance objectives were bucketed into two categories: organizational (the division) and project (the government contracts/accounts) levels. Figure 1.10 defines the performance objectives in their three categories. The managers worked to ensure that there was some alignment (balance) between the division-level performance objectives and the account/project level objectives:

- Project/account objectives **A** and **B** align with and support the achievement of division objective **2**.
- Project/account objective **C** aligns with and supports the achievement of division objective **4**.

The managers also recognized that progress toward division objective 3—automate performance measurement collection, analysis, and reporting—would probably have to be deferred until there was an incremental budget for technology investment.

The division president was so happy with the outputs of the workshop that she decided to give the team the afternoon of the third day off to go skiing or shopping, but she told the account managers that she expected them to have a defined strategy for achieving the objectives and defined performance measures by the end of the following month.

Goal Articulation Criteria	Improve Client Satisfaction with Service and Deliverables in All Projects	Improve Communication	Reduce Process Deployment and Maintenance Costs by 5% Per Year	Capture and Reuse the Knowledge and Learning of Our Employees; Reduce the Cost of Relearning and "Reinventing"	Reduce Average Product and Work Product Delivery Schedule by 10%	Improve Employee Morale
The goal supports the organization's strategy and vision	Yes	Yes	Yes	Yes	Yes	No
The goal is aligned with the organization's core business and core competency	Yes	No	Yes	Yes	Yes	No
The goal is achievable and neither unrealistic nor mediocre	Yes	No	Yes	Yes	Yes	Yes
There is a consensus understanding among the goal stake holders of the meaning of the words used to define the goal	Yes	Yes	Yes	Yes	Yes	No
Achievement of the goal is measurable and/or observable	Yes	Yes	Yes	Yes	Yes	Yes
Individuals in the organization have a personal stake in goal achievement	Yes	No	Yes	Yes	Yes	Yes
The goal is specific enough to deconstructed into plans for actions, tasks, projects, or jobs with defined start and end dates, and resources	Yes	No	Yes	Yes	Yes	No

Figure 1.9 Putting it into practice: initial candidate performance objectives evaluated using GAC.

Goal Articulation Criteria	Improve Client Satisfaction with Service and Deliverables in All Projects	Improve Communication	Reduce Process Deployment and Maintenance Costs by 5% Per Year	Capture and Reuse the Knowledge and Learning of Our Employees; Reduce the Cost of Relearning and "Reinventing"	Reduce Average Product and Work Product Delivery Schedule by 10%	Improve Employee Morale
The goal can be communicated, and can be easily articulated by every one in the organization	No	No	Yes	Yes	Yes	Yes
The goal identifies what must be accomplished and perhaps by but, not how	Yes	Yes	Yes	Yes	Yes	Yes
The goal can be prioritized with other goals	Yes	No	Yes	Yes	Yes	No
The business benefit(s) resulting from the goal's achievement can be identified and articulated	Yes	No	Yes	Yes	Yes	No
The products or deliverables that would result from goal achievement can be identified	Yes	No	Yes	Yes	Yes	No
Individual Goal Score Totals	11	4	12	12	12	5

Figure 1.9   *(Continued)*

ACC Federal Division 3-year performance objectives:
1. Improve client satisfaction with service and deliverables in all projects
2. Reduce process deployment and maintenance costs by 5% per year
3. Automate perfomance measurement collection, analysis, and reporting
4. Capture and reuse the knowledge and learning of our employees; reduce the cost of relearning and "reinventing"
5. Reduce average product and work product delivery schedule by 10%

Project/account performance objectives:
A. Reduce average process tailoring effort/cost by 10% per project
B. Reduce peer review and work product review iterations and duration
C. Capture and review lessons-learned in each phase (not at end of project)
D. Improve project communication (but reduce email and meetings)

Figure 1.10 Putting it into practice: ACC Federal Division performance objectives.

In the weeks after the off-site workshop, the account and department managers conducted several meetings to develop an improvement strategy. As they discussed the division and account/project objectives, it became clear that these objectives would have to be accomplished primarily through process improvement, rather than through changing the workforce (offshore labor) or technology. As a result, the managers decided to enlist the help of the division's engineering process group (EPG) to develop the strategy and plans for process improvement measures. See Chapter 2 for the continuation of this "putting it into practice" story.

Do's and Don'ts

Here is a summary list of things you should do and things you should not do when establishing performance objectives and measures.

Do

1. Question your current beliefs and assumptions about organizational performance.

2. Recognize that, in an organization, improvement comes from one or more of only three sources: people, technology, and process.
3. Remember that the only good reason to improve process is to improve performance.
4. Think about derivative effects and unintended consequences of implementing improvements.
5. Use Whyagnostics to get to the real performance objective.
6. Use criteria to evaluate and prioritize performance objectives.
7. Define, collect, and use only measures that indicate achievement of performance objectives.
8. Use a construct or a standard to define performance measures.
9. Plan and manage the establishment of performance objectives and measures as a project (projectize the work).

Don't

1. Initiate process improvement without understanding the expected effects on performance or without seeking an ROP.
2. Assume that the only way to achieve performance improvement is through process improvement.
3. Delegate establishing performance objectives or goals to subordinates.
4. Define measures that won't be used to determine goal achievement.

Reflect and Plan: What Did You Learn? What Will You Do?

Congratulations! You made it through the first chapter. But remember: Reading is learning, but it is not doing; you can't realize a positive return on your investment in reading until you apply the learning to your work. Use the information presented in this section as a mental checklist to think about and plan actions to implement your learning from this chapter.

What?

1. Does your organization already have performance improvement objectives? If so, what are they?
2. Does your organization already have process improvement objectives? If so, what are they?
3. Do the process improvement objectives clearly align with and support the organization's performance objectives?
4. What is the relationship between the performance objectives and changes in people (skills), technology, and process?
5. What, if any, performance measures are currently being collected?
6. How are those measures used to determine the achievement of performance objectives/goals?

Who?

1. Who are the people or which roles are best suited to establish the organization's improvement strategy or objectives?
2. Who are the right people or what are the right roles to determine the focus of an improvement (people, technology, or process)?
3. Who are the right people to determine the process improvements that need to be made to contribute to goal achievement?
4. Who are the right people to define performance measures?
5. Who should serve on the project team to establish (or update) performance objectives, process improvement objectives, and measures?

6. Who are the customers and stakeholders of the outputs of the project to establish objectives and measures?
7. Who will be accountable for demonstrating a positive ROP when the process improvements are implemented?

When and How Much?

1. What is the schedule for establishing (or updating) performance objectives and for defining performance measures?
2. In terms of the organization, what is the scope for the defined objectives and measures?
3. What are the resources—people and technology—that will be allocated to this project?

Endnotes

1. And here's a good time to talk about a phrase I use often in this book: "Definition is everything." In both my personal and professional lives, I have often been involved in (suckered into, more like it) very lengthy (and annoying and distressing and exhausting) discussions about the meaning of something. Many people will argue for hours, days, or forever on the meaning of something and, in the process, will introduce opinions, mental models, individual understanding or interpretation, nonfacts, unobservable observations, skewed information, and just plan false information. In all cases (100 percent), resolution of the differences or disagreements could have been achieved much more quickly and with less energy had the participants defined (written) the meanings of the words and phrases they were using to make their case and could have worked to achieve understanding prior to using those undefined words and phrases in their arguments.
2. Deming, W. Edwards, *The New Economics*, MIT Press, Cambridge, MA. 1993, Chapter 9. Dr. Lloyd S. Nelson invented this demonstration made popular by Dr. W. Edwards Deming. The aim of this experiment is to demonstrate the losses that are caused by "tampering": action on a system without action on the fundamental cause of a problem. A funnel is suspended

over a table. A target is marked and marbles are dropped through the funnel. Their final resting positions can be marked on the surface. Different rules of moving the funnel can be tried. The patterns of attempts to increase the accuracy of drops can be compared.

3. Davenport, Thomas H., *Process Innovation: Reengineering Work through Information Technology,* Harvard Business Review, Boston, 1992.
4. I was invited once to facilitate a workshop developed by my consulting firm called Effective Performance Measurement (EPM) to a now defunct group in NAVAIR then known as the NAVAIR Software and Systems Support Center (NSSC; don't know what happened to the third "S"). This was a team of people who supported NAVAIR management and engineering organizations with facilitation, Team Software Process (TSP) coaches, CMMI "experts," and organizational development. Part of the EPM workshop is to use defined criteria for developing performance objectives for a team. I guess I wasn't entertaining enough, because the client group didn't want me to give them the information about criteria to use in developing objectives; they just wanted to dive right into brainstorming the objectives. Among the "performance objectives" that came out of that session were statements such as, "We will not fear" and "We will have fun." Your tax dollars at rest.
5. Shapiro, Stephen. *Best Practices Are Stupid: 40 Ways to Out-Innovate the Competition,* Penguin Publishing, New York, 2011.
6. www.wiktionary.com
7. In three instances of organizations that achieved a CMMI maturity level, I had the opportunity to ask senior managers about the measurable or observable performance improvements they could correlate to the CMMI-based process improvement effort. In two of these three cases, the leadership could not articulate any business performance improvement associated with the maturity level.
8. Frazer, Mark, "Attracting Investment in Process Improvement through Strategic Positioning," SEPG Europe Conference presentation, Porto, Portugal, 2010.
9. From *The Balanced Scorecard—Measures That Drive Performance, Harvard Business Review on Managing Corporate Performance,* Kalpan Robert S. and David P. Norton, Harvard Business Review, MA, 1992.

10. Bogan, Christopher E. and, Michael J. English, *Benchmarking for Best Practices: Winning through Innovative Adaptation,* R. R. Donnelley & Sons Company, Chicago, 1994.
11. McFeeley, B., "IDEAL[SM]: A User's Guide for Software Process Improvement," Technical Report CMU/SEI-96-HB-001, Carnegie-Mellon University, February 1996, Pittsburgh, PA.

Chapter 2

Real Process Improvement

I hope that when companies start getting excited
again about process improvement, they resist one
method for doing so. A hybrid, combined approach
is really the only approach that makes any sense.
In religion many people worship only one god, but
in process management we should all be pantheists.

—Tom Davenport

What Do You Think? What Do You Believe?

Take a minute and answer the questions in Figure 2.1. Then,
once you've finished reading this chapter, complete the
section at the end ("Reflect and Plan: What Did You Learn?
What Will You Do?") to find out how much this information has helped you with your own process and performance
improvement work.

1. Process performance objectives:
   a. Should identify all the procedures that need to be updated
   b. Are aligned with and support business performance objectives
   c. Establish the date for achieving a CMMI maturity level
   d. Can be both qualitative and quantitative in nature
   e. B and D
   f. C
   g. All of the above
2. True or false: Process improvement only involves improving the organization's defined processes and adding things to the PAL.
   a. True
   b. False
3. Three proven ways to improve process performance are:
   a. Accelerate process performance
   b. Improve process performance efficacy
   c. _____
4. True or false: Senior management is the customer of the processes, so the processes and procedures should be defined to please them.
   a. True
   b. False
5. When using the CMMI for process improvement, performance improvement can be achieved at:
   a. Maturity level 2
   b. Maturity level 3
   c. Maturity level 4
   d. Maturity level 5

Figure 2.1   What do you think and what do you believe about real process improvement?

Establishing Process Performance Objectives

Chapter 1, "Real Performance Improvement," provides the organization guidance for establishing business performance objectives that are achievable and measurable (or at least observable). The focus in this section is to understand how to establish process performance objectives that, when achieved, will contribute to the achievement of the business performance objectives.

People like you and me, who have spent much of our professional lives in the process world, have a hard time coming to grips with the realization that process improvement by itself is not something we should do; we don't like the idea that process improvement should be subordinate to higher level purposes such as improving business performance. But the sooner you reconcile the place—a supporting role—of process work within the context of the rest of the working world, the better off you'll be.

Many organizations that believe they are implementing a balanced score card (BSC) simply try to figure out all the measures that need to be reported against the objectives, and then force-fit those measures into the wide variety of work performed by different divisions or departments. This rarely works very well because if you're a manager of a division, unit, or team and you're told to report certain measures, you're going to find a way to do so even if the work of your unit doesn't naturally produce those measures.

One powerful concept of balanced score cards (a la Kaplan and Norton) that is frequently overlooked is the idea of the cascading strategy. When the organization's strategy—and the performance objectives aligned with those strategies—are thoughtfully cascaded from the top of the organization to the bottom, the lower divisions and units have a say in whether or not their units can even contribute to the performance objectives and, if so, how.

A Story of an Unbalanced Scorecard

For the sake of illustrating this situation, let's use, for example, a typical product development company. As with many companies, it is internally organized by various functional departments such as Marketing and Sales, Finance and Accounting, Human Resources, Engineering, Service and Support, Operations/IT, and Purchasing. I am the CEO and, along with other executives, have come up with our 3-year strategy and the organizational performance objectives for achieving the strategy. One of the performance objectives is to "offer customers the most feature-rich product for the best price." No one challenges me or the other execs on this goal (see "Getting to the Real Performance Objective" in Chapter 1.) One day I hear about this thing called a "balanced score card." Without much reading or investigation, I decide that a BSC is the "silver bullet" to achieving all the corporate objectives, so I mandate that all departments tell me how they are going to achieve "the most feature-rich product for the best price" and report measures against that objective every month. After issuing the edict, my attention quickly turns—as it often does—to the next thing to keep the Board happy.

There are two dimensions to this goal of offering the most feature-rich product for the best price: (1) increasing the features per product offering or release, and (2) driving down the price customers pay for the product. Some of the departments can contribute to the second dimension of the objective— driving down the price (by driving down the per-unit or per-feature cost), but only engineering can really significantly contribute to the "feature-rich" dimension of the objective. Additionally, if neither the executives nor the departments are mindful of the law of unintended consequences, a department's "contributions" to the objective could actually diminish or even prevent the cumulative achievement of the objective by the whole organization. Table 2.1 identifies the dimension of the performance objective to which each department

Table 2.1 Analysis of a Mandated Performance Objective That Isn't Thoroughly Thought Out

Department	Performance Objective Dimension Contribution	Possible Unintended Consequences
Sales/Marketing	None	
Finance and Accounting	None	
Human Resources	Lower product price	HR can find and outsource work to lower labor cost. However, lower cost engineering labor may not have the capability to increase feature richness.
Engineering	Lower product price Increase feature richness	Pressure to integrate more features into a product release could increase defect density and defect removal, driving up the product cost and thus price (or reduce margin).
Service/Support	None	Support for more feature-rich products could drive up product cost and thus price (or reduce margin).
Operations/IT	Lower product cost	
Purchasing	Lower product cost	Acquisition of lower cost materials could lower product and price, but lower quality materials could cause more defects, which would drive up product cost/price.

realistically can contribute, and how, and it also identifies potential unintended consequences that could work against achievement of the objective.

Look at the conflicts and contradictions I have inadvertently set in motion—with the best of intentions—by mandating that all my departments implement improvements toward achieving the objective of offering customers the most feature-rich product for the best price, and reporting measures against the achievement of that objective. The people in Sales and Marketing, Finance and Accounting, and Service/Support cannot have good effects toward objective achievement, but they'll try to do something because they want to please the boss. They'll ultimately fail, but it was really I, their leader, who failed them. Human Resources will find lower cost labor and report those cost improvements, but who will measure the potentially diminished engineering capability resulting from the lower cost labor? Purchasing will proudly report cost reduction in parts and materials, but who will measure the potentially corresponding and offsetting increase in cost resulting from defective materials and components?

The problem is that I cascaded an organizational performance objective without thinking systemically and without balancing the contributions toward the objective and designing the performance measures accordingly.

As it turns out, the only department I should have reasonably levied the objective on was engineering. They can improve their product development tools and processes—using many available methods and approaches—to produce more features in a product release using current labor resources (no corresponding increase in cost) and to produce the same or better quality. And because the product development processes are almost wholly owned by engineering, they can design the appropriate measures needed to determine achievement of the objective and the effects of any unintended consequences.

One of your qualities as a leader is thinking your actions and decisions all the way through to their conclusions, and realizing all the possible consequences. It's not that you don't take risks; rather, it's just that you've learned to manage and mitigate the effects of unintended consequences. You do this by thinking holistically or systemically. In improvement initiatives, you need to realize that everyone in every functional role will want to contribute to your requests; they want to be noticed and recognized. If you know that an individual or team cannot possibly contribute to the achievement of one of your objectives, let them know that up front and find ways to recognize them for the contributions they make to other aspects of the organization's viability.

From the Strategy to the Performance Objective to the Process Performance Objective

In his book on process innovation,[1] Thomas Davenport defines five activities to develop a process vision:

1. Assess existing business strategy for process direction
2. Consult with process customers for performance objectives
3. Benchmark for process performance targets and examples of innovation
4. Formulate process performance objectives
5. Develop specific process attributes

Davenport's advice is mostly as valid and insightful now as it was in 1993, but the business of process improvement has learned a few lessons since then, which enables me to elaborate and refine Davenport's work.

Strategic Process Alignment

In an SEPG (software process engineering group) conference presentation,[2] Mark Frazer, then director of corporate strategy at Welch Allyn, recognized that executives don't really pay attention to process improvement (a "how"); rather, they pay attention to business performance results (the "why"). Frazer also provided some sound reasons for aligning process improvement with the organization's strategies, primarily because

- Process improvement is usually a long-term investment, and the achievement of a strategy also usually takes a long time.
- There is a lag between the investment in process improvement and realizing the return on that investment, just as there is with a strategy.
- The leadership of an organization can and frequently does change. One leader might support process improvement, but her successor might be opposed to it. Strategies, however—especially those strategies sponsored by the shareholders or driven by the customers or market base—can survive changes in leadership.

Performance Objective Process Alignment

In Chapter 1, this book addressed how to develop business performance objectives. That chapter and, specifically, Table 1.1 also provide guidance on how to determine in which dimension—people, process, or technology—to focus an improvement initiative. So, at this point in the book we have figured out why we want to align process improvement with a strategy, and we have defined business performance objectives. In Davenport's five key activities, we have mostly completed the first activity. Now it's time to define the process performance objective.

Note use of the phrase "process performance objective" instead of the simpler "process objective." This is intentional because—as previously articulated—it is the performance of process that affects business performance, irrespective of how processes are defined or even if they are defined.

Davenport suggests ways to define a process vision because his book is thematically aimed toward very large-scale, technology-driven process changes. In defining a process performance objective, I have found it useful to be tool or technology agnostic; in other words, how can I improve the way work is performed irrespective of the technology?

From the business performance objective, we can easily narrow down the short list of processes we need to change in terms of performance. Table 2.2 identifies some sample performance objectives and the corresponding processes that are candidates for improvement.

As a manager, you are either the critical point of success or the critical point of failure in establishing and maintaining a strong linkage between performance objectives and process improvement work. It is your job constantly to question the process improvements proposed by your staff to verify that the improvement can reasonably be expected to yield results that will align with and support the organization's performance objectives.

Table 2.2 Sample Performance Objectives and Candidate Processes for Improvement

Sample Business Performance Objective	Candidate Processes Performance Improvement
Deliver customer fixes and enhancement requests faster	Requirements development process Project scope management process Product design and development processes Product release and delivery process
Reduce call-to-closure service request lapsed time by 20 percent	Help-desk processes Call transfer and escalation processes Call record capture processes and tools
Reduce the cost of learning (COL) by 10 percent per year	Lessons-learned process Lessons-learned capture and access process Training acquisition and delivery process
Increase name and brand recognition by one million customer potentiates per year	Content management process Employee brand promulgation process Media content development and delivery process
Reduce carbon emissions by 15 percent per year	Energy consumption policy and process Carbon recovery processes Remote work policy and processes

Understanding Defined Process versus Performed Process

It happens almost everywhere and almost all the time: In the name of "process improvement," a team is formed and they immediately begin writing process and procedure documents. (Read more on this topic in "Process Design and Development" in Chapter 5, "Improving Process Improvement.") The processes and procedures usually read like an extrapolation of the practices in the CMMI (capability maturity model integration) or the standards in ISO 9001 or AS9100. When these improvement teams—usually called an engineering process group (EPG) or software engineering process group (SEPG)—have filled several 3-inch binders with paper, they celebrate their success in having "improved" the process. Have they really?

At best, creating or updating your written processes and procedures has improved the defined process, but you haven't necessarily had any effect on the performed process (next section).

This idea that you have improved your processes simply by defining your processes—writing them down in a way that mirrors a model or standard—is replete with logical fallacies, but the primary two are

1. Performance improvement is achieved by improving process performance, not necessarily process definition. You could define what appears on paper (or on your display) to be the most efficient and effective processes the world has seen, but how have you improved performance if no one in the organization follows or uses those defined processes, or if people perform the processes differently than the way they are defined? If you can demonstrate some fidelity between the performance of your processes and their physical representation, then and only then can

you legitimately make a connection between improving the defined processes and resulting business performance improvement.

2. Even if we could correlate performance improvement to improving the defined processes, how does creating processes that simply meet the intent of CMMI practices or International Organization for Standardization (ISO) or Aerospace Standards (AS) standards make them effective and efficient? The CMMI practice or ISO or AS standard is nothing more than an academic abstraction of something someone once thought was a good thing to do. Does that make it the "high bar" for performance? People often refer to the practices in the CMMI as "best practices." But to paraphrase Stephen Shapiro, author of *Best Practices Are Stupid,* calling something a best practice is like saying a giraffe has the best neck in the world. It's not necessarily the best neck in the world—it's just the best neck for the giraffe.

Also, if people still believe that both the defined and the performed processes have a positive effect on business performance, why aren't they asking themselves the obvious question: Which of the two—defined processes or performed processes—has the greater positive effect on project or organizational business performance? If we investigated this question, and if it turned out that it is only the performed processes that have an effect on business performance, irrespective of how the processes are defined (or even whether they are defined), then why would people focus so much energy on creating or changing their defined processes?

That is not to say there are not valid business reasons for improving the defined process, but all improvement of the defined process should be for the sole purpose of improving the performance of those processes and, consequently, improving business performance.

If you're on the team in your organization that is responsible for process improvement (e.g., an EPG or SEPG), it is critical that before you start doing anything, you and your colleagues understand what you're talking about when you use the phrase "process improvement." You will need to communicate clearly to stakeholders and your bosses whether your team is improving the defined processes, the performed processes, or both, and the level of fidelity between the two. (Also see "Synchronizing the Defined and Performed Processes" in this chapter.)

Improving the Performed Process

Based on the argument presented in the previous section, this section addresses approaches to improving the performed process. As with business performance, in looking at process performance it is more important first to start thinking about what needs to be improved and why before figuring out how to make the improvement.

With process performance, the major performance characteristics that can be improved are

■ Speed (or efficiency)
■ Efficacy
■ Output or results quality

Notice that there is no mention of "compliance" as a performance characteristic. That is because causing process performance to be in compliance with a standard or a model can increase performance or decrease performance, but there is no compliance measure that can be used as an indicator of having improved process performance.

Accelerating Process Performance

Process performance speed is, at its core, a very simple concept: How fast is the process performed? Improving process performance speed means: Can we make a change that will enable us to perform the process faster?

Speeding up the process often involves automating some or all aspects of process performance with technology. A Ford Focus makes it through the assembly line process a lot faster than did a Model T for many reasons, but primarily due to how much faster software-driven robots can assemble cars than can humans. There is nothing wrong with speeding up a process with automation through the application of technology, but doing so without first speeding up the process itself can inadvertently hide inefficiencies in the process. Technology may be able to execute an unnecessary task faster than a human can, but it's still an unnecessary task.

Increasing the speed of process performance is a tricky thing because just focusing on and affecting process performance speed is rife with risk and unintended consequences. As it turns out, faster sometimes becomes slower, and slower sometimes becomes faster. If performing process tasks or steps faster introduces defects or errors (i.e., waste), which then later requires rework to remove or correct, we may have inadvertently slowed the overall process performance.

There could also be an unintended net-zero effect on speed. If I accelerate the performance of subprocess A, but subsequent subprocess B cannot use the outputs of subprocess A any faster, then I have invested in process improvement, but have not had a positive net effect on overall process improvement; my return on process (ROP) is negative.

There are a number of ways to increase process performance speed, including:

1. Reduce the number of tasks or steps
2. Reduce lag time or wait states between tasks
3. Perform tasks in parallel or concurrently

Reducing Process Performance Tasks

It's ironic that with all the methods available to us to reduce the number of tasks in a process, so many organizations embark on "improvement" initiatives that end up adding tasks to a process, often making their processes less efficient, not more efficient. This behavior is commonly driven by enslavement to being compliant with a model or standard: "If we're not doing a practice in the CMMI, then we have to add a task or process to make sure we do so."

Probably the most common approach to reducing the number of tasks in a process or subprocess is value stream mapping (VSM). In the VSM technique, a process or subprocess is decomposed into its lowest level tasks—tasks that cannot be further decomposed. Each task is then evaluated for "value"—typically, value to the organization, value to the customer, value to the process, or value to the product. Tasks that do not add value to the organization, the customer, the process, or the product are eliminated.

The success of VSM, of course, is highly dependent upon the participants in a VSM session to have a shared perception of what constitutes "value." I am human; therefore, I am biased. If a particular task is what I do for a paycheck, then I'm probably going to declare that its performance has value to the organization.

Many organizations, especially those operating in the defense contracting or government sectors of the economy, often find themselves in an inescapable trap between efficiency and compliance. The government or the Department of Defense (DoD) wants them to maintain some form of standard registration (ISO 9001 or AS9100), or a CMMI maturity level. The government also wants its contractors to deliver products and services as efficiently as possible. For the contractor, this is a paradox; for the taxpayer, this is a money incinerator. The defense contractor must maintain a CMMI maturity level in order to bid on defense contracts; the choice is to maintain CMMI compliance or go out of business. The contractor feels compelled to add a task to its configuration management (CM) process to conduct configuration audits (CMMI-DEV CM SP 3.2). So the contractor adds the task to conduct configuration audits into its process. But the contractor provides products to the Navy—specifically, Naval Air Systems Command (NAVAIR)—and according to NAVAIR's Airspeed program,[3] the contractor also is required to implement Lean initiatives vis-à-vis Six Sigma. So a team forms to conduct value stream mapping on the processes and, lo and behold, when they evaluate the configuration management process, they determine that the task to conduct configuration audits does not add value to anything or anyone. In fact, what is found in the VSM evaluation is the same thing that is "discovered" in lots of organizations: The CM systems perform the digital equivalent of integrity and configuration audits constantly, 24/7—no human intervention needed or desired.

Reducing Process Performance Lag or Wait States

Another way to accelerate process performance is to reduce the number and size of process performance lag or wait states, which I describe as intervals of time or states in which work is not being performed, but should be.

The best current methods for addressing process performance lag or wait states can be found in the volumes of literature on Lean and Six Sigma, and there is essentially no reason to try to repeat or even summarize that body of knowledge here.

The concept that is important to understand is that if you can reduce or eliminate situations or conditions in the performance of a process in which someone or something has to idle (do nothing) while waiting for something else to happen, then you can accelerate process performance. Alternatively, if you can fill a lag or wait state with work, even if it is not in-line work—work directly related to the previous or subsequent tasks, but still work within the overall process—then you have also accelerated process performance.

Working or waiting is binary; there is no null or zero state in which you are neither idling nor working, or idling and working at the same time. So if waiting is a –1 and working is a +1, then whenever an organization converts waiting to working, it's a +2 gain.

Parallel Process Performance

Parallel process performance is perhaps one of my favorite topics, and it has a strong connection to improving the defined process (see "Improving the Defined Process" in this chapter). In most product development and service delivery organizations, there are many processes that can be performed in parallel but often are not because they are represented as serial or sequential. And the reason they are represented as serial or sequential is usually because so many process systems employ last century's information representation: text-based narrative. As Philip Armour correctly noted in *The Laws of Software Process*,[4] textual notation, by its immutable nature, can only define ideas or tasks serially. One word has to follow another, one sentence has to follow another sentence, one paragraph follows another; there is no way truly to represent parallel process performance using text. You can write: "Perform the tasks in this section in parallel with the tasks in the next section," but first the agent or performer of the process must serially read the two sections and then (hopefully) remember that they can be performed in parallel.

Imagine a process for developing a project plan. The process calls for building multiple subordinate plans— effort and cost estimates (or spending plan), schedule, resource plan, stakeholder involvement plan, configuration management plan, quality assurance plan, product integration plan, test plan, etc.—and then integrating all those multiple subordinate plans into the project plan. Even though the project manager may be ultimately responsible for developing the project plan, she very likely assigns other project team members or support teams to develop the individual subordinate plans for which they have subject matter expertise, coordinates reviews of the subplans, and then integrates all the planning information into a single document or a web page. The process, represented in text as usual, takes 2 weeks when performed as defined, serially. However, when the process is performed in parallel—all the subordinate plans developed by different individuals and teams almost concurrently—the process takes 1 week: a 50 percent schedule savings. Note that it's probably not an effort or cost savings, but we have accelerated the schedule (clock time) for performing the process. In Figure 2.2, a portion of the project planning process is depicted. The solid line connectors depict tasks that are performed sequentially, and the dashed line connectors depict the tasks that can be performed in parallel, a process representation that is extremely difficult to describe in textual notation.

Process Representation

Of the three types of process performance improvement, speed is most closely related to how the defined processes are represented. The provable, observable fact is that performing text-based narrative is slower than performing graphically oriented instructions. A text-based narrative process description essentially inherently creates process performance inefficiencies (depicted in Figure 2.3).

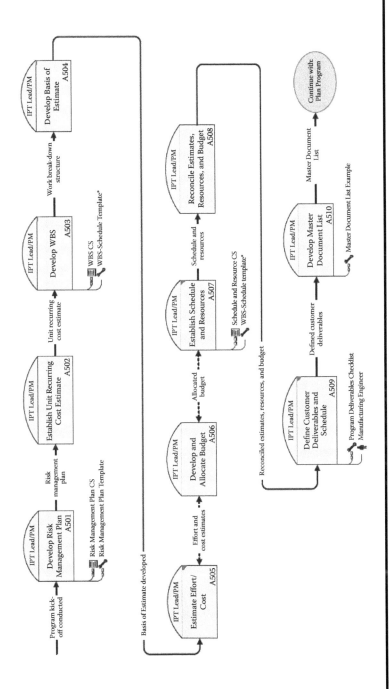

Figure 2.2 Sample project planning process graphically depicting parallel process performance.

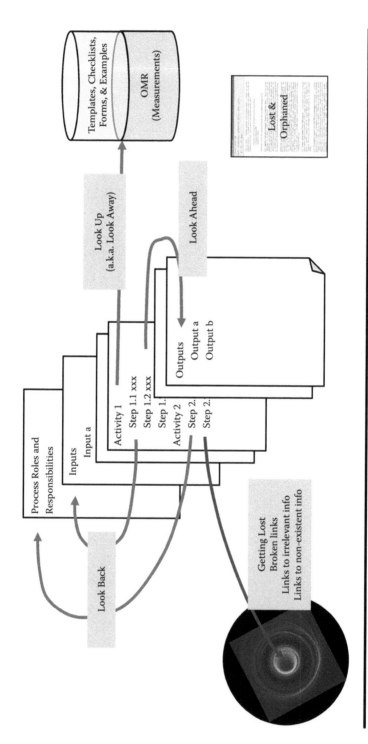

Figure 2.3 Process performance inefficiencies inherent in text-based narrative process descriptions.

Let's say you start reading a 35-page process description for creating a software design document. By the time you get to page 10, which defines the activities and steps, you've forgotten the roles and responsibilities and have to flip pages (or scroll) back to the beginning of the document to refresh your memory (look back). Or, the activities/steps reference outputs that you have to flip/scroll forward to in order to familiarize yourself with the outputs and how each one relates to an activity/step (look ahead). Then, right in the middle of the activity/steps descriptions, there is a reference to a template you're supposed to use, but you have to leave the document to locate it in a repository (look up or look away). Some links to assets or referential information are broken and either take you nowhere or take you to the wrong item (getting lost). Much to your frustration, the intuitive navigation techniques that you're accustomed to (e.g., back (←) and forward (→) buttons) don't work in all systems.

Also, it is always awkward—and mostly impossible—to use textual narrative to compel parallel or concurrent process performance, the third way to accelerate process performance. These process performance efficiencies slow down process performance. So, you might find out that one of the most effective ways to accelerate process performance is to change the way the defined processes are represented.

Sentiment Can Ruin Efficiency

I fly a lot, and I am a lifelong loyal customer of Delta, indicated by my many years as a Platinum Medallion flier. I love Delta, so it pains me to point out to them the sweet but thoughtless practice performed—and I suspect, institutionalized—by their flight attendants every day. Although Delta has made dramatic improvements in on-time arrivals, stuff like weather happens, and sometimes flights are very late—way behind schedule. When this happens, the flight attendants will inevitably make an announcement during taxiing to the gate about passengers with "tight connections" (imagine figuring that phrase out if you don't speak English), and they will plead with all of us to stay seated and let those with "tight connections" get up and run like hell for their next flight. The spiel goes something like this:

> If X (the airport at which we are arriving) is your final destination (oh God, please don't let Grand Junction ever be my FINAL destination!), we would appreciate it if you would stay seated and let those passengers with tight connections get off the plane and have a chance to make their connections. We're certain that someday you'll want them to return the favor.

This never works. The airplane comes to a stop at the gate and the "ding" bell sounds for people to stand up, gather their things, and move into the aisle. And then, those flight attendants, whom I'm sure have been told to make that sweet, thoughtless announcement, get busy doing other things and don't notice that this tactic *never works!*

Why? Because, statistically, and depending on the equipment, one-half to two-thirds of those passengers with tight connections are sitting either in a middle seat or a window seat. They can't get up without all of us "final-destinators" also standing up to let them into the aisle. Then we're in the aisle and still between them and the exit door. Did I mention: *This never works!*

Why are the passengers in the middle and window seats the travelers late for their connections? Because, in general, the more experienced fliers are in the aisle seats because they go to seatguru.com and know how to select their seats online; they know airports and the transfer time between concourses and thus know how long they need for a connection when they book the flight.

What would be far more effective in speeding up the deplaning process would be if the flight attendant would announce:

> Because we're late, a bunch of you have to run for it. We'd like the rest of you to run also, at least to the top of the jet-way. You've been sitting for 3 hours, and you need the exercise. Move it!

Then, when the get-up-and-run "ding" sounds, they need to play will.i.am's "I Like to Move It" really loudly over the PA system. That would work much better.

The status reports and the monthly program reviews are never going to tell you what's really going on in the organization; they're only going to give you the good news that your subordinates think you want to hear. You could be the captain of a ship with a 20 by 10 foot gash in the bottom of the hull, but by the time the message gets up to you on the bridge, it's a humidity problem.

Get out there! Go be the product going through development. Go be the customer making a request of your organization. Go live one day in the life of one of your workers. Go be "Undercover Boss," and you will find out what is really going on.

Simply following the rules or the process can expedite situations. How many times have you driven to a four-way stop and had two or three drivers sit there and just look at each other or wave for another driver to proceed. On the surface, the driver who arrived first but wants to wave others through the intersection seems like he's being courteous. But those of us who actually read the rules on right-of-way don't trust the waving driver, and we're going to stick to the rules because doing so won't necessarily keep us out of accidents, but it may help us from being charged with the fault. The rules pretty much obviate the need for courtesy, which, although much needed in society these days, has more function and provides more efficiency at a party than it does at a four-way stop; rules are better for driving.

Improving Process Performance Efficacy

In everyday language, "efficacy," as it relates to process performance, is making every action count and adding value toward the end deliverables of the process. If an action doesn't result in the creation of a work product or the change of state of a work product (note that "change of state" can include being observed, measured, or monitored), then the action has resulted in nothing; there has been no effect and therefore no efficacy.

Reasons why an action isn't effective vary, but there are three common reasons:

1. The process is not defined or represented in a way that makes it clear what people are supposed to do and what those actions should yield.
2. People perform processes, procedures, or tasks that do not result in the creation of a work product or the change of state to a work product.
3. The process was developed and deployed in an organizational culture in which activity equals work, and the pervasive attitude is that if people are busy and doing

things—meeting, talking, looking up stuff on the web, traveling to a meeting, texting people, etc.—then work is being performed when it really is not.

In improving process performance efficacy, it's much easier to address the first two causes. (Addressing the third cause warrants its own book, but I partially address it in 'Activity is Not Work' in Chapter 4, "Small changes, Big performance Improvement.") solution to addressing process ineffectiveness reasons 1 and 2 lies in process definition and how process is structured or represented. Assuming that individuals and teams are performing the processes as they are defined (see "Synchronizing the Defined and Performed Processes" in this chapter), then the cause of ineffective process performance might be how "process" is structured and represented. Figure 2.4 shows two different representations of the same task.

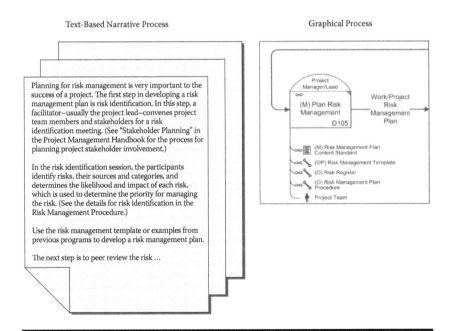

Figure 2.4   Two sample representations of developing a risk management plan.

In the first example, the task of developing a risk management plan addresses a lot of information about risk management planning that some process performers will find useful but many others will find not useful and even distracting. Why? Because much of the information in the narrative representation might be informative, but not executable—it doesn't really compel anyone to *do* something. It's challenging to cull from the text the imperatives versus the informative. Reading and learning aren't bad activities in which to engage, but they are not *doing*.

In the graphical representation, people who have been trained to understand the meaning of the simple symbolism know that this task compels the project manager to develop a risk management plan, and the output of performing that task is a risk management plan. The syntax of the task is: *Agent role* (project manager) performs *imperative verb* (develop) to create *object of the verb* (risk management plan). There is no ambiguity in what action must be performed, by whom, or the result of the action. Note there are assets linked to the graphical task for developing the risk management plan that provide enabling "how-to" assets exactly where they are needed, with no cross-references to go look in other locations for the things needed to perform this task.

Thus, there are two places to look for and address process ineffectiveness: (1) in the defined process, and (2) in the performed process. You can examine the organization's defined process and, as you do so, ask and answer these questions:

1. Is it clear and unambiguous what action is being compelled?
2. Is it clear and unambiguous who (which functional role) is supposed to perform the action?
3. Is the result of performing the action—the creation of a work product or the change of state to a work product—clear and unambiguous?

4. Is performing the action necessary? Is the reason for performing the action—the value—obvious, intuitive, or otherwise clearly expressed?

My advice in examining defined processes as prescribed before is that you have people other than the authors/developers of the defined processes perform this examination. The process authors/developers are inherently prejudiced because it's very difficult for a person to be critical of his or her work. If I'm trying to examine a process that I developed, my mind will fill in understanding for the preceding questions just as it did when I was creating the processes. I won't apply the same scrutiny that others will. Ideally, use people who have to perform the processes to examine them and ask and answer the efficacy questions.

When the performed process for efficacy is examined, efficacy questions 1 and 2 are not so important; the fact that the process is being performed indicates that the performers know which action is supposed to be performed and by whom. However, efficacy questions 3 and 4 are still important:

1. Is there a physical outcome of performing each and every action—the creation of a work product or the change of state of a work product? If not, then
2. Why is performing the action necessary? What value does it add to project or organizational performance, the product or service, the process, or to the customer?

Even in the organizational culture with the pervasive attitude that activity equals work, a true leader

with the courage of conviction and the mind for
improvement will make it clear to the workforce
and to her own colleagues that everything called
"work" will result in an output, and that activities not resulting in an output will not be called
"work." Think about it...even a meeting should
result in documented minutes, decisions, and
action items; even online research should result
in documented findings and observations; even a
text to a colleague should result in documented
input on something you're thinking about or trying
to decide. Why should any activity that you or
someone who works for you is charging for result
in nothing?

Improving Process Performance Output and Results Quality

If we subscribe to the argument presented in the previous section that every performed task or activity should count toward
creating a work product or changing the state of a work
product (i.e., add value), then we can logically conclude that
another way to improve the performed process is to ensure
that process performance increases the quality of the process outputs. Process performance provides two approaches
for improving output quality, as defined in the following two
subsections.

Before an organization—specifically, its leaders—initiates
effort to improve process performance to improve the quality of outputs, it must first decide what the acceptable level
of quality for its products or services is, beyond which
there is no appreciable effect on business performance. In
other words, what level of quality is "good enough"? Then,
in order to reap a positive ROP, the organization must estimate the cost of the process improvement for quality and

compare that with the estimated business performance benefits from the improvement to establish a business case for the improvement that answers the question, "Will it be worth it?"

Preventive Quality Process Improvement

In plain language, preventive quality improvement is ensuring that the work performed produces exactly the desired outputs at exactly the desired quality; in other words, work is performed in such a way that it does not create or introduce errors or defects. Preventive quality improvement can also include process performance that reduces the impact or cost of a defect downstream in the process.

To illustrate the concept of "produces exactly the desired outputs at exactly the desired quality," I'll use a chemical process analogy. I can predict with some degree of certainty that if, in the context of our current three-dimensional understanding of the universe, I combine hydrogen with oxygen via combustion, the resulting output will be water that meets my quality standard for water: H_2O.

As it turns out, the business of service delivery or product realization is somewhat more complex than even the most complex chemical reactions. If I integrate or compile software components in the same integration environment in which they were last integrated and if none of the software components were changed since I last integrated them, then I can reasonably expect the same integration output. Nice analogy, but no one sells software products that don't have new features or functionality introduced since the last release. So if I introduce a change, either in the integration sequence or environment or in one of the integrated units, and if I didn't understand all the components and their relationships in design and development, then I cannot accurately predict the quality of the integration results. Nature was perfect with the simple design for water, but our human endeavors and our technology are prone to error and lapses in understanding. Preventive quality improvement may be one of the best arguments for consistency. Remember that the pursuit of consistency for its own sake is an immature view of process improvement, and we're better than that. However, consistent process performance can provide a statistically viable sample of process performance data, which can be used to identify process performance improvements and then to implement those improvements.

Let's use a simple product development example to illustrate preventive quality improvement.

An Example of Preventive Quality Process Improvement

My organization develops software applications for a county government. We were awarded the contract based on several criteria, but one major factor was that we were CMMI-DEV maturity level 3.

Among the many things we must do in our software development projects is establish and maintain requirements traceability (REQM SP 1.4), which is a good practice that we would always do even if it weren't in the CMMI. We use dynamic object-oriented requirements system (DOORS) to maintain traceability between customer requirements and derived software requirements, hardware requirements (which a different organization implements), design specification, the software module or object, and test cases.

Even though our applications usually make it through our own system testing with very few defects, we often get a lot of trouble tickets right after the application is released to the customer. After some investigation, we realize that most of the problems are related to the customer not using the application in the same version of the operating system (OS) in which we built the product. Our product transition and implementation team tries to ensure the customers are always on the same versions of operating systems as our product but, as with most customers, we can't force them to comply. When a customer reports a problem with the application, there is a high cost to address the trouble ticket. The most costly activities are

- Collecting configuration information from the customer
- Analyzing the problem to determine if it's an operating system mismatch or some other cause
- Managing and reporting status on the problem from submission to closure
- Helping the customer upgrade his or her OS and then reinstalling the application (if the problem is a retro-grade OS)

The cost of taking customer support actions to resolve their problems was high, about $600 per call in labor, and we were averaging four such calls per week. In addition to the product support cost, our organization suffers a growing customer satisfaction problem because the customer per-ceives our applications to be defective.

In collaboration with the customer's leadership, we implement several process improvements to address this situation. First, we negotiate with the customer that we will support two versions of the operating system: the most current version and the prior version. In reciprocation, the customer agrees to enforce a policy among its workers that they will always accept updates to their workstations' operating system, so long as there are not more than six OS upgrades per year. We will also update our require-ments traceability matrix (RTM) to trace product features and fixes to specific versions of the operating system. This will ensure that we run test cases on the two then-currently supported OS versions prior to release to the customer. Finally, we agree to add software to our application's install shield to check the workstation's OS version and suggest to the user first to upgrade it if it is not current or supported. Note this last improvement is a technology improvement, not a process improvement, so it doesn't count toward the ROP.

The nonrecurring cost of implementing the preventive quality improvements, not counting the install shield tech-nology improvement, was about $4,000, and the recurring cost—incremental effort per release—is $200 per release. Since we were spending but are now saving (not spending) about $9,600 per month in resolving services calls related to this issue, the improvement more than paid for itself in the first month of implementation, and the ROP was positive thereafter. Additionally, our latest customer satisfaction survey results are indicating an upward trend in satisfaction, particularly with the quality of our applications. This is particularly important since we are approaching contract renewal.

One could make the argument that the preventive quality process improvement described here was really corrective, that what the organization really did was correct its mistake for not addressing operating systems in the product's release requirements in the first place. To that charge I plead no contest; it's a valid point. But no one and no organization ever gets everything right the first time, and the value of being smarter today than yesterday is realized only if that knowledge is applied.

Corrective Quality Process Improvement

Corrective quality improvement through process improvement is essentially finding and removing defects at the point of the best value cost-to-benefit ratio (lowest cost to highest benefit). In product development, improving corrective quality improvement is usually achieved by improving peer review or inspection processes, or by improving testing processes. In service, corrective quality improvement is achieved by correcting a service issue so that it doesn't grow in magnitude or get escalated further.

My favorite quality process improvement is peer reviews or inspections, especially when they are focused on early life cycle (product development or service) detection and removal of defects or issues. If you take away nothing else from this book, then take away the idea that carefully planned and well executed peer reviews are probably the best return on process you can get.

When Peer Reviews Yield a Positive ROP

Peer reviews and inspections can yield a high, positive ROP when

- They are carefully planned using historical peer review measures to focus the reviews on the right work products at the right point in the product or service life cycle.
- There is a defined standard or basis for identifying defects or issues.
- Only people with expertise—true peers—are involved in the review or inspection.
- The work product being reviewed, and the standard against which it is to be evaluated, are provided to the reviewers some time in advance of an inspection or review meeting (if one is held).

When Peer Reviews Might Not Yield a Positive ROP

I have witnessed some very good implementations of peer reviews, as well as some very poor implementations. Poor implementations of peer reviews that are more likely to yield a negative ROP than a positive one have one or more of these characteristics:

- The organization mindlessly peer reviews everything, throwing effort and thus cost at peer reviews without giving thought to or collecting measures that define the payback.
- The role of "peer" is assumed but not defined in terms of knowledge, skill, or experience, so peer reviews involve people who cannot contribute to improving the work product being reviewed.
- The organization has not defined standards for each work product or type of work product that is peer reviewed, so peer reviews focus on non-content-related "defects" such as typographical errors, punctuation, format, word choice, and style—findings that will have relatively low impact on the overall quality of the work product.

Simultaneous Corrective and Preventive Process Quality Improvement—A Real-World Example

My wonderful neighbor and friend, Chris Hammaway, is sales and marketing director for the Montage Resort in Deer Valley, California. If you're not familiar with Montage—as I wasn't—it's probably because it's a very high-end resort for people with a lot more money than most of us have. It is known for excellent quality accommodation and guest service, and it is the choice for many celebrities and dignitaries.

Soon after meeting Chris and his wonderful wife, Jennifer, they invited us to dinner at the Montage. It was winter, and we checked our coats at the entrance to the restaurant, Apex. After a truly fine dinner, we handed our coat-check tags to the seating host to retrieve our coats, but the coats that were brought back were not ours.

I looked at the cheesy tag for just a few seconds, which Chris instantly noticed, and asked to see it. It was a cheap cardboard circle with handwritten numbers, with a different number on each side!

Chris immediately addressed the situation, with great professional aplomb and grace. He asked the restaurant manager to order some quality coat tags that represent the Montage brand, and that was the end of it. Now the tags are beautifully etched and stained wood rounds with the number on one side and the Montage symbol on the other; no more tags bearing two different numbers. In an instant, Chris corrected a quality issue, but it wasn't just a one-off correction; it was also an action that would prevent the quality issue from recurring...ever!

Imagine how much that one simple act paid forward for Montage. If you're someone who is paying $1,500 or more per night for a room and dropping close to a grand for four people to have dinner, you're going to be disappointed having someone else's coat brought to you or your dining partner. It might not drive you over to the St. Regis, but then again it just might.

If your organization is going to be known for quality, then quality has to be persistent and omnipresent; it has to be apparent in everything said, done, and shown in your organization. Chris's simple, professional, corrective and preventive action saved effort and money, maintained customer loyalty, and protected the Montage brand. THAT is real process improvement.

Improving the Defined Process

Process engineer: Read this before doing **anything!** It is very likely that you have been hired into a position that your manager and you believe involves defining processes and procedures. Your boss is going to tell you that the work of process improvement is defining (writing) processes and procedures, and I'm going to tell you that you should first focus on the performed process instead of the defined process. Who are you going to listen to...the author of a book or the person who controls your paycheck? If I were you, it would be the person who controls my paycheck. So since I'm not going to influence your priorities and since you're going to start down the path of creating or revising your organization's defined processes, at least get that part of your job approximately right and pay close attention to the concepts in this section. If you learn from another's lessons, that makes you the smart one.

Having improved the performed process (previous section), an organization may want to ensure that its defined processes accurately portray the performed processes. There are many good reasons for having fidelity between defined and performed processes; the major reasons are

- If the defined process and the performed process are not synchronized with each other, people can change (read: tamper) with one, without knowing or being able to understand the effects or consequences on the other.
- Measures of the performed process cannot be useful for determining what, if anything, should be changed in the defined process.

However, assuming that the organization comes to understand the value of synchronizing the defined process and the performed process, there are numerous ways to improve the defined process. The more effective ways to improve the defined process are

- The process is a product.
- Build the process for its users.
- Design the process for the way users work.
- Establish process design standards.
- Provide meaningful process tailoring.
- Design to the "-ilities."

The Process Is a Product

Treat your process as you do your products because, by almost every imaginable definition, it *is* a product. The defined process has users and customers who have needs and requirements for the process. The defined process should be founded upon an architecture or design, for which there are design standards. The defined process can and should have interfaces to exterior processes or systems. The defined process should be updated and maintained to resolve users' problems, to provide new features or enhancements, and to stay synchronized with the performed process. Doesn't all this sound like a product?

But thinking of process as a product is a big mental shift for some of us in the process business. Some of us start thinking of our processes, which we have worked so hard to develop, as existing for their own sake and not for the benefit of our customers—the process users. But shift we must if we are to elevate process to a strategic perspective in our business.

What does treating process as a product entail? It means

■ Aligning process development initiatives with higher level strategies and initiatives

■ Understanding the customers of the process and their needs and wants

■ Planning, managing, and executing process development and definition projects just as you would product development projects (see "Planning and Managing the Performance and Process Improvement Project"), using a skilled team of professional process designers and developers (not just your underemployed tech writers)

Build the Process for Its Users

The Apple iPhone and iPad are phenomena. These wondrous devices were not designed using input from focus groups, customer surveys, or customer requirements. You simply cannot ask most people to tell you what they want or need and then expect them to describe things they can't and never will imagine. The "i-things" were built based on the imagination of a visionary: Customers didn't create the iPad; the iPad created customers...the market "need" to fill did not exist. As one of my friends likes to say, the iPad should have been called the Apple Orgasm...something everybody wants but can't really explain or justify why they want it.

But whereas business processes, industrial processes, product development processes, and service processes are products, they are not and don't need to be the iPad. If we want customers for our defined processes, we can and should build the process product such that users want to adopt it and use it, instead of being forced to use it by policy or fiat. Our processes should earn customers and should be deserving of their attention.

In almost every organization I have engaged, the organization's existing manifestation of process was hundreds or thousands of pages of narrative text replete with the word "shall"…"you shall," "they shall," "he or she shall," etc. "Shall" is a stern word, one that implicitly carries with it the ominous consequences if you don't comply with the "shall" commandment.

And because many organizations suffer a culture of distrust—management's distrust that workers will do the right thing and workers' distrust that management is always getting in the way of their doing the right thing—organizations often believe that their people are constantly trying to bend or break the rules and dodge the "shalls." Management thinks that the people in the organization have a "no cop, no stop" attitude and, just because it is paranoia, doesn't mean it's not true.

In such cultures, what does management do to solve the "problem?" Well, the "solution" is clear…either write even more procedures and rules with more "shalls" liberally sprinkled among the words, or establish the "process police" to catch people breaking the "shalls" and write tickets, or both. The sad irony of this approach is that it doesn't work, and it is horrifically wasteful.

Think about it…if you define processes full of implied threats and people still find ways not to comply, then even more threats are not likely to make a difference. And if you have to keep adding staff to police process compliance every time you create more "shalls," then you have a system that is in what Peter Senge would call an addiction loop—the more you apply the wrong solution, the more the problem worsens.

What if you could build and give to your workers a process system that, upon seeing and touching, makes people say, "I will," "I will perform that," "I will execute that," "I want to follow that process because I can see how it will help me do my job better"? If you could create a process system in an environment in which workers say, "I will," when it comes to performing and complying with the standard processes, would you really need a thousand or a million "shalls"? Can an organization really emerge from the process dark ages just by adopting a new attitude and approach to the way its processes are represented?

We can and should build better process systems than we have in the past. Our software and systems developers use the most advanced development tools to create products and provide services, and yet we expect them to follow processes using last century technology—the written word. When we know that about half the people on the planet understand some types information represented graphically better than they do text, why are so many of our processes and procedures still represented via text-based narrative? Why do we think defining processes and procedures is just locking a bunch of people and tech writers in a room to create volumes of text? We can do better; we must do better.

Building the process for users goes way beyond just identifying who the users are or their functional roles. Building the process for the users also means

■ Defining user preferences for information representation for different types of information: instructional, referential, educational, etc.
■ Understanding the users' learning modalities: reading, watching, doing

- Understanding and defining the range of user and potential user knowledge, skill, and experience in performing the process
- Defining not only what users want in the process, but also what they don't want
- Defining—based on the preceding information—the range of realistic use cases

If you're responsible for process design and definition, always work with the process user in mind. Even better, staff the project team responsible for developing or changing the defined processes with people who are or will be its users. Give them a chance to provide their input early and often; in fact, get them to take ownership of the defined processes. Once deployed, it will become much more difficult for people to complain about the defined processes if they were the people who built them.

Design the Process for the Way Users Work

Look around you and observe how people interact with each other and with technology. Watch someone surf the web. Go buy a grill and pull out the assembly instructions. Watch someone navigate and drive around in a foreign country. What do you see? You see people reading some words, but mostly "reading" pictures and symbols, graphical representations that have meaning.

Yet when we define processes or procedures, we traditionally represent process with text-based narrative and, occasionally, throw in the gratuitous static flow chart or block diagram. So, outside the process, the engineer, the project manager, and the call center operator can quickly navigate through and digest information, but when they try to follow the process, they have to slow down and read words.

Designing the process for the way users work involves the following:

- Creating new process representations or changing existing process representations so that people find them more adoptable, adaptable, and helpful
- Making process representations more accessible
- Making process representations more intuitive (which does not mean ignoring the fact that all things new need to be trained)
- Making process representations easier to change with changes in the business
- Changing the process representations such that people comprehend them more quickly and can use them more effectively and efficiently

In my consulting practice, I have developed advanced process systems for clients that incorporate all the innovations described in this section, but the topic is deserving of its own book (future project).

Establish Process Design Standards

Maybe the reason processes have clung to text is because we hold onto the belief that the words we use have the same meaning for everyone else as they do for us; in other words, when we write textual process descriptions, we have *de facto* standards such as the English language and grammar.

The problem is that such beliefs are provably unfounded in today's world. As the cultures within our work organizations have transformed from homogenous societies—mostly white men, with similar upbringing and backgrounds—to multicultural, multigender people with widely varying backgrounds, one word or one phrase will have different meaning in different contexts for different people. You can test this for yourself. Gather up five people in your organization and ask them to write a definition for the word "process" without speaking to each other or accessing glossaries or dictionaries. See how many different definitions you get.

The point is that we have easy-to-learn and easy-to-remember standards all around us. No matter what country you drive in, a red light means stop, a green light means go, and a yellow light means yield or caution. The circle with the diagonal red line through it means don't do whatever action the picture beneath the circle displays. After initial interpretation, some standards, especially graphical standards, become part of our subconscious; they are institutionalized and we don't have to interpret them each time we encounter them. Standards make following a process "second nature" to us; we don't have to think too much.

Thus the problem with purely text-based process descriptions: Whereas we may have once had standard understanding of words and sentences, our language is now full of jargon, colloquialisms, and microcultural context. Take the phrase, "answer the mail." It could mean respond to a written letter, respond to an e-mail, take action on an explicit or implicit request or demand from a co-worker or boss, or respond to a customer request or requirement. If you transported Aunt Bee from yesterday's Mayberry into today's organization and asked her to "answer the mail," she would likely fail with her first three attempts, give up, and go bake a pie.

Regardless of whether your processes and procedures remain text based or evolve to a graphical representation, an audio representation, a video representation, or some hybrid of representations, you should establish internally consistent design standards to make process learning, adoption, and implementation more effective and efficient.

Design standards also make new process development and process maintenance easier and more efficient because the standards serve as the building blocks of the process system. Here, again, definition is everything. Do you really want to spend dozens or hundreds of hours arguing with someone over the differences between a "process" and a "procedure" or the difference between a "template" and an "example," when you could get agreement on those definitions up front before using them as the building block for your process system?

Almost any useful process system, regardless of how its information is represented, will be built of components— information entities that will need consistent meaning in order to work together in the integrated system. Following is a list of some of the information entities that serve as building blocks common to most process systems:

- Process
- Procedure
- Task or step
- Role
- Input
- Entry criteria
- Output
- Exit criteria
- Tool
- Guide
- Template
- Training
- Reference
- Standard
- Predecessor
- Successor

In the process systems I have designed and built for client organizations, each of these process entities has had a slightly different definition because there is no one right definition for every organization, just as there is no single process system that will work in every organization. The meaning of these entities must be relevant within the context of the organization and culture.

Other design standards are needed. For example, if I'm developing a predominantly text-based narrative process system (which, by the way, I would never do), I want to design the voice in which it is written—passive, active, imperative—so that reader-users don't get confused when trying to perform the process. If my process system is graphically represented or a hybrid of graphic and text, then I want to develop design conventions for how the building blocks are graphically represented. In a graphically represented process, I need design standards or conventions for all of the process entities previously listed and for

- Shapes
- Colors
- Links
- Lines: color, width, solid/dashed, etc.
- Ordination and subordination
- Task/step labeling (I always use imperative verb + object of the verb; e.g., "develop test plan")

Yet other process system design standards should be established, long before developing the process system. Regardless of the nature of the process system's representation, there are usually structural design standards to establish, including standards for

- File formats and versions for all the process entities
- Interface or system access from the users' perspective (e.g., application or browser)

- Process system hosting platform(s)
- Process system interfaces and protocols

Provide Meaningful Process Tailoring

Meaningful tailored performance of the organization's standard defined process is a powerful way to increase ROP because, when appropriately planned and implemented, tailored process performance enables projects/work units to perform the right amount of work to achieve their goals: not too much work and not too little.

One of the challenges for organizations trying to achieve compliance with standards or models is that they succumb to the notion that compliance requires one standard organizational process or set of processes that somehow must fit all projects or units of work. The CMMI is particularly challenging because, whereas it provides for process tailoring (GP 3.1s, OPD SP 1.3, and IPM SP 1.1), hapless tailoring and, in particular, tailoring out work performance can cause difficulty for projects in producing evidence needed for achieving capability or maturity level ratings in a CMMI appraisal (SCAMPI [standard CMMI appraisal method for process improvement] class A).

The principles of meaningful process tailoring are

1. Tailoring is in process performance, not in process definition.
2. Process tailoring is tailoring of the organization's standard processes, not tailoring of nonstandard processes.
3. Tailoring is based on business need and defined criteria and rationale.
4. Systemic and measured tailoring provides insight into the performance of the organization's standard processes and identifies opportunities for changes and improvements to the defined process.

A few of these principles require more explanation, which is provided in the following subsections.

Tailoring Is a Process Performance Activity

There seems to be some prevalent idea—especially in organizations using the CMMI—that a project's or work unit's "tailoring" involves the project or work unit redefining or rewriting the organization's standard processes.

Not quite. The misperception is born of the misnomer; thus the word "tailoring" misrepresents what we really want to do. If we look at the clothing analogy, "tailoring" is indeed changing by redefining the suit, the shirt, the skirt to fit our wearing of the garment. My 42-inch suit coat needs to be shortened in the sleeves and the waist because most standard men with a 42-inch chest are taller than me.

But in terms of process tailoring, the clothing analogy doesn't—pardon the pun—fit. Whereas the purpose of tailoring clothing is to make the standard suit fit, the purpose of process tailoring is to apply a standard process that was built for a typical scenario to a nonstandard scenario. The more appropriate clothing analogy for process tailoring is application. It's not raining, but I'm walking through the gardens of Clos Luce in France in which there are lots of pigeons in the tree branches above the paths, so I should wear my rain gear. Or, I can have an easily removable item such as a tie that, in the midst of my client meeting, I can remove—under the guise of ulterior premises—if I perceive an excessive application of formality for the environment. In the process world, "variable but controlled application" of the standard process is a more accurate descriptor than "tailoring" for what we're trying to accomplish.

How do you determine what is the "standard" process versus the nonstandard or variant process? You will say the standard process is the one we've defined, but you will be only partially correct. The "standard process" is the one that is defined, but its definition is based on the process that is most often performed. When you begin to think of a standard process in the same context as we think of work practices or habits—those things that most of the people do most of the time—then you will understand and be able to identify the standard process in your organization. And, until you can characterize the standard performed process, you cannot define a standard process, and you cannot detect what is variant and can be tailored. (Also see "Synchronizing the Defined and Performed Processes" in this chapter.)

The concept of projects tailoring the organization's standard set of processes (OSSP) is defined in the CMMI. Process tailoring is known to be a capability/maturity level 3 concept based on its appearance in the model in the organizational process definition (OPD) process area (PA) in specific practice (SP) 1.3, "Establish Tailoring Criteria and Guidelines." It is important to note that OPD SP 1.3 follows OPD SP 1.1, "Establish Standard Processes," because it would be difficult to tailor the performance of an undefined process. Additionally, OPD as a maturity level 3 PA is subject to generic goal 3, which includes generic practice (GP) 3.1, "Establish a Defined Process."

That being said, most organizations find it difficult if not impossible to "institutionalize a managed process" (generic goal 2) without first defining their processes. As a result, organizations often begin addressing the concept of process tailoring even as they are defining and developing processes consistent with the maturity level 2 process areas.

Tailoring criteria and guidelines are used by projects during project or work unit planning. A project performing capability/maturity level 3 processes consistent with the practices in integrated project management (IPM) implements SP 1.1, "Establish the Project's Defined Process." The project's defined process (IPM SP 1.1) is established by using tailoring criteria and guidelines (OPD SP1.3) to tailor its implementation of the OSSP (OPD SP 1.1). Lots of people take the language of the CMMI too literally and too prescriptively, and they think that the "project's defined process" needs to be some kind of a rewrite or revision to the organization's standard process. This line of thought causes a lot of unnecessary waste of time and effort, and a negative ROP. An efficient and effective way to enable projects and work units to define their tailoring of the organization's standard processes is to allow them to define their planned tailoring in work products they usually have to create anyway, such as the project schedule. If the starting point for a project schedule is a WBS (work breakdown structure) that identifies all the tasks, activities, and work products in the organization's defined standard process, then tailoring process performance becomes a natural aspect of project or work unit planning, and process performance is integrated into project/work unit plans.

The relationships between CMMI components that support process tailoring are illustrated in Figure 2.5.

Tailoring Is Based on Criteria and Rationale

Tailoring is based on criteria and rationale that, in turn, are based on historical data, measures, and information from projects and work units having tailored their performed

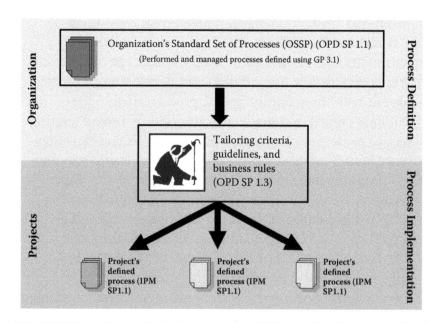

Figure 2.5 Relationships of CMMI components that define and support process tailoring.

process. Too often, organizations, especially those in a hurry to achieve a CMMI maturity level, will allow projects and work units to tailor process performance simply because they want to or because they perceive performance of the standard process to be too onerous, even though they haven't really bothered to understand the work that the standard process entails. Here are some of the reasons (read: excuses) I have heard used to justify ad hoc process performance:

■ Our project is so important (critical, politically sensitive, urgent, high risk, blah, blah, blah) that we can't be burdened by the standard process.
■ Our project is so unique that standard processes won't work for us.
■ Most of the standard process don't apply to the type of work we do.
■ We just sort of tailor as we go.
■ The tailoring criteria don't make any sense.
■ We use Agile processes (oxymoron, emphasis on the "moron"), so we don't really have a standard process.
■ We don't tailor; we just follow the standard process (so long as it's convenient to do so).

One of the reasons projects and work units will spend effort and time coming up with excuses for not tailoring their implementation of the standard process is because the well-meaning process group doesn't provide reasonable and useful tailoring criteria and guidelines. They make tailoring of the process a perfunctory task to "check off" so that there is evidence of some CMMI practices come appraisal time.

So from where do meaningful tailoring criteria and guidelines come? They come from time, patience, and many runs or cycles through the process by projects with process performance data overlaid and correlated with attributes about the projects or units of work that performed the process.

If you're an organization in a hurry to achieve a CMMI maturity level, time and patience are not abundant commodities. Let's say that your organization develops a product, that you have three products, and that the average project duration—start to release—is 9 months. That means that in a 4-year span, the organization has 12 projects that start and finish, or 12 instances of performing the standard product realization process. Are 12 data sets a statistically viable data population to formulate statistically meaningful process performance data and meaningful tailoring criteria? Probably not, and 4 years is way longer than your bosses gave you to get the organization to maturity level 3.

What do you do? How do you reconcile not having enough information to build processes and assets for a reasonable implementation of OPD SP 1.3 and IPM SP 1.1 with the schedule to get to CMMI-DEV maturity level 3?

Well, if you're like other organizations in the same quandary, you punt: The organization issues a mandate disguised as a tailoring guideline that decrees no tailoring of the standard process is permitted. Problem solved.

CMMI problem solved, but serious negative ROP problem incurred. What inevitably happens—and becomes institutionalized—under this scenario is that projects or work units will gratuitously perform actions to gratuitously generate evidence for a CMMI appraisal or an ISO/AS/TL audit. When you perform an action or create/change a work product and the energy and resource spent don't add value, then by definition it constitutes waste. It diminishes, if not obviates, your ROP.

The following subsections provide you with additional ways to think about and structure process tailoring using criteria and rationale.

Define Types of Tailoring

There are essentially four types of process tailoring, which are further defined in Table 2.3: (1) no tailoring, (2) tailoring down, (3) tailoring up, or (4) replacement tailoring.

Table 2.3 Tailoring Types and Associated Risks and Benefits

Type	Description	Risks	Benefits
No tailoring	Work unit's performed process is same as the standard defined process; no process is tailored	• Standard defined process "force-fit" gives work unit no performance flexibility • Work unit may incur unnecessary process performance overhead	• Performance of work unit's process is more easily monitored • Work unit can use ready-made standard work products and assets
Tailor down	Work unit's performed process omits some standard defined processes, activities, steps, or process assets	• Work unit incurs risk of skipping critical activities and work products • Work unit may not produce evidence required for a CMMI appraisal or ISO/AS audit	• Work unit can perform only most critical processes and thus save effort, cost, and schedule that might otherwise be spent on unnecessary process overhead • Work unit's process performance data adds to organizational body of knowledge in project performance and tailoring

(Continued)

Table 2.3 (*Continued*) Tailoring Types and Associated Risks and Benefits

Type	Description	Risks	Benefits
Tailor up	Work unit's performed process adds processes, activities, steps, or work products that exceed the standard defined process or process assets	• Work unit may incur excessive process performance overhead • Work unit may need to use unproven processes and work products	• Work unit has flexibility to perform processes required by customers • Work unit's process performance data add to organizational body of knowledge in project performance and tailoring • Work unit can pilot new processes, activities, steps, or process assets
Replacement	Work unit's performed process invokes substitutes for standard defined processes, activities, steps, or process assets	Work unit may need to use unproven processes and work products	• Work unit's process performance data add to organizational body of knowledge in project performance and tailoring • Flexibility and adaptation help the organization discover "best practices" • Work unit can pilot new processes, activities, steps, or process assets • Projects have flexibility to use processes and/or tools as requested by customers

For each of the four types of process tailoring defined in Table 2.3, and for each level of tailoring described in the next subsection, the organization needs to have decision criteria or business rules that work-unit managers or leads can use to tailor the performance of the standard defined processes.

Organization Levels of Tailoring

There are multiple levels at which the tailoring of organizational standard processes can be defined and performed. Levels of tailoring usually fall into one of two major categories—organizational level and process level—and there are sublevels of tailoring within each category.

In organization-based tailoring, the tailoring of standard processes is determined based on three major factors:

1. The organizational unit (within the larger organization at which level the standard processes are defined) that is defining and performing the tailoring
2. The line of business (LOB) in which the tailoring organization operates
3. The extent to which the tailoring organization is involved in various systems delivery life cycle phases

Organizational unit tailoring means simply defining and performing of an organization's standard defined processes in subordinate organizational units within the organization at which the process has been defined. For example, within a large company that has an enterprise-wide standard process, process tailoring can be executed at the division, group, team, or project level. In some cases, if a division or group engages in fairly homogenous projects, it may be more economical to tailor process performance at the division level and have the same tailoring apply to all projects within that division. In such cases, the division has essentially established its own standard process, which is a tailored version of the parent organization's standard process.

If, based on the CMMI, a typical OSSP will provide processes and process assets for all aspects of product or service development and delivery. However, some LOBs do not perform processes that are typical to product realization or service delivery. For example, an organization such as a project management office (PMO) that provides project management support and services to a customer organization may not be involved in processes related to the engineering, such as defining and managing requirements or developing technical solutions (i.e., the process areas within the engineering category in the CMMI).

Some typical generic LOB classifications that can be applied to organizational units include:

- Product development
- Product maintenance/sustainment
- Research
- Integration and testing services
- Information technology (IT) services
- Project management
- Marketing and sales
- Purchasing and contracting

The key to defining reasonable tailoring criteria and guidelines based on LOBs is first obtaining a thorough understanding of the nature of the business performed by the unit or team that needs to tailor its performance of the standard defined processes. The activities performed and the work products created in each LOB need to be known and defined. Once an organizational unit's or team's LOBs are characterized, the organization can establish a high-level design for process tailoring such as the example shown in Table 2.4.

Characterizing the organization's LOBs is an important performance factor in tailoring. However, even before tailoring, understanding the magnitude or amount of work the organization spends in each LOB is an important factor

Table 2.4 Example of LOB-Based Process Tailoring

Standard Organization Process	Related CMMI Areas	Lines of Business within Organization			
		Product Development	IT Services	Purchasing and Contracting	Marketing
Requirements development and management	REQM, RD	No tailoring	No tailoring; service requests = requirements	Tailor down	Tailor down
Project management	PP, PMC, RSKM, IPM	No tailoring	Tailor down	Tailor down	Tailor down
Acquisition and contracting	SAM	Tailor down	Tailor down	No tailoring	Tailor down
Software development	TS, PI	No tailoring	Tailor down	Tailor down	Tailor down
Peer review process	VER	No tailoring	Replacement tailoring	Replacement tailoring	Replacement tailoring
Configuration and data management	CM, GP 2.6	No tailoring	No tailoring	Use DM process only	Use DM process only
Testing	VER, VAL	No tailoring	Tailor down	Tailor down	Tailor down
Quality assurance	PPQA, GP 2.9	No tailoring	No tailoring	Tailor up	Tailor down
Performance measurement	MA, PMC GP 2.8, GP 3.2	No tailoring	No tailoring	Tailor down	Tailor up

in designing standard processes. For example, let's say that an organization knows that it spends 80 percent of its effort performing acquisition and contracting work. It should be obvious that such an organization should design and construct its standard processes to provide processes and assets related to acquisition and contracting, not some other LOB such as product development.

Somewhat related to LOB-based process tailoring is life cycle-based tailoring. In some situations, such as very large-scale systems development—the Joint Strike Fighter, for example—multiple organizations are involved in developing and delivering the product or system. In such cases, any single organizational unit may have responsibility for only one or a few phases of a typical end-to-end software or systems life cycle. This concept of a software/systems life cycle being divvied up among multiple organizational units is illustrated in Figure 2.6. In the conceptual diagram illustrated in this figure, Organization X is responsible for most of the common

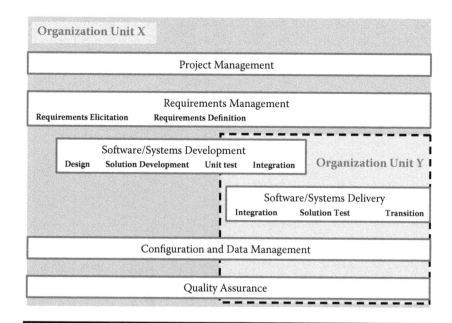

Figure 2.6 Conceptual illustration of life cycle-based tailoring.

life cycle activities, such as project management, requirements management, product development, etc. However, Organization Y has primary responsibility for system integration, testing, and transition to the end user or customer.

In our illustrated example, both Organization Unit X and Organization Unit Y will need to tailor the standard processes according to the phases of the life cycle for which they are respectively responsible. Organization Unit X will tailor out those standard processes related to the product integration (PI) and validation (VAL) process areas of the CMMI-DEV, and Organization Y will probably tailor out most of the standard processes, but has business rationale for performing the processes related to the CMMI components PI, VAL, CM, and PPQA/GP 2.9.

Process Levels of Tailoring

The previous subsection describes tailoring of the organization's standard processes based on organizational factors. Another level of tailoring is based on the level of the standard defined processes at which tailoring can be defined, planned, and performed. Using the four types of tailoring defined in "Define Types of Tailoring" in this chapter, process tailoring can be performed at different levels of the standard process, such as

- Policy level
- Process level
- Procedure level
- Work product level

For process-level tailoring to be meaningful and executable, the organization needs to have clearly defined (i.e., an OSSP architecture or design) the various levels of processes and process assets. Process-level tailoring cannot be defined if processes and procedures exist but the difference between these two classes of process assets has not been defined.

In policy-level tailoring, an organizational unit such as a project or division may tailor the standard defined processes at the policy level. Such tailoring would typically involve changing the scope or applicability of standard process implementation. For example, if the standard process (or parts of it) applies to a project, but the project has business reasons or rationale for not using the standard process, it might seek to have the policy waived. The line of business-based tailoring illustrated in Table 2.4 provides an example of policy-level tailoring because LOB rationale can be used to determine the scope of standard process implementation.

Wherein policy-level tailoring described in the previous paragraph typically addresses the "why" questions about standard process scope and applicability, process-level tailoring typically addresses the "what." In other words, an organizational unit might invoke process-level tailoring to not perform one or more of the standard processes if it has reasons for doing so. An example of process-level tailoring would be a project in which an external organization is contracted to perform the testing, and thus the project would tailor outperforming the standard defined process related to testing. Table 2.5 illustrates an example of process-level tailoring.

Tailoring can also be performed at the procedural level, assuming the organization's standard defined process clearly distinguishes between a process and a procedure. (In many organizations, a process defines simply what is to be performed, and a procedure defines how to perform a process, but process design and classes of processes require greater definition than this.) Table 2.6 illustrates an example of a project defining procedure-level tailoring for the organizational procedure that defines various procedural options for estimating work product attributes and project effort.

Process asset-level tailoring is similar to procedure-level tailoring in that the person or team planning and performing the standard process tailoring makes decisions regarding how to implement a process. In this type of tailoring,

Table 2.5 Example of Process Level Tailoring

OSSP Process	Project X Tailoring and Rationale
Requirements development and management	Project X performs only requirements development; requirements are managed by the Integrated Product Development Team.
Project management	Project X performs project planning. Project monitoring, control, and reporting are performed by the PMO.
Performance measurement	Measurements are collected and reported by Project X. The Measurement and Analysis Group performs measurement analysis and generates performance measurement reports.
Configuration management	Project X identifies and manages project documentation. Source code and compiled code are managed by IT.

the implementation choices are based on which process asset or tool is used to implement a process. Table 2.7 illustrates an example of work product-level tailoring in which there is a choice of two tools that can be used for estimating project effort.

Tailoring Criteria and Guidelines

Tailoring of standard processes should always be based on defined criteria and guidelines. (Also see "Tailoring Principles.") In order for tailoring to be institutionalized as a managed and defined process, people performing OSSP tailoring need information that helps them consistently make reasonable decisions regarding what to tailor and how to perform tailoring.

Typical Tailoring Criteria

Tailoring criteria are parameters that characterize the work to be performed upon which you base decisions about tailoring organizational standard processes. At a unit of work that

Table 2.6 Example of Procedure-Level Tailoring

Estimating Activity	Choice	Procedural Options	Tailoring Rationale
Estimate attributes	No	Estimate project documentation page count	Due to 80 percent reuse of previous project documentation, effort estimate known
	Yes	Estimate software function points	FP count will be based on an estimate of 60 percent reuse
	No	Estimate thousand lines of code (KSLOC)	Customer wants FPs used for estimates
	Yes	Estimate project complexity	Complexity will be based on number of project stakeholders
Estimate effort	Yes	Estimate person-hours	Will use defined standard of 25 percent overhead
	No	Estimate person-days	Not needed
	Yes	Estimate person-years	Required by customer; roll up of person-hours

Table 2.7 Example of Work Product-Level Tailoring

Estimating Activity	Choice	Work Product/ Tool Options	Tailoring Rationale
Estimate project effort	No	COCOMO (constructive cost model)	Tool is not sufficiently calibrated for UML development
	Yes	OSSP Wideband Delphi Estimating Workbook	Will reuse estimates in prior project's workbook

is planned and managed, such as a project, typical tailoring criteria include parameters such as

- Size or magnitude of the work, which is typically characterized in terms of effort hours, schedule duration, cost, or size of work products/products to be created
- Complexity of the work, which is typically characterized in terms of parameters such as number of product/system interfaces, number of different destination environments/platforms, number of different development languages or environments, or number of project stakeholders
- Difficulty of the work, which can be characterized in terms of amount of new technology or new knowledge or new skills required to perform the work
- Risk of the work, including technical risks, political risks, and risks due to cost, resource, or schedule constraints
- Criticality of the system being delivered (e.g., a system backup status reporting application may be able to tolerate some errors resulting from loose process rigor, but a life-support application project may need to control errors tightly through process rigor)

Where Do Tailoring Criteria Come from?

Tailoring criteria are most effective when they are derived from historical work or project performance information; criteria are rarely useful when arbitrarily defined.

So where do tailoring criteria come from? The answer is that the organization needs to start collecting and analyzing information about projects and project performance even before people really know what to do with that information. When organizations attempt to establish process tailoring criteria without historical measures and other information, they typically fail to define criteria that are relevant or meaningful to the work being performed.

Relevant and useful tailoring criteria are derived from the analysis of correlations between project parameters and process implementation. For example, let's say we examine 10 completed projects by plotting schedule performance against project size, measured in terms of total effort hours (the chart on the left in Figure 2.7). We examine a different set of 10 projects by plotting schedule performance against project complexity, measured in terms of number of stakeholders (the chart on the right in Figure 2.7).

When we analyze these two plot charts, we can see that project size (in effort hours) has relatively little correlation with schedule variance. We see projects ranging in size from 50 to 600 hours, yet the schedule performance only varied between –6 percent (the project completed under schedule) and +8 percent (the project completed over schedule). However, in the plot chart on the right showing the correlation between project complexity (number of stakeholders external to the project team) and schedule variance, there appears to be a correlation. With eight or fewer external stakeholders, schedule performance varies only by 7 percent (–1 to +6). When the number of external stakeholders is nine or more, there is significant schedule variance.

Note that correlation does not prove causation, and we know that there are always other variables that affect the performance of something such as a project's schedule. Nevertheless, when an organization needs to find tailoring criteria based on

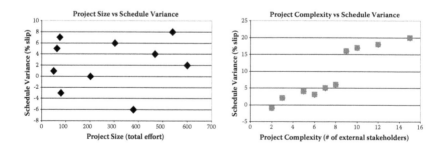

Figure 2.7   Example of analyzing historical information to derive tailoring criteria.

rationale, this type of analysis of historical information at least provides a reasonable basis for those criteria. Almost any fact-based rationale is better than guessing wildly at criteria.

Here's the rub: Many organizations, especially those that use the staged representation of the CMMI, don't start thinking about process tailoring until they start addressing the maturity level 3 process areas. So by the time these organizations realize they need historical project parameters and data to identify and rationalize tailoring criteria, they usually don't have the data because when they started process improvement they didn't know they would need those data in the future, and they haven't collected them.

So if your organization didn't look ahead into the future and didn't collect the information that it would then later need to define tailoring criteria, what do you do? Talk to people. Even when people haven't recorded information, they often retain a lot of knowledge, which can be elicited through questions.

Tailoring Guidelines

Tailoring guidelines are based on defined criteria; thus, criteria must first be defined. A tailoring guideline suggests decision or action given that a criterion is met. Tailoring guidelines can be considered business rules for using and performing the organization's standard defined process. A tailoring guideline can be in the form of an "if–then" statement (e.g., "if criterion X is met, then do Y") or could offer a range of decisions or actions based on criterion satisfaction.

Tailoring guidelines can be rigid and prescriptive, or they can flexible and serve as suggestions.

Design to the "-ilities"

Designing a process system that workers will want to adopt and perform requires designing a system that provides "-ilities" such as those defined in Table 2.8.

Table 2.8 Process System "-ilities" to Accommodate in Design

Process "ility"	Questions to Answer to Define and Design "-ility"
Accessibility/ usability	How easy or difficult is it for process performers to access the process system and acquire the information they need to perform the work they are currently performing?
Adoptability	How easy or difficult is it for process performers to modify their work practices and behaviors to adopt the process system and use it to perform work?
Adaptability	How easy or difficult is it for process performers to integrate use of the process system with the work they perform? How easy or difficult is it for process performers to understand how the processes and process assets apply to their jobs and deliverables? How easy or difficult is it for process performers of varying levels of experience and expertise to apply the process to their work?
Flexibility	How easy or difficult is it for process performers to adapt the process to different situations, different tasks, or different work environments?
Extensibility	How easy or difficult is it for process developers or process performers to apply the process to new types of work or new business needs?
Maintainability	How easy or difficult, or how cost effective, is it for process developers to implement and deploy changes and improvements to the process system?
Auditability	How easy or difficult is it to monitor or audit process performance accurately against the defined processes and process assets? How easy or difficult is it to capture variability between the performed and the defined process?
Measurability	Can process performance measures be defined and implemented that will provide accurate and actionable information on the defined process (providing there is high fidelity between the defined and the performed process)?

The value of first defining -ilities and then designing the process system to provide them is that the organization then has a way to test and measure improvement. For example, let's say an organization is about to embark on improving its standard defined processes. To understand the extent to which the current processes provide the -ilities, it designs and conducts a survey that asks performers of the current processes questions similar to those posed in the right column of Table 2.8. Each survey question is structured to provide respondents with choices on a difficult-to-easy scale for each question—for example: very difficult, difficult, easy, or very easy. (Remember! When using a scale for survey questions, always use an even number of choices that straddle a midpoint. This disallows the respondent to be a "fence-sitter" by making the null choice of the middle.)

The organization then defines requirements for each -ility in terms of requirements for the process representation (text, graphical, hybrid), hosting platform, process asset file format and structure, user interface, etc. The requirement derived from the -ilities can then be used to develop test cases or scenarios to test the process system before release or deployment. When the improved processes are being piloted or deployed, the same -ility survey that was conducted on the legacy process system can be administered for the improved process system, and the before-and-after survey results can be compared.

Additionally, some of the -ilities can be used to derive process performance measures. For example, the intuitiveness of the process system's navigability (an aspect of usability) can be measured by the length of time it takes a process performer to navigate to a particular location in the process system. The intuitiveness of a search function (also an aspect of usability) can be measured by the number of search attempts or variations of the search criteria a user executes to get the information he or she is seeking.

Don't Define Inconsequential Processes

Numerous states have spent millions of dollars passing legislation that makes it unlawful to text while driving, which is an abysmal waste of legislators' time and taxpayers' money because there are not enough law enforcement officers on the planet to enforce such laws. Drivers themselves won't voluntarily adopt no-texting driving because most won't see it in their self-interest to do so…they either like texting while driving or they are simply addicted to texting. These laws are a nice sentiment and represent the best of intentions (including my own) toward protecting people on the roads, but are enacted at a high cost and to zero effect because they are not and cannot be systemically enforced.

The same principle applies to process definition. If the defined process isn't perceived by workers as adding value to their jobs and thus enticing enough to adopt voluntarily, or if the defined process is something that cannot or will not be compelled, then there was no point in defining it to begin with.

As a CMMI Institute-certified Lead Appraiser, I have found myself drawn into fruitless and unwinnable debates with personnel in client organizations that want or need to achieve a CMMI maturity level. Typically, an EPG or SEPG operating at the organization level will define standard processes that mirror the practices in the CMMI. Inevitably, at some point in the process of collecting and evaluating evidence of process implementation, I'll get into a discussion with someone that goes like this:

Me: Your process says the output of performing this procedure is a ____ (fill in the blank with your own thoughts on the least useful work product you have to produce).
Client employee: Why would we do that?
Me: Because the rules of conducting a CMMI appraisal require physical evidence as an indicator of process implementation.

Client employee: Well, we don't do that; it doesn't add value.

Me: OK. Do you agree that having a CMMI maturity is valuable to your organization?

Client employee: Yes.

Me: And do you agree that I must diligently follow the rules for conducting a SCAMPI appraisal?

Client employee: Yes

Me: So what do you propose we do about the evidentiary requirements for this practice?

Client employee: Well, we're not going to do something just because it is in the CMMI.

Me: OK.

This is the trap of the CMMI. There is a huge difference between using the CMMI as guidelines for improving your processes *and* wanting a maturity level. If you just use the parts of the CMMI that will provide real benefit and ROP, you can choose not to adopt the practices you don't perceive as yielding performance results. But the day you or someone in your organization decides to pursue maturity levels, you have no choice but to adopt and implement practices even if they really don't add value. In that case, you will define processes that have no business consequence other than generating evidence for a SCAMPI appraisal.

Remember! People will always do what you want them to do so long as what you want them to do is what they want to do.

Synchronizing the Defined and Performed Processes

Remember that all performance improvement that can be attributed to process improvement can only come from improvement in the performance of process, and that we can only affect process performance through process definition improvements if and only if there is a high fidelity between the defined process and the performed process.

Thus, before you can improve process performance by improving the defined process, you need first to establish defined process–performed process fidelity, and this takes time. You might think that you take a few measures or conduct a few process audits and establish defined–performed fidelity, but such uncontrolled checks will not give you an accurate characterization of the state of fidelity. A good mental model for thinking about the defined and the performed processes not being aligned is to visualize two asynchronous sine waves, as illustrated in Figure 2.8.

In Figure 2.8, your perception of whether your defined and performed process is in synch is dependent upon the timing of your measure or observation. You could be lucky and conduct an audit of an activity or work product at some point in time that would seem to indicate people are performing the process as defined. However, you could just as easily not be fortunate and make your observation at other points in time that would indicate the process is not being performed as defined.

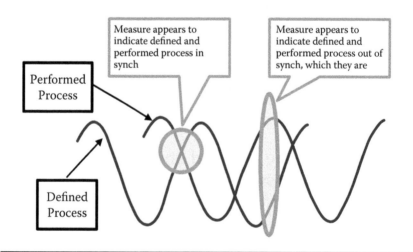

Figure 2.8 Mental model for thinking of asynchronous defined and performed process.

There is a logical life cycle to synchronize the defined and the performed process as depicted in Figure 2.9 and described later. There is not a typical or predetermined amount of time that it takes to work through one cycle of this life cycle, as there are many influencing variables, such as the volume of defined processes and process assets, the duration of process performance, and the number of opportunities for process performance and measurement.

For the purposes of explaining Figure 2.9, let's assume that your organization is just starting out not having the certainty of facts or measures about the fidelity between the performed process and the defined process. This is the hard reality for most organizations, whether or not anyone wants to admit it. Those of you who work in organizations that have achieved CMMI maturity level 3 will say, "Well, that's not us because we're maturity level 3," and I say, "OK, whatever lets you sleep at night." The truth is that

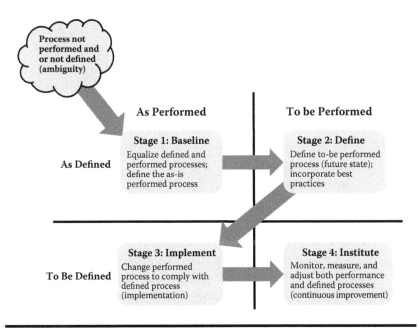

Figure 2.9   Defined and performed process synchronization life cycle.

a CMMI appraisal such as a SCAMPI will check to see if you have defined processes that address the model, and it will check to see if projects and work units produce outputs that look like they meet the intent of CMMI practices, but the appraisal method simply doesn't provide for the rigor it would take to look for defined–performed process fidelity. However, after reading and understanding the following sections that describe the stages in this life cycle, you can decide if your organization is already in one of the stages and start there.

Stage 1: Equalize the Defined Process with the Performed Process

Too often, teams such as SEPGs, EPGs, (process improvement groups [PIGs], process action teams [PATs], whatever you call yourselves) will skip this stage altogether and start with stage 2. You'll read some literature or you'll get some advice from a friend that essentially says you should just start writing procedures (or develop an OSSP and a process asset library (PAL), or write a quality management system [QMS]) that "satisfy the requirements" in the CMMI or ISO or AS9100. Stop and think! If you pursue this well-worn path, then you have further widened the chasm between the reality of the performed process and the fiction of the defined process, and you have set your organization up for failure in stage 3.

Starting off in a state of ambiguity about the defined–
performed process fidelity, you first want to equalize them by
defining what is currently performed. This is not yet improvement because at this point you don't concern yourself with
whether what is performed is good or bad, efficient or inefficient, effective or ineffective. You're simply modeling the as-is
performed process and, in fact, the term "process modeling" is
often used to describe such activities.

Process modeling is a more appropriate descriptor than
"process definition" because what you're really doing is describing the performed process at a level of abstraction, a model.
For example, let's say you find that in the performance of a
process or subprocess, person A performs steps 1, 2, and 3;
person B performs steps 2, 1, and 3; and person C performs
steps 3, 1, and 2. In process definition, you would try to find
out which of those sequences of performance is "correct" or
the best way to perform the process and then define that. In
modeling, you would abstract the three steps to a model of
what is performed—not how—and what the outputs of that
performance are. If the outputs are generally consistent regardless of the sequence of steps, then you have a model for the
task, process, or subprocess that comprehends those steps.

Example Modeling

Let's say we want to model decision making processes in
an organization. To do this, we will carefully design an
interview script and then use it to interview a cross-functional
representation of the employees and ask them questions about
how they make decisions. In one of the questions, we asked
respondents to identify how frequently they made five
different types of decisions, choosing from a subjective scale
of frequently, sometimes, seldom, or never. Figure 2.10 shows
the results for this interview question.

From these data, we can deduce that the process model
should, at a minimum, accommodate making staffing decisions

Decision Type / Use	Staffing or Personnel Selection	Alternative Design or Solution	Make vs. Buy	Make vs. Reuse	Tool or Technology Selection
Frequently	7	3	2	4	3
Sometimes	2	6	3	3	3
Seldom	1	1	2	2	3
Never	0	0	3	1	1

Figure 2.10   Example data collection for modeling a decision process—types of decisions.

and making decisions to choose from alternative designs or solutions. This direction forward is based on looking at the number of people who either frequently or sometimes make one of these two types of decisions: nine and nine.

We can also find out by asking what outputs are recorded when these decisions are made. To this question, we get the results shown in Table 2.9.

With the information in Table 2.9, we can use a threshold to establish the minimum content for decision outputs and records. If, for example, we could say that a particular information element is recorded for any two of our four types of decisions, then recording that information element is required or mandatory for all types of decisions. Or, we could say that only the information elements that are usually recorded for all four types of decisions are the mandatory minimum.

So now we have the basis for our process model: (1) an action to be performed—"make decision"—with two ways to perform it, and (2) a standard for the minimum information that must be recorded as an output of performing the action. Our process model for this example would look something like that shown in Figure 2.11.

The key to moving through this stage efficiently is constantly to be vigilant about getting bogged down into too many details, personal preferences, and the need to be

Table 2.9 Example Data Collection for Modeling a Decision Process—Decision Outputs

Decision Output	Staffing	Alternative Design	Make vs. Buy	Make vs. Reuse
People involved in the decision		✓	✓	✓
Decision makers' roles			✓	✓
Decision stakeholders				
Type of decision	✓		✓	✓
Criteria evaluated	✓	✓	✓	✓
Evaluation method(s)		✓	✓	✓
Decision method	✓		✓	✓
Decision made	✓	✓	✓	✓
Follow-up on decision implementation results	✓	✓		

"perfect." You want to exit this stage with a process model that accurately reflects the process as it is "typically" performed without being so detailed that it only describes a narrow subset of all process performance instantiations.

Stage 2: Define the "To Be" Process

Once we have equalized the two parts of our process system by modeling or defining the performed process, we can assume the two will remain in synch—reflective of each other—for a while. After all, we built the model based on what people have been doing all along, and there's no reason—other than paranoia—to believe that people will

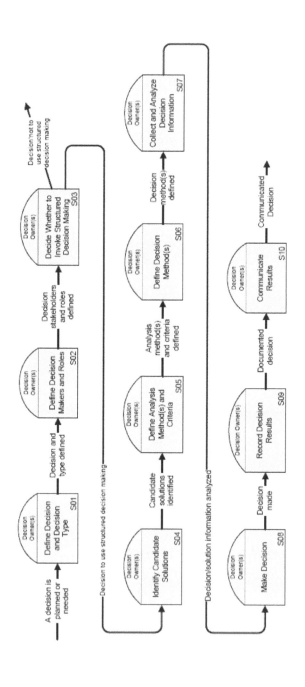

Figure 2.11 Example model for decision process.

immediately change their work process and practices right after we observed and defined them.

In Stage 1, you defined your process world the way it is; in Stage 2, you define it the way you want it to be. Stage 2 is the heart of improvement through process definition work; it is here that teams such as engineering process groups or process improvement teams can really make a difference and add value…but only if they make appropriate decisions followed by brilliant execution.

Here's where you get to invent, innovate, imagine… and steal like a thief in the night! This is where bodies of knowledge, models, and standards come into play by providing you with a wealth of ideas and practices you can incorporate into your defined processes. Here's where you can conduct analysis of your defined processes and Lean or streamline using techniques such as value stream mapping (VSM).

It is this stage of synchronizing the defined and performed process in which teams such as SEPGs and EPGs can excel and demonstrate their worth, but only if you consciously decide up front that you and your colleagues are not going to have blind faith in models and standards. You will have read or heard that the CMMI is a collection of "best practices," a reputation that is not even claimed either within the model itself or by its authors at the SEI. It is a collection of practices that many organizations have found useful, but that doesn't mean they are best practices for your organization. For example, if you didn't bother to define or model what is currently performed, then perhaps you didn't find out that your organization's testing department employs very sophisticated automated testing software that essentially performs tasks equivalent to the practices in the validation (VAL) process area of the CMMI. So you and your fellow process improvement colleagues will go off and write some procedures for performing VAL, only to find out in stage 3 that procedures written for humans to perform are completely unnecessary. Congratulations, you've already encumbered a negative ROP for the organization.

And—to borrow again from Tom Davenport, one of the best minds in process reengineering and innovation—be a "pantheist" in your use of models and standards. For example, to improve your defined project management practices, you could use the practices in the CMMI process areas project planning, project monitoring and control, integrated project management, and risk management. However, if you look in the Project Management Institute's (PMI) Project Management Book of Knowledge (PMBOK),[5] you'll find a collection of practices and work products that are significantly more robust than the CMMI in the area of project management.

The bottom line for this stage is that models, standards, and bodies of knowledge are all process improvement, but not all process improvement can be found in the models, standards, and BOKs... much of it should come from mining your own good minds and the lessons learned in your own organization. Process improvement could have been right under your nose all along.

When it comes to improving the defined processes in an organization, there are lessons that have been incurred by many organizations in all sectors of the economy, but they aren't lessons learned unless and until an organization applies them and incorporates them into its process improvement work. Table 2.10 defines some of the lessons I have observed, learned, and applied toward achieving a positive ROP.* (Also see "Learn One, Learn All" in Chapter 4, "Small Improvement, Big Performance Improvement.")

Stage 3: Perform the Defined Process

With newly defined process, the next stage in the defined–performed process synchronization life cycle is to deploy and implement the new or revised processes and process assets. If you designed the processes and assets for the users, based on their input, better yet; if the process users helped design and build their own processes, it should be a very hard sell to get people in the organization to adopt.

To have any real chance of success in implementing new or revised processes and process assets in an organization, here are some practices that have proven helpful:

- Have executive or senior management establish and communicate rewards or incentives for process adoption; publicize those teams and individuals who are early adopters.
- Communicate (in summary form, not nitty-gritty boring details) what has changed in the processes and what has not changed.

---

* Oh, I know…your organization is different; unique. Other organizations' lessons don't apply to your organization. You're wrong, and it is this line of thinking that will start you down the path of negative ROP right from the beginning.

Table 2.10 Lessons in Process Definition That You Should Consider

Process Definition Lesson	*ROP: Why Implement the Lesson?*
Use models and standards as guidelines, not as prescriptions for improvements to defined processes.	If you use models or standards as prescriptions, you will end up defining processes that your business doesn't need to perform, resulting in waste in both process definition and attempts at implementing unnecessary process.
Get the right people involved in process development and definition (also see "Building the Process Definition Team" in my book, *Real Process Improvement Using the CMMI*).	We love only what we know, and we don't love what we don't know. If you only use people who love tools, all you'll get is tools. If you only use people who love people, all you'll get is a lot of socializing, but not much process. If you only use people who love the CMMI, all you'll get is the CMMI. Use people who deeply understand "process" at all its levels of abstraction and detail.
Innovate, but not too much.	Don't be afraid to try new things…new visual representations of information, new process technologies, etc. But don't adopt something just because it's new to you or your organization.
Process definition is not just writing processes and procedures.	Read "Improving the Defined Process" in this chapter.
Focus on enabling work products, not the process (also see "Critical Factor 5: Focus on Process Implementation Assets" in Chapter 5 in my book, *Real Process Improvement Using the CMMI*).	Remember! The purpose of performing a defined process is to create or change the state of a work product. (The purpose of performing a process is not to perform the process.) If you give workers process assets such as templates, checklists, examples, and easy, efficient ways to create and update work products, you have made them far more efficient than you have when you just make them read a process or procedure. Work is doing, not reading.

Table 2.10 (*Continued*) Lessons in Process Definition That You Should Consider

Process Definition Lesson	ROP: Why Implement the Lesson?
Define the process definition language (also see "Establish Process Design Standards" in this chapter).	Save countless hours arguing with other people about the difference between "process" and "procedure," between "form" and "template," between "project" and "program." Just define the language—the building blocks of your process system—up front and reduce or eliminate the waste incurred by never-ending discussions on the meaning of words and phrases.
Know your process users, know how they prefer to receive and use information, and know their work habits. Build process systems they will want to perform.	The ROP in applying this lesson is that if you don't build a process system that process users will adopt and perform, the organization will spend excessive amounts of time and money trying to force, coerce, or entice the users to adopt and use the processes. Worst case, the process user community will "go underground" and develop their own processes that work for them, which they will keep secret from the people responsible for process management in the organization.

- Develop and communicate a policy that provides people with clear guidance on when and how to implement the new processes. For example, the policy might state that projects near the end of the life cycle do not need to adopt the new processes.
- Offer and publicize a period of quality assurance amnesty—a period during which process audits will be conducted for the sole purpose of acquiring information about how well the new processes are working, but any teams or individuals found to have deviated from the standard process are exempt from having to take

corrective action. (You can't expect people to adopt new processes and then immediately punish them for doing so...what are you thinking?)

■ The process management team (e.g., EPG, SEPG) should offer and publicize that they will provide hands-on coaching or mentoring to teams and individuals who are willing to adopt and try out the processes.

Note that I make no mention of providing guidance or help to people in tailoring their implementation of the new processes; you should not do this. Before you can build meaningful and useful process tailoring criteria and guidelines (also see "Provide Meaningful Process Tailoring" in this chapter), you first need to find out what works and what doesn't with the standard processes by having projects or work units try and succeed or try and fail. It will be the data you collect about the failures—Why did something fail? What were the characteristics of the project or work unit? What was the nature of the instantiation?—that will later inform meaningful process tailoring criteria and guidelines.

Stage 4: Institute Synchronization and Continuous Improvement

Once the organization has a statistically viable population of experiential information and data from process implementation in stage 3, it can embark on instituting a stable symbiosis between the defined and the performed process and can quantitatively manage continuous improvement and optimization of the process.

The body of experiential implementation data collected in stage 3 can be used in one of two ways:

1. Defined processes or process assets that did not work in any implementation environment or instantiation can be viewed as defects in the defined process, and corrections or adjustments should be identified and implemented.

2. Correlations between defined standard processes or process assets either not working or implemented differently than intended and characteristics of the projects/ work units or implementation environments or instantiations in which the variations or deviations occurred should be used to establish process tailoring criteria and guidelines.

It is exactly the work defined in the preceding—doing something with the information that identifies deltas between the defined and the performed process—that is so important to return on process, and yet, unfortunately, it is the point at which many process groups fail.

What happens all too often is that the team responsible for process improvement develops and deploys the defined processes (part of stage 2 but not all of it), and then monitors implementation and collects implementation outputs, but only for the purpose of having evidence for a CMMI appraisal or an ISO audit. More than once, I have even witnessed EPGs or SEPGs disbanded or dismantled immediately following the achievement of a CMMI maturity level. It's sad for the people on these teams, but it's also sad for the whole organization because its leadership came so close to realizing a positive ROP and then blew it.

Using Defined–Performed Process Variance for Improving the Defined Process

Remember that, in this stage, you're continually trying to bring the defined process and the performed process to be more closely aligned—representative of each other. The information you collect about variations between the performed process and the defined process will help you do this.

Let's say that since deploying the new or revised standard processes, 10 projects have attempted to perform the processes as they are defined. The information collected via process and work product audits shows that all 10 projects failed to perform one of the defined tasks or subprocesses. One of the reactions to this info—and one that is typical, at that—is for the EPG to think that the people on those projects are malicious, or "resisting" change, or—as one of my colleagues once whined to me—"just not doing what they know to be the right thing." A more constructive and progressive thought is this: Maybe, just maybe, there's a really good reason no projects performed the task…maybe that defined task really doesn't fit our business or our culture, or maybe it simply doesn't add value to overall performance. In this situation, assuming that the projects that performed the defined standard processes were "normal"—that is, they were representative of the work normally performed in the organization—the variance between the performed and the defined process should be considered a candidate for improving the defined process. In other words, the task that was consistently not performed should be evaluated for possible removal from the defined processes.

One organization I worked with found an innovative way to keep the defined process synchronized with the performed process in real time. The process descriptions were written as wiki pages. As process users performed the process, they were able to add their own notes to the relevant wiki to provide process performance detail, "how to" tips and techniques, and example work products they used to perform the process more effectively and efficiently. Thus, at any point in time, the defined process and the performed process were very closely aligned, if not a true representation of each other.

Using Defined–Performed Process Variance for Improving the Performed Process

The previous section addressed how to use defined–performed process variance to improve the defined process, but different types of variance information in the synchronization stage can be used to improve the performed process.

Let's use a slightly different scenario than the one used in the previous section, and say that of the 10 projects that attempted to perform the defined standard processes, six of them performed a task that the other four either did not perform or performed in a way that significantly deviated from the way the task was defined. In this case, we can use our newfound knowledge in process tailoring (see "Provide Meaningful Process Tailoring" in this chapter) to identify characteristics or attributes of the six projects that did perform the task, and the characteristics or attributes of the four projects that did not perform the task or performed it in a highly variant way. We then analyze and abstract those characteristics/attributes to define tailoring criteria and guidelines so that future projects having similarities with the four don't waste time struggling with thinking or deciding about the task, or expend effort trying to conceal or disguise the nonconformance or variance.

Continuous Improvement, Synchronization, and ROP

Where's the continuous improvement and ROP in synchronization? That's pretty easy to figure. If you keep it simple, you can measure the effort and cost of doing the analysis of the defined–performed variance information and either changing the defined process or developing the process tailoring criteria and guidelines. It is also reasonably easy to estimate the value of the performance gained when projects don't have to stop and come up with all the reasons and ways for not performing a task. When you multiply that value by the number of future instantiations—projects performing the defined process—you can determine the ROP: performance value minus cost of process improvement.

The CMMI and Process Improvement

In my previous book and in this one, it may appear to some readers that I am overly critical of the CMMI; I am not. In fact, I am a CMMI aficionado. There is not anything inherently wrong with the CMMI, and it does not purport to be anything other than what the SEI or the CMMI Institute claim it to be: guidelines for improving process. What goes terribly wrong with the CMMI and what gives it a bad reputation in some communities and organizations is how people misappropriate the CMMI's purpose and how they misuse it.

If your first assignment in "process improvement" was to go take CMMI classes at Carnegie-Mellon University and perhaps then become a certified lead appraiser, it is very easy—almost seductive— to adopt the worldview that the CMMI is all process improvement and that all process improvement can be found in the CMMI. Neither is true, but we love what we know, and we either ignore or discount what we don't know. You've come to cherish the feeling you have about yourself when you are intro- duced as a "CMMI expert." I know; I was once you.

I will offer you some friendly advice: The more you become a CMMI expert, the more likely you are not to open your mind and learn about the bigger world of process improvement. Read some books other than the CMMI, like books about proj- ect management, books on Agile, books on Lean and Six Sigma. Join online discussion groups related

to process improvement (but be skeptical enough
to parse opinion from fact-based statements). For
each process area, such as risk management, in the
CMMI, you'll find collections of books just on that
topic that provide a deeper, richer understanding of
the topic.

Perhaps your bosses have told you that your job
is to get the organization to a certain maturity level,
so that's what you will have to do. But that doesn't
preclude you from examining each CMMI practice to
be implemented and figuring out how its implementation can really improve something. You'll inevitably
come across CMMI practices that may not yield performance improvement, but you won't know unless
you apply critical thinking and curiosity.

Ways to Think about Best Practices

I'm a member of several professional collaboration sites, one
of them being a CMMI discussion group on Linked-In. After
a year of observing a few useful but mostly inane discussions
on this site, I can make the supportable observation that most
people using the CMMI or thinking about using the CMMI
consider it a collection of "best practices."

For the sake of instigating thought, let's suspend our
critical thinking for a moment and assume that the CMMI
(or Information Technology Infrastructure Library [ITIL] or
the PMBOK) really is a collection of best practices. In his
book, *Best Practices Are Stupid*, Stephen Shapiro gives us
a compelling, rational way to frame the appropriate relevance and importance of "best practices" in a business.
He writes:

> I play golf—not well, but I play golf. My handicap
> is in the double digits. For me to shoot par would
> be a dream. But for Tiger Woods, par would be a

nightmare. I am reminded of this comparison when I see companies are satisfied to focus on their understanding of "par," otherwise known as best practice. It was once an admirable aim, but it is not sufficient today. Par won't keep you alive in the current environment. Once something becomes a best practice, it is really no longer a best practice.

So, if your organization and all of your competition have implemented what you believed to be the best practices in the CMMI, then you are all shooting the same score—par—and none of you is really winning. The organization that innovates and achieves real process and performance improvement will shoot way under par, and will win.

If, however, I haven't dissuaded you from thinking of models, standards, and BOKs as best practices, then at least consider their appropriate place and application in business performance improvement. Read "The Place for Best Practices in Performance Improvement" in Chapter 1.

Where Improvement Begins in the CMMI

One of the reasons the CMMI is often maligned is because people want to believe that all of the practices in the model, when implemented, will yield instant improvement and hence instant gratification and immediate ROP. When I started out in model-based improvement with the Software CMM in the early 1990s, many organizations pursued CMM maturity level two as if it were the penultimate representation of a mature organization. Then, as now, once so many organizations had achieved CMMI maturity level 2 (maturity level saturation in the market place), that maturity level became passé, and organizations became convinced they had to achieve CMMI maturity level 3. Now, maturity level 3 is boring and quotidian, and organizations pursue maturity levels four and five so that they can "stand above the rest."

I fully expect some defense contractor to make an appeal to the CMMI to invent a maturity level six so that they can be the first to achieve it before all their maturity level 5 competitors. The belief that the minute you start implementing CMMI practices is when you also start improving and reaping a positive ROP is a complete misinterpretation of this model and a debasement of the meaning of "improvement." The process areas and the practices defined in maturity levels 2 and 3 (capability levels 1 through 3) are foundational for improvement, but are not yet improvement themselves. The practices defined in maturity levels 2 and 3 create work practices and a stable process, which can then be measured and improved, but their implementation is not necessarily in and of itself improvement. The simple act of implementing a work practice that you did not previously perform is not inherently improvement. In fact, doing so can be anti-improvement—negative ROP—if you add process cost to product or service delivery without adding value.

Don't believe me? Just read. In maturity level 2, your organization has somehow managed to perform a "managed process," whether or not that process yields business performance improvement. In maturity level 3, your organization performs its defined processes, but, again, has not necessarily improved processes that yield performance improvement. It isn't until you come to understand the practices defined in maturity levels 4 and 5 that you see the real "improvement" components of the CMMI; however, an organization must first build the foundation—maturity levels 2 and 3—upon which improvement can be implemented.

It is only after you have taken the time and energy and have made the investment to build a process foundation that thoughtful use of the CMMI's practices in maturity levels 4 and 5 can enable process performance improvement. Let's take a look at how the CMMI can bring real process improvement to an organization *after* it has achieved CMMI maturity level 3.

Look at what you have to have in place before you even begin addressing CMMI-DEV maturity level 4 practices. Let's say you want to implement specific practice (SP) 1.1 in quantitative project management (QPM), which is to establish and maintain the project's quality and process performance objectives. From what do you think those project performance objectives are derived? The most likely source is the organization's performance and measurement objectives that you established and have been measuring from the measurement and analysis (MA) process area in maturity level 2.

How would you implement QPM SP 1.2—"Using statistical and other quantitative techniques, compose a defined process that enables the project to achieve its..."—if you didn't already have a plethora of historical project process tailoring data and performance measures (see "Provide Meaningful Process Tailoring" in this chapter) that you could analyze to compose that defined process? How could you adequately "compose a defined process" if you had not already learned about process design and definition in maturity level 3?

And how would you "select subprocesses and attributes critical to evaluating performance and that help to achieve the project's quality and performance objectives" (SP 1.3) without having a statistically viable population of historical subprocess performance data and measures from many cycles through subprocesses? How indeed would you select subprocesses if your organization never defined—as a maturity level 3 organization—the distinction between processes and subprocesses? (Also see "Establish Process Design Standards" in this chapter.)

The same argument is valid for the other maturity level 4 process area, organizational process performance (OPP). For example, how would you establish quantitative process performance baselines (SP 1.4) if you had not been operating at maturity level 3 for quite some time and had lots of historical process performance measures and measurement data?

The point of all this is that, yes indeed, implementing processes and practices consistent with the practices in maturity levels 4 and 5 *can* yield improvement, but cannot reasonably be undertaken without a significant amount of history implementing, monitoring, and measuring the processes defined and managed as a maturity level 3 organization. And, by the way, implementing maturity level 4 practices still might not get you quantized improvement; rather, it may only yield information, data, and analysis that you need to implement the maturity level 5 practices reasonably to get real improvement.

This being the situation, when you achieve CMMI maturity level 5 and the leadership is looking to claim a positive ROP to buttress or support the maturity level achievement, does it subtract all of the cost of process improvement, even the cost of getting to and operating at maturity level 3, or does it calculate only the cost of the investment in achieving maturity levels 4 and 5? My guess is that if using total cost of CMMI implementation doesn't yield a positive ROP, some leaders will manipulate the ROP formula to yield what they want it to yield.

Putting It into Practice

As you may recall, in "Putting It into Practice" in Chapter 1, the Federal Division managers at Ascendance Consulting Corporation decided to enlist the help of the division's EPG to develop the strategy and plans for process improvements improvement measures. The EPG, having read this chapter, "Real Process Improvement," are ready to get to work to implement its concepts to achieve performance improvement objectives through process improvement.

Putting It into Practice: Defining Process Performance Objectives

Remember that the account/project objectives derived from Federal Division performance objectives were (see Figure 1.10 in Chapter 1) to

- Reduce average process tailoring cost/effort by 10 percent per project
- Reduce peer review and work product review iterations and duration
- Capture and review lessons learned in each phase (not just at the end of the project)
- Improve project communication (but reduce e-mail and meetings)

The division EPG decides to make process improvements to address the first three of the preceding four process improvement objectives at the division, but let the accounts and projects take on the fourth objective at the account or project level.

(To meet the intent of providing an example, the remainder of this "Putting It into Practice" section applies the concepts and practices in this chapter just to the account/project performance objective to reduce peer review and work product review iterations and duration.)

The EPG has years of peer review data but, unfortunately, they cannot be holistically examined or analyzed. According to the division standard process for conducting peer reviews, accounts and projects are allowed to collect whatever data they deem appropriate and to archive or store them in any format and location they choose. The EPG doesn't even know where all the peer review data are, so its first order of business is to try to gather up and consolidate as much historical peer review data as possible.

To do this, the EPG enlists the aid of the division president. They develop for her an e-mail for broad distribution, calling for all peer review data (the dreaded "data call") from all projects or accounts over the past 3 years. The EPG builds a one-page guide that goes out with the president's e-mail that defines what is meant by "peer review data."

Concurrent with the data call, the EPG decides to collect additional as-performed process information by observing a representative sample of peer review sessions, or by conducting structured interviews with people who conduct peer reviews. They use this observation and interview information to model the as-performed peer review process; the model reflects the most commonly occurring inputs, tasks or steps, and outputs.

It takes the EPG several weeks just to parse and organize all the data they have collected in a way that makes analysis even possible. Their analysis of the data and information collected yields these observations about the performance of peer reviews:

■ There are three types—or subprocesses—of peer reviews performed: (1) formal inspections, (2) structured walk-throughs, and (3) collaborative redlining (also called "off-line reviews"). The reason these three types of reviews are considered "subprocesses" of the peer review process is because the process activities conducted prior to any of these three subprocesses are generally the same and because the classes or types of outputs from all three subprocesses are also consistent.

■ The most commonly used peer review subprocess is structured walk-throughs.

■ Most peer review and work product reviews are conducted in software design and development.

■ Requirements and project plans are rarely peer reviewed.

■ The "defects" found in most documents are related to formatting, typographical errors, spelling, or grammar—not technical content.

- There is no consistency in the data, information, or measures that are recorded from conducting peer reviews, nor is there consistency in how is they are recorded and stored.
- Peer reviewers are frequently not given enough time in advance of the peer review to review or become familiar with the work product.
- Peer reviewers are generally not selected based on their knowledge of the item being reviewed.
- There are no consistent definitions used for "defect," types of defects, or severity of defects.

When the EPG evaluates these observations against the current defined peer review process, they notice that the performance improvements can be categorized in one of three categories:

1. The defined process or process asset needs to be improved to compel the intended process performance.
2. Process performance needs to be improved to align more closely with the defined process.
3. Both the defined process and the performed process need to be improved.

Putting It into Practice: Improving the Defined Process

There is a lot of work for the EPG in improving the defined processes and process assets related to peer reviews. Here are the process definition changes the EPG makes:

- Definitions for defect, defect type, and defect severity are developed and added to the peer review checklists.
- For each type of work product to be peer reviewed, the functional roles that serve as the most appropriate "peer"

are defined, and this information is added to the peer review process.
■ The peer review process is updated to specify a minimum number of business days by which reviewers must receive the peer review package prior to the peer review.
■ Standard peer review performance measures and measurement data are defined. A centralized SharePoint list with an .htm data entry form is established for collecting all peer review performance data and information. These data include:
   – Name and type of item reviewed
   – Life cycle phase in which peer review was conducted
   – Number of reviewers
   – Number of effort hours expended planning and conducting the review, and removing defects
   – Number of defects captured by type and severity
   – Estimated downstream cost saved by removing defects

The EPG develops new peer review training material to enable more efficient and effective training on the revised peer review process and process assets. New process quality assurance assets and processes are also developed to help the EPG monitor the deployment of the new peer review process and assets.

Putting It into Practice: Improving the Performed Process

Although the current defined peer review policy states that peer reviews should be conducted early in the product development life cycle, there is no particular incentive—positive or negative—to motivate projects to do so. The EPG works with senior managers and project managers to address this performance weakness in two ways. First, senior managers are mentored to ask project managers about peer reviews of requirements and project plans in project reviews and status reports. Second, the project managers are coached to add tasks, resources, and schedule to their WBS/schedule for conducting peer reviews of requirements work products and plan work products.

Another performance improvement implemented immediately via first policy and then later changes to the standard processes is that all documents to be peer reviewed are first edited by a technical writer or editor prior to a peer review. This inexpensive improvement removes most of the noncontent "defects" from work products, prior to expending more expensive resources in a peer review to find those defects, and makes peer reviews more efficient and effective because it enables the reviewers to focus on finding technical content defects.

Putting It into Practice: Synchronizing the Defined and Performed Process

In aggregate, many of the improvements to the defined process and process assets reflect what the EPG considered "best practices" when they observed peer reviews being performed and interviewed peer reviewers, so the changes to the defined process are not completely new to some of the projects.

When ready for piloting, the EPG asks account managers which projects can be used to pilot the new peer review process and assets. The EPG meets with the project managers and senior managers of the selected projects and provides them with help to build tasks, resources, and schedule into their project plans that will enable them to conduct the process piloting work, which includes:

■ Providing training or orientation on the new/revised processes and process assets
■ Providing process performance feedback and measures to the EPG
■ Planning and conducting peer reviews that the projects may have not performed in the past

The EPG also negotiates with the managers for their commitment to conduct the pilots and provide the measures and other information needed to evaluate the efficacy of the new processes and assets. In reciprocation, the EPG commits to provide the pilot efforts with close-in consulting and support.

Putting It into Practice: Measuring the Process Improvement

In the course of piloting or implementing the process improvement, the EPG knows it needs to capture process performance measures to be able to demonstrate that improvement has indeed been effected and to have performance measures to understand the contribution of the process improvement to the division's performance improvement objectives. So even before the piloting of the new and improved peer review process begins, the EPG plans the measurement collection and analysis.

Remember! In order to show improvement quantitatively, there must be baseline measures against which the results of the improvement implementation can be compared. Table 2.11 shows both the baseline peer review performance (before improvement), based on the data collected via the data call and analysis, and the effects of implementing the peer review improvements. (Also see "The Most Important and Most Overlooked Measure: The Performance Baseline" in Chapter 1.)

Putting It into Practice: Progress toward Higher CMMI Maturity Levels

In "Putting It into Practice" in Chapter 1, the CEO of Ascendance Consulting Corporation directed the Federal Division president to improve her division's performance, but he also wanted the division to move from CMMI maturity level 3 to maturity level 5 because he believed that would give the Federal Division a competitive advantage in bids for government contracts.

Table 2.11 Putting It into Practice: Peer Review Performance before and after Process Improvement

Peer Review Performance Dimension	Baseline (Before Improvement Implementation)	Performance (After Improvement Implementation)
Average number of peer reviews conducted per project	8	10
Percentage of peer reviews conducted on requirements work products	2 percent	18 percent
Percentage of peer reviews conducted on project planning work products	3 percent	14 percent
Average number of peer review iterations on the same work product	3	1
Average number of defects captured and removed per peer review	25	35
Percentage of technical or content defects detected in peer reviews	11 percent	45 percent
Defects removed in first peer review of a work product as a percentage of all defects eventually removed through subsequent iterations	45 percent	85 percent
Average peer review effort per reviewer (planning, conduct, and follow-up defect removal)	5.5 hours	5.8 hours

Table 2.11 (*Continued*) Putting It into Practice: Peer Review Performance before and after Process Improvement

Peer Review Performance Dimension	Baseline (Before Improvement Implementation)	Performance (After Improvement Implementation)
Average number of people involved in a peer review	6.5	3.5
Average person-effort per defect captured and removed	4.5 hours	6 hours
Average downstream savings per defect removal	No baseline; will estimate based on peer review literature and benchmarks	

Although the division's focus—the president, the senior managers, the EPG, and the practitioners—has been on performance improvement, they have made some progress in implementing practices in CMMI-DEV maturity levels 4 and 5. The EPG didn't even have an objective to "implement the CMMI" to move the organization up in maturity levels. Instead, they focused on improvement, referring to the CMMI only for guidance and not for prescription. Table 2.12 identifies the CMMI-DEV practices the EPG feels confident that they have implemented.

At this point in time, the only QPM practice that can be reasonably addressed is QPM SP 1.1, "establish and maintain the project's quality and process performance objectives." The remaining specific practices in this process area require the establishment of a process model, which has not yet been established (see the entry for OPP SP 1.5 in Table 2.12. Nevertheless, this progress toward higher CMMI maturity levels is good news for the division president—news that she is happy to report to the CEO.

Table 2.12   In Practice: Progress toward Higher CMMI Maturity Levels

PA and Practice	Practice Description	Evidence of Implementation
OPP SP 1.1	Establish and maintain the organization's quantitative objectives for quality and process performance, which are traceable to business objectives.	In "Defining the Process Performance Objectives" in this "Putting It into Practice" section, four process performance objectives were defined. Of those four, two are either already quantified or could easily be quantified: (1) Reduce average process tailoring cost/effort by 10 percent per project, and (2) reduce peer review and work product review iterations and duration. Also, recall that these process performance objectives were derived from the Federal Division account/project objectives, which, in turn, were derived from the Federal Division performance objectives (see Figure 1.10 in Chapter 1).
QPM SP 1.1	Establish and maintain the project's quality and process performance objectives.	Federal Division projects always have standard performance objectives such as schedule performance index (SPI), cost performance index (CPI), earned value (EV), on-time deliverables, and customer satisfaction. These project-level performance objectives were cascaded from the account-level performance objectives, which, in turn, were cascaded from the division-level objectives. With the implementation of improvements in the peer review process, all projects also added the objective to "reduce peer review and work product review iterations and duration," and each project had performance targets associated with that objective.

OPP SP 1.2	Select processes or subprocesses in the organization's set of standard processes to be included in the organization's process performance analyses and maintain traceability to business objectives.	The selection of the peer review process for improvement is based on the analysis of the data collected about peer reviews. Three peer review subprocesses are defined, and the historical data collected can be used to analyze the three subprocesses separately if necessary.
OPP SP 1.3	Establish and maintain definitions of measures to be included in the organization's process performance analyses.	The organization's leadership, in collaboration with the EPG and others, defined an organizational measurement definition document using the approach described in "Establishing Performance Measures" in Chapter 1.

(Continued)

Table 2.12 (Continued) In Practice: Progress toward Higher CMMI Maturity Levels

PA and Practice	Practice Description	Evidence of Implementation
OPP SP 1.4	Analyze the performance of the selected processes and establish and maintain the process performance baselines.	With the division president's help, the EPG put out a data call and collected historical peer review performance data from multiple years and multiple types of projects. They normalized and analyzed these performance data and established the process performance baselines defined in the second column in Table 2.11.
OPP SP 1.5	Establish and maintain process performance models for the organization's set of standard processes.	Having implemented improvements in both the performed and the defined peer review process, the EPG now wants to stabilize and institutionalize the improvements and to monitor the synchronization between the performed and the defined process. The EPG correctly decides that they simply don't yet have enough performance measures to establish a process model, so they plan a point in the future to do so when they perceive they will have a sufficient population of data.

See Chapter 3, "Getting the Return on Process (ROP)" for the continuation of this "putting it into practice" story.

Do's and Don'ts

Here is a summary list of things you should do and things you should not do when working to improve process.

Do

1. Make sure you define process improvement goals that align with and support the achievement of the organization's performance objectives.
2. Focus process improvement effort and investment on the performed process.
3. Define, collect, and use process performance measures that align with project or organizational performance measures.
4. Realize that not all departments, units, teams, or individuals can contribute to every performance objective.
5. Improve process performance through speed (efficiency), efficacy, and output quality.
6. Improve the defined process only after you understand the fidelity between the performed process and the defined process.
7. Create meaningful process performance tailoring criteria and guidelines from historical performance measures and work/project characteristics.
8. Plan, manage, design, build, and deploy standard processes and process assets as you would a product or system; execute process improvement as a project.
9. Apply a disciplined approach to synchronizing the defined and the performed process.
10. Use models and standards to guide your process improvement efforts.

11. If using the CMMI, ensure implementation and institution-alization of the practices in maturity levels 2 and 3 before applying the high maturity practices for real process improvement.

Don't

1. Initiate process improvement work without under-standing how it will affect project or organizational performance.
2. Assume that models or standards are "best practices."
3. Assume that implementing processes that conform to models or standards always constitutes process improvement.
4. Try to improve the defined process without first under-standing or measuring process performance.
5. Try to show improvement without a baseline or pre-improvement measures.
6. Assume that the way your processes and procedures have always been represented is the best or only way.
7. Design or redesign processes and process outputs without input from process users.
8. Create feckless and inconsequential processes—processes that no one uses.

Reflect and Plan: What Did You Learn? What Will You Do?

Congratulations! You made it through the second chapter. Remember: Reading is learning, but it is not doing, and you can't realize a positive return on your investment in reading until you apply the learning to your work. Use the information in this section as a mental checklist to think about and plan actions to implement your learning from this chapter.

What?

1. What are your organization's process performance or process improvement objectives, and how do they map to higher level performance objectives?
2. What, if any, process performance measures have been or are being collected?
3. How are those measures analyzed and used to understand process performance?
4. Which process measures give you information about the defined process? Which ones give you information about the performed process?
5. What work is currently being done to improve process performance?
6. What is the level of fidelity between the performed process and the defined process?
7. What work is currently being done to improve the defined process? How will those changes affect process performance? How do you know?
8. Which models, standards, or bodies of knowledge is the organization using or trying to be compliant with? What is the defined relationship between those models or standards and the process improvement work that is planned or under way?
9. What are the deliverables or outputs from the process improvement project(s)?

Who?

1. Who is responsible for process improvement in your organization, and what are their specific (defined) responsibilities?
2. Who is responsible for defining process improvement or performance objectives and ensuring they align with project or organizational performance objectives?

3. Who is responsible for defining, collecting, analyzing, and using process performance measures?
4. Who—which projects, work units, or teams—will perform or pilot process improvements and provide performance measures?
5. Who is responsible for creating or revising the defined processes? How does management know they are the right people with the right knowledge, skills, and experience to be effective in that role?
6. Who is ultimately responsible or accountable for the investment in process improvement to yield a positive ROP? Is he or she aware of that accountability?

When and How Much?

1. How much effort, money, and time will be invested in process improvement work, and how is it allocated or budgeted?
2. How much of the investment will go toward improving the performed process and how much will be applied to improving the defined process?
3. How much value needs to be generated by process improvements to yield a positive ROP?
4. How much money and time can be spent doing work that does not yield a positive ROP?
5. By when does leadership expect to see results from process improvement? Is that enough time compared to similar efforts in similar environments?
6. How will the valuation of process improvement be calculated?

Endnotes

1. Davenport, Thomas H., *Process Innovation: Reengineering Work through Information Technology*, Harvard Business Review, Boston, 1992: "Creating a Process Vision."

2. Frazer, Mark, "Attracting Investment in Process Improvement through Strategic Positioning," SEPG Europe Conference presentation, Porto, Portugal, 2010.
3. In 2003, NAVAIR chief, Admiral Wally Massenberg, initiated "Airspeed," which was NAVAIR's name for Lean/Six Sigma. What was the compelling business case? A single aircraft depot maintenance shop (North Island) that learned to keep tool bins where they are needed and an obviously slick pitch from the George Group. Under Airspeed, many hundreds of government employees were put through Six Sigma green belt, yellow belt, and black belt training at the taxpayers' expense. What was really missing though were enough Six Sigma projects in NAVAIR to keep all those black belts busy. To look useful, many of them simply became facilitators of meetings and recorders of meeting minutes, not learners of process.
4. Armour, Philip G., *The Laws of Software Process: A New Model for the Production and Management of Software,* CRC Press LLC, Boca Raton, FL, 2004.
5. The Project Management Body of Knowledge (PMBOK) is an online repository of project management information. This repository is maintained by the Project Management Institute (PMI). For more information, go to www.pmbok.com.

Chapter 3

Getting the Return on Process (ROP)

It's a process. It's a process. It's a process.

—Brad Pitt as Billy Beane in *Moneyball*

What Do You Think? What Do You Believe?

Take a minute and answer the questions in Figure 3.1. Then, once you've finished reading this chapter, complete the section at the end ("Reflect and Plan: What Did You Learn? What Will You Do?") to find out how much this information has helped you with your own process and performance improvement work.

1. True or False: Once you begin process improvement, it's management's responsibility to maintain visibility into whether or not the performance objectives are being met.
   a. True
   b. False
2. Process improvement includes:
   a. Implementing DOORS
   b. Only changing the performed process
   c. Only changing the defined process
   d. Implementing project portfolio management
   e. B only
   f. All of the above
   g. It depends
3. If my process improvement accelerated process performance, the performance improvement was:
   a. Process output quality
   b. Efficacy
   c. Efficiency
4. If the process improvement removes tasks that don't need to be performed or that do not result the change of work products, the performance improvement is in _____.
5. The value of using the CMMI or a standard for your processes is:
   a. Performing work practices that can prevent problems or mitigate risks
   b. Guarantee cost savings and improved schedule performance
   c. Achieve maturity levels to be able to bid on defense or federal contracts
   d. Leverage knowledge that other organizations have already learned
   e. A and B
   f. A, C, and D
   g. B and C
   h. B only

Figure 3.1   What do you think and what do you believe about getting a return on process?

Measuring the Effects of Process Improvement on Performance

If you don't ask for the return on process improvement in your organization, you will never know what it is. Perhaps a year or two ago, either with some coaching or because you're a born leader, you did all the right things as a sponsor of the process improvement initiative. You fought for the investment budget, you helped set the process improvement goals, and you established the incentive structure. But then you quickly became busy with other, more urgent matters...the annual budget cycle, perhaps a business development project, or you had to help save a big customer... the daily "emergencies" and operational problems. You used to meet with your engineering process group (EPG) to get the status on the improvements, but you ended up canceling the last three scheduled meetings to deal with what you perceived to be more important things. You know that somewhere in the hundreds of e-mails in your in-box, there are status and measures from the EPG on the process improvement efforts, but you always have to respond to the notes from the CEO first. But in always dealing with the day-to-day issues and ignoring that big investment in process improvement, you are likely creating for yourself a really big future problem: being passed over for promotion or even losing your job. What happens on the day when your boss suddenly remembers the investment in process improvement and comes to you and says, "Show me the money"? What response will you have? How will you explain why you didn't manage the investment? Will those explanations be accepted by your boss? Don't think about these things then; think about them now. That's what a leader does.

So, if you have been applying the concepts in this book as you've been reading it, if you've been working it instead of just reading it (which is my hope), then by now you are ready to realize the return on process. If, in fact, you have been integrating the concepts herein into your process improvement work, the ROP won't be as elusive for you as it is for so many others.

Sometimes, we've been working at something for so long that we lose sight of the "why." I remember a memorable vignette from my job on the Xerox software EPG (SEPG) many years ago. My colleagues and I had been working on improving the defined process (without knowing much about the performed process) for several years. We were in a conference room one day conducting a walk-through of one of our process definition documents when suddenly someone in the group asked, "Would somebody tell me again why we're doing this?" It's funny to me when I think about this now, but it wasn't so funny at the time because none of the rest of us around the table had a very good response to the question.

My lesson learned from the incident is for you to ask yourself every day, "Why am I doing this?" If you can't quickly come up with an answer—one that traces your current actions and decisions to the improvement objectives established perhaps quite some time ago—then pause what you're doing until you figure it out.

To understand how to measure the effects of process improvement on business performance, go back to the initial reasons for undertaking process improvement; go back to the thoughts you had when you read "Learn What to Improve and Why" in Chapter 1, "Real Performance Improvement."

When you read Chapter 1, what were the business performance measures you defined when you read, "Establishing Performance Measures"? When you read Table 1.2 in that chapter, what areas of improvement did you identify that would address business problems or achieve business objectives?

What were the business performance objectives you or others defined after you read "The Place for Best Practices in Performance Improvement"? For the sake of exploration, let's assume that you haven't yet read the section,

"The CMMI and Process Improvement," in Chapter 2, "Real Process Improvement," and that you accept bodies of work such as the CMMI (Capability Maturity Model Integration), ITIL (Information Technology Infrastructure Library), and the PMBOK (Project Management Book of Knowledge) as collections of best practices. If this is your thinking, then you should also remember and apply one of the primal rules of business: There is a right place, a right time, and an appropriate application for all knowledge, tools, and skills.

In the book *Best Practices Are Stupid,* author and consultant Stephen Shapiro gives us a simple and insightful way to think about our business called the innovation targeting matrix (ITM). My extrapolation of Mr. Shapiro's ITM is shown in Table 1.3 in Chapter 1. The ITM helps leaders focus on where to emphasize innovation in the organization and essentially explains why it is only in an organization's differentiatiors—those capabilities that set you apart from your competition—that you should innovate.

Shapiro further makes the case that it is only in the core and support capabilities where best practices are useful. A logical take-away from this line of thought is that the adoption of best practices is *not* innovating.

Changing Process and Measuring the Effects

Always report to your management or executives your and your colleagues' status and progress in the process improvement efforts and always report the ROP, even if it's not always good news. Your

management or executives might forget to ask for
status or the measures, but that doesn't relinquish
you from the obligation to report that information.
Inevitably, your bosses will renew their interest in
process improvement as the deadline approaches
for achieving a CMMI maturity level or renewing
International Organization for Standardization (ISO)
or Standards Australia (AS) registration, and they'll
start asking questions such as, "Will we be ready
for our appraisal or audit?" You have to answer
such questions, but when you do so, also provide
information they didn't ask for, such as data and
measures that indicate the ROP.

When we change our process, we want to understand the
effects of the change on business performance. In order to do
that, we need either to understand the effects of other influencing phenomena such as changes in worker knowledge/skill
or changes in technology, or to limit those effects. When we're
honest with ourselves, we can only give the credit to process
that it deserves and not let it take credit for improvements contributed by other factors.

To generate further understanding of how to think about
and analyze situations in which there is a mix of factors
seemingly contributing to performance improvement, I'll
provide three such scenarios—all actual experiences from my
consulting engagements—and elaborate on how to parse the
primary contributors to the performance improvement.

My consulting firm has been supporting a Naval Air
Systems Command (NAVAIR) organization for about 6 years,
helping them implement process improvements. Sometime
in the 2007 to 2009 time frame, the Navy established IBM's
SharePoint as the standard document management and collaboration platform for all NAVAIR organizations. As with many
similar and sweeping enterprise technology changes, there

were and still are many organizations that have failed to adopt and use SharePoint fully. This situation persists even today, likely due to the Navy not recognizing that the successful institutionalization of any change requires leadership to address institutionalization factors overtly. For example, there was little to no follow-up and monitoring done by the Navy to ensure that SharePoint was being used in all organizations for its intended purposes. And if an organization did not implement SharePoint appropriately, there were no consequences.

In 2012, the organization we were working with had a goal to improve its document management processes, including file naming conventions and use of SharePoint versioning to store and retrieve documents and maintain their integrity. Personnel in the organization had never learned much of SharePoint's basic functionality, such as versioning, inherited site/subsite and folder permissions, document flow, lists, and autonotifications.

The biggest challenge to change in this organization was also one of the biggest ironies: Individuals responsible for process improvement, a.k.a. the organization's "change agents," were among the most reluctant to relinquish their old practices for new, more efficient and effective practices. For example, in the effort to develop file name conventions or standards, one of Natural Systems Process Improvement (Natural SPI)'s consultants tried to show how a document's version or date should not be part of the file name because SharePoint assigns and records the version of the document and the date it was posted to a site. Proper use of the SharePoint environment not only obviates the need to include version numbers or dates in a file name, but having such information in the file name will also cause risk of regression and confusion among people using the work product. One of our clients even argued that the file name for a version of a document had to include all the information that makes a version of the document unique. Again, in the SharePoint environment, as in other document management systems, a file's uniqueness does not have to be encumbered entirely by the file name; uniqueness can and should be a unique combination of the file name and other attributes such as the version assigned to it by the document management system.

As the organization gradually began changing its document management processes and work practices, which included allowing file versioning to be performed automatically and accurately by SharePoint, performance improvement was observed even if not measured. For example, people had more confidence that they were downloading the latest version of a file and didn't have to spend time asking around for the latest version.

At first glance, it would seem that the primary contributor to the performance improvement was the adoption of technology, that being SharePoint functionality. But the technological improvement had been in place for quite some time; it was the change to processes, practices, and individual work habits (changes that can be considered process improvements) that paved the way to let the technology do its thing. In this scenario, it was the process improvement that was the biggest contributor to the performance improvement.

By contrast, technology can be and often is the major contributor to performance improvement, even when the adoption of the technology requires workers to change their processes. Over the past 30 years, quantum leaps in product and service delivery performance have been achieved through the appropriate adoption and implementation of systems used for

- Requirements development, management, and traceability
- Communication and meeting facilitation and management
- Configuration and data management
- Document management
- Work collaboration
- Customer support and service management
- Automated product and product component integration and testing
- Supply chain management and inventory control

- Automated manufacturing
- Enterprise performance monitoring and measurement
- Project portfolio management
- Finance and accounting
- Customer contact and sales automation
- Decision support

In many technology changes, the cost of educating the workforce to make efficient and effective use of the new tools and systems is minor compared with the cost performance gained by implementation of the technology. We also all know about or have our own personal stories of technology replacing workers when the cost of equipment and systems is lower than the cost of labor over the long term; you can amortize capital equipment, but you cannot amortize a person. It is usually in-your-face obvious when technology improvement is the primary contributor to performance improvement, and it is easy to determine the return on technology (ROT).

Technology change, when implemented for the wrong reasons or when implemented poorly without supporting policy or cultural changes, can and often does result in anti-improvement and diminished performance. If most of your workers are using the company's work collaboration system to conduct meaningless and useless arguments with each other, you've lost productivity, not gained it. If your workers use Facebook or Twitter to socialize with friends or to solicit opinions from others on topics in which you hired them to possess knowledge already, the organization will experience anti-improvement and diminished performance results. When you invest in tools and systems that, for a myriad of reasons, are not used for their designed purpose* or are not used appropriately, you will have anti-improvement and negative ROT.

When your improvement appears to be the result of two or more contributing areas of improvement, a simple way to determine the primary contributing improvement is to ask "how" of each contributing improvement. How did the process improvement change performance? How did the technology improvement change performance? How did the knowledge and skills improvement change performance? It goes back to understanding and defining the relationship between process improvement and business performance. (Also see Table 3.2 later in the chapter.) Table 3.1 shows an example of answering how various process improvements contributed to a business performance improvement.

To elaborate further how to determine the primary contributor to performance improvement, I'll analyze the second item in Table 3.1, in which the improvement was defining the test procedures. In this case, there was both a process definition improvement and then a process performance improvement because, prior to the definition improvement, test procedures were missed (not performed) because they were not defined. (Had the newly defined test procedures not been performed, there would have been no improvement.) So, I can see the obvious relationship between the process improvement and

---

* I had a client that was proud of the number of PhDs employed in the organization, who were, for the most part, pretty bright people. But they were using dynamic object-oriented requirements system (DOORS) as a repository for their glossary—terms and acronyms and their definitions. Given the cost of a DOORS license, which would be needed by everyone just to look up a glossary term, this represented an abysmally inappropriate use of the technology. A simple SharePoint list or a wiki would have been easier to use and far less expensive.

Table 3.1 Example of Answering How Process Improvement Contributed to Performance Improvement

Business Performance Improvement	*Process Improvement*	*How Process Improvement Contributed*
Projects perform within estimated budgets	Improve project risk management practices	Effective risk management practices mitigate the impact of risks that cause overspending
Reduce the number and density of defects in released products and subsequently increase customer satisfaction	Define test procedures	Defined test procedures ensure test steps are performed and improve defect capture in test
Reduce the cost associated with rework in product design and development	Develop a standard for product requirements and use that standard to review requirements	Reduced design and development rework that was caused by poor requirements
Reduce operating costs	Introduce standards for conducting meetings	Reduced waste/loss cost associated with meetings that did not result in defined decisions, actions, or outputs
Reduce operating costs	Implement an organization-wide lessons learned	Reduced waste/loss cost caused when individuals and teams learned things that had previously been learned by others

the performance improvement. I can also ask other questions to gain confidence in my premise that process improvement was the primary contributor. I can ask, "Was there a technology change that occurred in the same time period as the process improvement? If the answer is "no," then I can eliminate technology improvement as having had an effect. I can ask, "Other than familiarizing testing personnel with the newly defined test procedures, did we increase the test personnel's skills?" Again, if the answer is "no," I can also eliminate a skill/knowledge improvement as a factor.

Measuring the Performed Process Changes

Remember! All performance improvement that comes from process improvement is a result of improvements in the performed process, which may or may not correlate to improvements in the defined process. So, the first place to look for and measure ROP is in the performed process. Also remember that in "Improving the Performed Process" in Chapter 2, you learned that the major process performance characteristics that can be improved are

- Speed (or efficiency)
- Efficacy
- Output or results quality

You also learned that in terms of speed—accelerating process performance—there are essentially three ways to increase process performance speed, including:

- Reduce the number of tasks or steps
- Reduce lag time or wait states between tasks
- Perform tasks in parallel or concurrently

You also learned from Chapter 2 that improving efficacy basically means making every process action count, that it results in either the creation of a work product or the change to the state of a work product, and that process performance output quality comes in two forms: preventive quality improvement or corrective quality improvement.

With this base of knowledge in process performance improvement, you're ready to take measures to determine if you've achieved the process performance objectives that were established.

Measuring Process Performance Speed

Measuring process performance speed assumes that accelerated performance is one of your organization's process improvement objectives. Remember! Don't have objectives for which you have no intention of measuring the accomplishment, and don't collect measures that are not related to any objectives.

Also, in measuring process performance speed, be cognizant of what exactly you are measuring, and be very specific with your measurement definitions. Process performance speed is so easily manipulated. For example, let's say you have a process that currently requires one full-time person a week to complete. A manager in your organization has figured out that the man-month myth is actually not mythical up to a certain point and applies two full-time people to the process; now it gets completed in 3 days. Did the organization really accelerate process performance *and* achieve a positive ROP? "Yes" to the first part of the question and, probably, "no" to the second part. Process performance accelerated, but at the cost of using more resources, so now someone has to figure out if the calendar time gain for the process outputs was worth the additional cost, a question that will inevitably lead to lengthy political discussions, further diminishing the ROP from the "improvement."

When measuring process performance speed, it's important to measure the same postimprovement phenomenon using the same units of measure that you used to characterize the baseline performance. So, if we're measuring what we believe to be an improvement in process performance speed, we need to measure the same process that served as our baseline measure. In other words, the process measured after the improvement and the process(es) that established the baseline performance measure should have all the same attributes (except for performance time/duration), including:

■ Inputs (quantity and quality)
■ Scope—how much process was performed
■ Outputs (quantity and quality)
■ Resources spent or consumed in performance
■ Skill level of process performers
■ Technology used

All other attributes being equal, if the improvement results in faster process performance (shorter duration or less effort for process completion), then we are getting close to our ROP measure. The problem with only pursuing and capturing process performance speed improvement measures is that it is sometimes challenging to translate time into other units of value. Sales or Marketing might tell you that the ability to release the new features in June instead of August meant the difference between capturing three new customers—easily assigned a monetary value—versus their going to the competition, but no one can ever know with certainty the veracity of such statements or relationships.

There are ways to convert accelerated process performance indirectly into more solid measures of value. If the same (as baseline) effort was applied to complete a product or work product faster, then the logical and arithmetic conclusion is that, with the time savings, those resources can complete or partially complete more output. Going all the way back to Chapter 1, our working definition for performance is "the amount of useful work accomplished compared to the time and resources used." If process performance produces more output with the same quality as the outputs of the baseline performance and using the same (as baseline) resources, then the value of the ROP is the value assigned to the increased output, whether that is closing/resolving more service calls or producing more product. If the preceding discussions about converting time saved to other measures of value don't help, revisit how process performance speed was increased:

- Was the number of tasks or steps reduced?
- Were lag time or wait states between tasks reduced or eliminated?
- Were tasks or steps performed in parallel or concurrently?

Relate the ROP measures to what was changed. The approach used to increase process performance speed will lead you to an appropriate approach to deriving value for the process improvement. If the number of tasks or steps performed was reduced, then it is not likely that the same (as baseline) effort was expended to complete the process or subprocess. So unless the people performing the process intentionally sandbagged it to sabotage the results, the same or more work was performed with less effort. If this is the situation, then the value of the improvement is the amount of effort saved (not expended to perform the process) multiplied by the fully burdened rate of the person or people performing the process.

If tasks or steps were performed in parallel or concurrently— versus being performed serially in the process(es) used for the baseline measures—and if the same resource expended the effort to perform two or more tasks/steps concurrently, then the estimated value of the ROP is the percentage of the parallel work multiplied by the fully burdened rate. In other words, if the product designer previously was able to produce two component designs serially with 16 hours of effort and the improvement (probably new reuse practices) enabled her to produce two component designs mostly concurrently in 12 hours, then the annualized value of the improvement is 4 hours multiplied by the number of designs usually produced multiplied by the fully burdened rate for product designers.

Of course, the final ROP is calculated by taking the value of the benefit and subtracting the investment. As with other business investments, the useful ROP number will be the annualized value projected to some reasonable point in the future—when the improvement will be retired or subsumed by other improvements—versus the investment. Some process improvements will incur one-time costs, whereas others will require ongoing effort to institutionalize the change. Those improvements requiring ongoing effort need to have that annual effort calculated into the investment side of the equation.

Measuring Process Performance Efficacy

Refer to "Improving Process Performance Efficacy" in Chapter 2. In that section, you learned how to improve process performance efficacy (many people use the word "effectiveness") by making every action count. If that was one of your methods of improvement, then that is what you should measure in terms of performance improvement.

Measuring process performance efficacy, as with all improvement measures, involves counting things before the improvement, counting those same things following the improvement, and then applying your chosen unit of value to the difference. Table 3.2 provides guidance on what to measure depending on the efficacy improvement the organization made.

Measuring Process Performance Output Quality

Refer to "Improving Process Performance Output and Results Quality" in Chapter 1 and remember that before undertaking the pursuit of greater quality, the organization should first determine the acceptable level of quality for its products or services, beyond which there is no appreciable effect on

Table 3.2   Measuring Efficacy Improvements

Process Efficacy Improvement	Postimprovement Measure
Work necessity	Tasks/steps that were not performed but needed to be performed and associated waste, rework, or lost value
	Tasks/steps that were performed but were not needed and associated waste
Work results	Effort and cost saved not performing actions that do not result in creation or change of state of work products
	Value of work products created or changed resulting from actions performed that previously did not yield results
	Value of work that temporally creates significant effort, cost, or opportunity savings later in time or in a product or service life cycle

business performance. In other words, if greater product or service quality beyond a certain threshold doesn't affect business value, then all effort toward quality beyond that threshold is waste…anti-improvement.

So measuring performance improvement resulting from process output quality improvement requires an understanding (and measures) of the cost of producing certain levels of quality prior to the improvement, and knowing that incurring quality improvement costs will result in incremental quality that is worth at least the improvement investment and preferably more.

Thus, improved process performance quality output could take these forms:

■ Lower effort or cost to produce the same (current) quality
■ Current effort or cost to produce higher quality
■ Increased effort or cost to produce higher quality, the value of which exceeds the increased effort/cost

Measuring the Defined Process Changes

If you remember only one concept from Chapter 2, it should be this: Performance improvement comes from improvement in process performance. Thus, the only way that improvements in process definition or representation can affect performance improvement is if and only if there is high fidelity between the performed process and the defined process (also see "Synchronizing the Defined and Performed Processes" in Chapter 2).

Overlay what you've learned from this in defined–performed process synchronization with what you or others in your organization are doing right now. Perhaps, like so many other people having similar responsibilities in process improvement, your or your organization's EPG/SEPG is diligently and with the best intentions making these mistakes:

- Writing or revising processes and procedures without knowing much about process performance
- Suggesting changes to process performance without knowing how the processes are defined or represented
- Writing processes which are not much more than a re-representation of verbiage in either the CMMI, ITIL, ISO, AS9100, or TL 9000
- Implementing "process improvements" without knowing what needs to be improved or why
- Implementing process improvement without knowing or characterizing the current state of process performance

To move forward, let's assume that you and your colleagues in process improvement are not doing any of these things and that, if you are, you'll have the courage to change course. Is there anything you can do in process definition to achieve measurable improvement?

No, not directly, but there is important work related to process definition that you and others with process improvement responsibility can do that will lay the foundation for process and performance improvement:

- Read, understand, and formulate your own plans to implement the concepts in "Improving the Defined Process" in Chapter 2.
- Read, understand, and formulate plans to integrate the concepts and practices in Chapter 5, "Improving Process Improvement."
- Develop process design standards and define process system entities, specifically those entities identified in "Establish Process Design Standards" in Chapter 2.
- Improve your acumen in process modeling.

By acquiring and applying new knowledge and skills related to process design and definition, you will positively affect the eventual ROP by reducing the resources, cost, and time needed for process development.

Making Claims of Performance Results from Process Improvement

In my search for case studies in which organizations achieved business results through process improvement, I found a collection of presentations and white papers on the Software Engineering Institute (SEI)'s website that were labeled "CMMI Case Studies" within the web pages titled, "Performance and Process Improvement." I downloaded the files (seven at the time) and began analyzing them. It's easy to be critical of other people's work without offering an alternative, and that's not the theme or intent of this book. However, it is important to learn from others, including lessons on what not to do. In this spirit of learning, here is a short analysis of some of the CMMI case studies. To be fair to the authors of these presentations and articles, it is not they who make the claim that their work constitutes cases studies; it is the SEI that categorized them as such.

"Aligning CMMI Implementation & Organizational Strategy for Better Competitive Advantages" was a presentation from Ron Radice and Madmuhita P. Sen at the SEPG conference in 2011. I have great respect for Ron Radice, and he has made some very original and good contributions to process improvement over the years, but there were no performance case studies in this presentation. In fact, the entire premise of the presentation was that an organization can "implement the CMMI," which is something we all should know by now cannot be done; we can implement processes but not a model. Slides 10 and 11 were titled "Sample cases...," but they only addressed the relationships between CMMI process areas at various maturity levels. There were statements that hinted at possible business performance such as "CAR removes the common causes of process variance after the assignable causes are removed at ML4, thus enabling an optimal process performance," but no actual instance or data of the optimal performance was cited. Slide 12 provided examples of presumed business performance enhancements by evolving to higher maturity levels, but the statements were replete with "could" and "should," indicating they were hypothetical or ideal situations, but not historical instances—not case studies.

"Benefits of CMMI within the Defense Industry" was a presentation developed by the SEI. It reported the performance improvements achieved through CMMI adoption and use in Raytheon, Harris, Northrop Grumman, AIS, Lockheed Martin, and the Armament Software Engineering Center at Picatinny, New Jersey. This presentation (which I attended at the 2010 NDIA CMMI Conference) reported improvements in schedule performance, rework cost performance, cost of repair, and quality performance as the organizations increased their CMMI maturity levels. So, these companies took performance measures when they were at various maturity levels, and the claim was that performance increased as the maturity level increased. The presentation certainly proved coincidence and intimated correlation, but in no way did it prove causality between the CMMI maturity level gains and the performance improvement. Did they factor in the effects of new technology or increased worker skill and expertise? I asked, and the response was "No." When they calculated the improved ROI from achieving higher maturity levels—some ratios astoundingly as high as 27.7 to 1—did they remember to subtract from the benefits the cost of the investment (the "I"), which would have been their total cost of developing and implementing CMMI-based processes from the time they began their CMMI journey? No. When I asked this question of the presenters, the answer was, "We would have had to do CMMI anyway."

In "How a Strong and Principled PPQA Overcomes Acute Challenges to Process Improvement," the authors reported the positive effects that implementing a team of principled process auditors had on implementing process changes. It was a good story and provided some excellent advice for establishing a quality function in an organization. Then, toward the end of the presentation, with almost no segue, there were slides showing performance improvement such as service stability and quality of change delivery. The reader was to presume that the implementation of the PPQA (process and product quality assurance) function and the change in process adoption caused these performance changes. In the interest of fair treatment on this, I exchanged e-mails with Sally Hannington, the co-developer and presenter of the slides. She said she really didn't have time to discuss the presentation with me and made a point to let me know that the organization was no longer pursuing CMMI maturity levels.

In 2002, the SEI published a document titled, "Using CMMI to Improve Earned Value Management (CMU/SEI-2002-TN-016)." Whereas the document did a good job of relating CMMI components to earned value management (EVM) standards, the closest this document came to "performance" was to address how EVM is integral to performance management systems. The document did not describe any instantiations of organizations achieving performance improvement from process improvement.

The reality of these and other experiences is that if you just give them a cursory review and don't dig a little deeper, they appear to be examples of business performance improvement achieved through process improvement. Some processes were improved and, in the same time frame, some performance improved, but that doesn't define a causal relationship. Performance improvement doesn't happen by accident or serendipity; it is planned, executed, monitored, and measured in a way that establishes and maintains a defined and preferably quantitative relationship between the process improvement and the performance improvement. If you think you see a relationship between process improvement and performance improvement, but you cannot define it using observations, facts, or measures, then the relationship is speculative at best.

If you cannot come up with fact-based answers to the following questions about process and performance improvement in your organization, then you may or may not have improved performance through process improvement:

- During the process improvement effort, what other changes—such as changes to tools or technology or changes to the work force—were made? What was the effect of those other changes on the performance improvement results?
- What were the measures defined and used to determine improvement in the defined process and, more importantly, the performed process? What is the relationship between those process performance measures and the business performance measures that were collected and used?
- If the correlation presented is between CMMI maturity levels and performance improvement, which process areas and practices were used to improve the processes, which processes were improved and how, and how did those changes affect performance?

Return on CMMI Use

Many organizations that adopt the CMMI as their guidance for process improvement will not achieve a positive, quantized ROP, especially organizations that end their CMMI adoption at maturity level 3. But that doesn't mean there isn't any value in adopting and using the CMMI; its use does provide value—qualitative if not quantitative—to many organizations.

One way to think about CMMI value is to view it as a collection of work practices that, if implemented, can serve as a "safety net" and help keep your organization from making mistakes or getting into trouble. Anyone who tries to argue that staying out of trouble doesn't have value will just look silly.

Think about a practice such as "adjust the project plan to reconcile available and estimated resources" (PP SP 3.2). It's not hard to imagine what happens when this practice is *not* implemented in a project. It's also not hard to envision that at least part of the evolution of a practice like this came from lessons learned: "Ouch! We ran out of resources before the project was complete...I wonder what we could have done differently?" Or: "Our release is 3 months late and we're way over budget paying for overtime...was there something wrong with our plan?" Whether or not you consider a practice like this a "best practice" is not as relevant as accepting this practice as something that sane people do and insane people don't do.

There is also value—sometimes quantifiable, sometimes not—in achieving and maintaining maturity levels, whether or not performance improvement was also achieved. Right or wrong, like it or not, the way defense and government contracting has evolved is that government agencies, program offices, and acquisition offices have established CMMI maturity levels and ISO registrations as overly simplified surrogates for capability and performance. As a result, the contracting entities get exactly what they ask for, which is often different from what they really want.

However, if you're the contractor and you know that the opening ante to play this game is a maturity level or an ISO registration, then achieving those things becomes part of your business strategy and objectives; you can't win if you can't play.

But just because an organization has to maintain a maturity level or compliance with a standard doesn't mean that it can't also enjoy real performance improvement and a positive ROP. After all, most organizations in this situation will have to undertake most process improvement work at their own internal cost: overhead. Overhead or indirect charges are always closely scrutinized and controlled because excessive overhead costs eat into profit and shareholder value. So, if you have to incur overhead to pay for process improvement, at least try to make process improvement pay for some of that overhead cost. Maturity levels or standards compliance and real performance improvement are not mutually exclusive.

Putting It into Practice

As you may recall, in "Putting It into Practice" in Chapter 2, the Federal Division EPG at Ascendance Consulting Corporation developed process improvement objectives and measures and then implemented improvements in both the defined and the performed process. Then, the EPG, in collaboration with several product development projects, piloted the improvements in peer reviews and compared the process performance measures with the baseline measures they collected and analyzed before implementing the improvements (see Table 2.11 in Chapter 2).

It has been 18 months since the Federal Division president conducted the off-site in Park City, Utah, with her management team, in which they established the division's 3-year performance objectives. Now the CEO is asking the division president for a status on the progress toward those objectives. He also wants to know how the division is progressing toward achieving CMMI maturity level 5.

Putting It into Practice: Deriving the Return on Process

The EPG now has enough preimprovement and postimprovement data to determine the value of the performance improvements that resulted from the peer review improvements. But before we can start doing the calculations for the value of the performance improvement, we have to parse the data from Table 2.11 in Chapter 2 into the cost of the improvement (investment) versus the benefits or savings or benefits resulting from the improvement; Table 3.3 shows a way to do this parsing.

When the EPG looks at raw data such as the numbers presented in Table 2.11, they realize that they can't just show these numbers to higher levels of management. Without providing contextual analysis, it's too easy for people to see only what they want to see, but not the whole picture. For example, if someone sees that the average per-reviewer effort went up by 0.3 person-hours, and that the average number of peer reviews per project increased by two, it would be easy to conclude that the average cost to the projects to conduct peer reviews increased. However, when you then consider that on average three people fewer were involved in a peer review postimprovement, the whole picture comes into view. The before-improvement average project cost of conducting peer reviews was

$$8 \text{ peer reviews/project} \times 5.5 \text{ effort-hours/reviewer} \times 6.5 \text{ reviewers} = 286 \text{ effort-hours}$$

The post-improvement average project cost of conducting peer reviews is

$$10 \text{ peer reviews/project} \times 5.8 \text{ effort-hours/reviewer} \times 3.5 \text{ reviewers} = 203 \text{ effort-hours}$$

So, one of the ROP messages the EPG delivers to management and the organization is an average per-project cost

Table 3.3   Putting It into Practice: Parsing Process Improvement Costs versus Benefits

Peer Review Performance Dimension	Improvement Cost	Improvement Benefit
Average number of peer reviews conducted per project	2	
Percentage of peer reviews conducted on requirements work products		16 percent
Percentage of peer reviews conducted on project planning work products		12 percent
Average number of peer review iterations on the same work product		1
Average number of defects captured and removed per peer review		10
Percentage of technical or content defects detected in peer reviews		34 percent
Defects removed in first peer review of a work product as a percentage of all defects eventually removed through all iterations		25 percent
Average peer review effort per reviewer (planning, conduct, and follow-up defect removal)	0.3 person-hours	
Average number of people involved in a peer review		Three people
Average person-effort per defect captured and removed	1.5 person-hours	

savings of 83 effort-hours, which, when multiplied by the fully burdened rate, is $8,300.00.

But the process performance cost savings is not the big story…the really big ROP story is in process efficiency and process efficacy as described in the following subsections.

Putting It into Practice: ROP Efficiency Gains

With the process improvements, peer reviews became more efficient, most prominently in structured walk-throughs. On average, the number of defects captured and removed in a peer review increased by 10. Also, the average number of peer review iterations on the same work product decreased by one, a savings that can be applied to project schedule performance.

These process performance efficiency gains correlate directly with the performance concept of speed. In ACC's Federal Division, the peer review process improvements have resulted in the same or more work output (more defects captured) with less work (less effort and less schedule to report the valuation of ROP in terms of efficiency returns, the EPG will report the increase in peer review efficiency as the increase in the number or percentage of defects captured per peer review (before = 25, after = 35), which is an efficiency gain of 40 percent. In addition, the EPG will report the efficiency gain represented by the reduction in the number of peer review iterations on the same work product (from three to one), which is a 200 percent efficiency gain.

Putting It into Practice: ROP Efficacy Gains

The EPG is feeling pretty good about the ROP. They are able to report positive results in terms of process performance cost savings and efficiency. With a little more analysis, they are prepared to respond confidently with a powerful ROP message when a senior manager or executive asks them to "show me the money," and that message is "efficacy."

The efficacy ROP measures come from two of the pre/postimprovement performance dimensions:

■ An increase of 16 percent in the peer reviews conducted on requirements-related work products
■ An increase of 12 percent in the peer reviews conducted on project planning work products

The EPG rationalizes that these are efficacy gains based on the prevailing literature that indicates defects removed early in the product development life cycle cost magnitudes less than removing them (or their derivative effects) later in the life cycle:

> Finding and fixing a software problem after delivery
> is often 100 times more expensive than finding and
> fixing it during the requirements and design phase.[1]

Also, refer to "Improving Process Performance Efficacy" in Chapter 2 to recall that one of the aspects of efficacy in terms of work results is the "value of work that temporally creates significant effort, cost, or opportunity savings later in time or in a product or service life cycle."

In other words, detecting and removing a defect in requirements or planning gives the organization "more bang for the buck" when it comes to its investment in peer reviews and peer review improvement.

The EPG has calculated that the postimprovement average cost per defect captured and removed via peer reviews is 6 effort-hours ($600 at the fully burdened rate). Since this figure is an average of defect removal throughout the product or service life cycle (up to delivery or release), then the SEPG conservatively applies this per-defect cost to the cost of finding and removing a defect at the beginning of the life cycle—requirements in product development or initial customer request in service delivery. This makes the cost of finding and removing a defect after product/service delivery

$60,000...ouch! With an aggregate increase in defect removal of 28 percent—16 percent increase in requirements and 12 percent increase in planning—the EPG estimates the peer review improvement has decreased the average cost of escaped defects (those needing to be found and fixed in the delivered product/service) by $16,800 per defect. There's the money.

Putting It into Practice: ROP Output Quality Gains

One of the observations that was supported by the historical peer review data collected by the EPG was that the "defects" found in most documents were related to formatting, typographical errors, spelling, or grammar—not technical content. (Refer to "Putting It into Practice: Defining Process Performance Objectives" in Chapter 2.)

The EPG—and everyone else—intuitively know that it is not good ROP to have highly paid engineers and managers look for and find spelling errors, and that their experts should spend more effort in peer reviews capturing technical or content defects. Punctuation and grammar "defects"—especially in internal, nondeliverable documents—don't have much of a cost, whereas technical defects have a much higher cost. As a result of the improvement that required all items subject to peer review first to be edited by a technical writer or editor, the percentage of those low-impact but high-cost nontechnical defects detected via peer reviews was reduced. (See "Putting It into Practice: Improving the Performed Process" in Chapter 2.) Thus, as shown in Table 3.3, the percentage of technical or content defects detected in peer reviews increased from 11 to 45 percent, an increase of 34 percent. The EPG doesn't have sufficient data on the cost of a technical defect versus the cost of a nontechnical defect, so it's difficult to evaluate this process output quality improvement. However, qualitatively, this change shows an increase in work product quality from the improved peer review performance.

Putting It into Practice: Progress toward Higher CMMI Maturity Levels

Recall that ACC's Federal Division has three peer review subprocesses: (1) formal inspections, (2) structured walk-throughs, and (3) collaborative redlining (also called "off-line reviews). (Refer to "Putting It into Practice: Defining Process Performance Objectives" in Chapter 2.)

Using historical data they collected plus measures from the piloting of the peer review improvements, the EPG was able to graph the defects detected per effort-hour for each peer review subprocess. Those measures are shown in the control charts in Figure 3.2.

The defects/hour data points are from 12 projects that implemented all three peer review subprocesses. Thus, the EPG now feels that it is making progress toward implementation of the quantitative project management process area in the CMMI as defined in Table 3.4.

The division president is under increasing pressure from the CEO to achieve CMMI-DEV maturity level 5, so she requests a meeting with the division EPG on the progress toward this goal. In the meeting, the EPG lead and the PMO manager tell the president that, although they probably have just enough evidence to achieve CMMI-DEV maturity level 4, they don't feel the newer practices are institutionalized, and they recommend spending more time measuring the processes and sub-processes and understanding the effects of the improvements.

She tells the EPG lead and the PMO manager how difficult it is for her to ask the CEO for more time to achieve CMMI maturity level 5. They sympathize with her and advise her to promote the very positive cost and schedule savings resulting from the peer review process improvements. They warn her that if the organization had to start preparing for a SCAMPI (standard CMMI appraisal method for process improvement) appraisal right now, it would hinder the improvement work under way and impede institutionalizing the improvements.

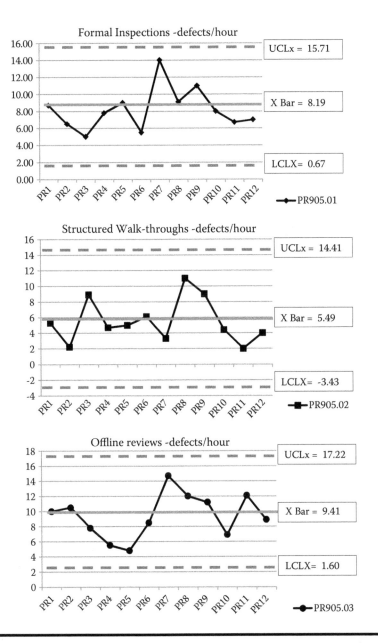

Figure 3.2   Putting it into practice: example subprocess control charts.

Table 3.4 Putting It into Practice: Progress toward Higher CMMI Maturity Levels

PA and Practice	Practice Description	Evidence of Implementation
QPM SP 1.1	Establish and maintain the project's quality and process performance objectives.	In ACC Federal Division, all projects now have quality objectives related to the performance of peer reviews. With the subprocess data shown in Figure X, projects can now establish measurement-based peer review performance objectives.
QPM SP 1.2	Using statistical and other quantitative techniques, compose a defined process that enables the project to achieve its quality and process performance objectives.	With the information shown in Figure X, ACC Federal Division projects can now use the organization's process tailoring assets (guidelines and a checklist) to define the project's peer review process, which will be a carefully planned mixed use of the three peer review subprocesses to achieve maximum peer review efficiency and efficacy.
QPM SP 1.3	Select subprocesses and attributes critical to evaluating performance and that help achieve the project's quality and process performance objectives.	The Federal Division EPG is in the process of establishing some new peer review guidelines, which will help projects select to use a peer review subprocess based on defined attributes, performance goals, and the type or class of work product being reviewed.

Table 3.4 (*Continued*) Putting It into Practice: Progress toward Higher CMMI Maturity Levels

PA and Practice	Practice Description	Evidence of Implementation
QPM SP 1.4	Select measures and analytical techniques to be used in quantitative management.	Projects are required to use performance measures and analysis methods currently defined in the division's measurement dictionary. Regardless of the peer review subprocess implemented, projects must continue collecting, analyzing, and reporting the peer review performance measures defined in Table X.
QPM SP 2.1	Monitor the performance of selected subprocesses using statistical and other quantitative techniques.	Control charts, such as those shown in Figure X, are used to monitor subprocess performance.
QPM SP 2.2	Manage the project using statistical and other quantitative techniques to determine whether or not the project's objectives for quality and process performance will be satisfied.	Based on discussions between the EPG and the project managers in the division's PMO, the division and account managers decided that there is not yet a large enough population of peer review performance measures and data (postimprovement) to design management practices for quantitatively managing project performance. They will continue to collect and analyze performance data and reconsider this in the future.

(Continued)

Table 3.4 (*Continued*) Putting It into Practice: Progress toward Higher CMMI Maturity Levels

PA and Practice	Practice Description	Evidence of Implementation
QPM SP 2.3	Perform root cause analysis of selected issues to address deficiencies in achieving the project's quality and process performance objectives.	As with the QPM SP 2.2, the organization doesn't believe it yet has enough statistical data to identify deficiencies in the process, much less perform meaningful root cause analysis. This, too, is deferred until there are substantially more measures and information.

She agrees and asks the EPG lead and the PMO manager to help her prepare her slides for meeting with the CEO; they happily agree to help.

Do's and Don'ts

Here is a summary list of things you should do and things you should not do when working to achieve and understand ROP.

Do

1. Measure the effects of what was changed.
2. Understand—quantitatively if possible—the effects of changes in process, technology, and people on performance.
3. Measure the results of process performance improvement and define the relationship between that performance and work/project or organizational performance.
4. Determine how to apply value (e.g., money) to performance improvement.
5. Do all the "Do's" in this book.

Don't

1. Make claims of "improvement" without being able to demonstrate or quantize the value of the improvement to organizational performance. You'll be the hero right up to the point at which someone asks you to prove it; then you're screwed.
2. Leave the word "improvement" undefined, unspecified, or unqualified.
3. Think that just because your leadership isn't constantly asking about ROP that it doesn't care; it'll care the moment you least expect it and are unprepared to respond.
4. Do any of the "Don'ts" in this book.

Reflect and Plan: What Did You Learn? What Will You Do?

Now review the following postchapter guide and think about what you've learned and how some of your views toward process and performance improvement have changed. Think about what you will do with the information you've learned (and how it makes you feel).

What?

1. What are the preimprovement and postimprovement process performance measures? Does it appear that process performance improved as a result of the changes that were implemented?
2. What are the measures that indicate improvement in process speed/efficiency?
3. What are the measures that indicate improvement in process efficacy?
4. What are the measures that indicate improvement in process output quality?

5. What are the measures that indicate improvement in the defined process?
6. What measures indicate that improvements to the defined process affected process performance?

Who?

1. Who is responsible for measuring the changes in process performance?
2. Who is responsible for monitoring the cost versus the value of process improvement?
3. Who is responsible for implementing changes in the performed processes or the defined processes?
4. Who is responsible for providing coaching or mentoring to the teams and individuals who are implementing process changes or improvements?
5. Who is responsible for calculating and reporting the ROP?
6. Who is responsible or accountable for demonstrating that a positive ROP was achieved?

When and How Much?

1. How long or how many improvement data points will you need to prove that the process improvements are positively affecting performance and ROP? Have you been given enough time?
2. How will the effects of concurrent improvements in technology and worker skills be valued and calculated in the ROP?
3. How much is the organization willing to risk losing? How much will it risk to win?

Endnote

1. Boehm, Barry and Victor R. Basili, "Software Defect Reduction Top 10 List," *Software Management,* January 2001.

Chapter 4

Small Changes, Big Performance Improvement

Even the largest avalanche is triggered by small things.

—Vernor Vinge

The Greatest ROP

What would yield the greatest return on process? Going back to our formula for determining ROP, the greatest ROP would come from making the smallest investment in a change that yields the greatest performance improvement…tiny changes that yield big performance results.

This chapter is about changes that can be easily implemented and institutionalized by individuals and teams at all levels of any organization. And here's what is really cool about these types of changes: They don't require some grandiose, sweeping change effort, nor do they require high-level policy changes or mandates from on high, nor do they require sophisticated tools, systems, or products.

But the real beauty of these changes is what I call the "tyranny of numbers." The tyranny of numbers means that the performance improvement that results from one person or one team implementing a change multiplied by the number of people, teams, or occurrences of change. If one person out of a thousand in your organization implements a change that saves 20 minutes per day, then all 1,000 people implementing the change can yield a daily savings of 20,000 minutes (333 hours per day or 42 business days per day), or the equivalent of 63 additional employees without hiring a single new person!

Here's a simple, practical example of implementing a tyranny of numbers improvement. In Microsoft Outlook, there is an e-mail Signatures and Stationary option that allows you to have Outlook automatically populate the bottom of all e-mail notes, including replies and forwards, with your contact information such as name, phone number, company or organization, credentials—really, anything you want. Thus, every time you send, forward, or reply to an e-mail, Outlook will automatically put this standard information in the bottom of your note. My observation of many years in office environments is that a very small portion of all modern workers use this Outlook feature. (As an aside—and explored in more detail later—very few people use very few of the features in MS Office tools that are designed to increase worker efficiency and efficacy. See "Use 20 to Do 80" in this chapter.)

For example, let's be really generous and say that 60 percent of the workers in our organization take advantage of this Outlook feature and that they at least have their phone number automatically populate in their e-mail signatures; 40 percent of our workforce does not use this feature. So the 40 percent create waste in one of two ways: (1) They take the extra time to enter their phone numbers manually in the signature, or (2) they don't include their phone number, so if recipients want to talk to the sender about the e-mail, they have to look up the sender's phone number or get up out of their office and go see the sender in person if they can.

Scenario caveats include the following:

1. Not every sender who doesn't use the Signatures and Stationary option is going to bother to enter his or her contact information manually.
2. Not every recipient of e-mails from the non-Signature-and-Stationary senders is going to bother to respond by phone or in person; he or she will simply reply via e-mail (or not respond at all to the "jerk" who refuses to learn how to use Outlook).

For the sake of illustrating the tyranny of numbers process improvement and resulting performance, we will assume the following:

1. Only half of the non-Signature e-mail senders in the organization (20 percent of the total organization's population) take the time to enter their phone number manually or (but could be "and") only half of the recipients of e-mail from non-Signature-and-Stationary e-mail senders look up the sender's phone number and call.
2. It takes about 10 seconds for non-Signature e-mail senders to enter their own phone number, or it takes about 20 seconds for a recipient to look up a sender's phone number in a corporate directory or online contact employee database. So we'll figure an average waste of 15 seconds per incident.
3. The average number of e-mails sent or received per day that cause waste is one per Luddite employee.

If all employees in the organization adopted the practice (a process improvement) of populating their e-mail Signatures with contact info, Figure 4.1 shows the daily, quarterly, and annual savings in employee effort.

Organization Size (# of employees)	Daily Savings (person-hours)	Quarterly Savings (person-days)	Annual Savings (person-days)
50	2.5	17.6	70.3
100	5.0	35.2	140.6
500	25.0	175.8	703.1
1000	50.0	351.6	1,406.3
10000	500.0	3,515.6	14,062.5
100000	5,000.0	35,156.3	140,625.0

Figure 4.1 Example of tyranny of numbers savings by adopting an MS Outlook feature.

By implementing and institutionalizing this simple tyranny of numbers process improvement, an organization of 100,000 employees would save 625 person-years per year! Want to see the money? Multiply these effort numbers by your organization's average fully burdened rate and take this to the board of directors or the investors if you want high-level sponsorship for your improvement idea.

Improvement initiatives do not have to be multi-million dollar ventures funding armies of process improvement "experts." Significant improvements in efficiency, efficacy, and productivity can come when one small behavioral change or one incremental work practice is implemented by a hundred or a thousand people every day. As the leader, you, more than anyone else, can influence tyranny of number improvements and results by first making

the change in your own work habits. In other
words, lead from the front by setting the example
rather than pushing from behind.

Use 20 to Do 80

Most of you know or at least have heard of the Pareto principle,[1]
although many of you will have learned some corporate
perversion of this principle that is no longer connected to its
origin. Here's the thing…every day, you and millions of other
workers will spend your whole work day (every day) in one
of two modes. You either

1. Spend 80 percent of your effort accomplishing only
   20 percent of what's important or
2. Spend 20 percent of your effort accomplishing the most
   important work, but then spend another 80 percent of
   your effort accomplishing the 20 percent of the work that
   is not important

In either case, you're wasting a lot of effort and not getting
much done. Some everyday examples follow.

I create something, such as a chapter for this book, a software program, an organizational policy, a new process, a
mechanical design, an article, or a technical paper. I spend
80 percent of my effort getting the content right. I check my
facts. I research and validate my references. I structure my
arguments in a logical manner. I check for internal consistency.
I undertake due diligence to make the creation compelling
and interesting. (Otherwise, it would be just another unqualified opinion disguised as information, like a blog or a tweet!)
Then I spend 20 percent of my effort on non-content-related
work such as spelling, grammar, format, etc. Then I send it to
"peers" for review and comment, but I fail to spend any time
carefully selecting those reviewers. Why? Because I live in an

organization like you in which the culture says that everyone's opinion is valuable, even when those opinions are uninformed or uneducated in the topic at hand.

I send my creation to 10 people whom I've been told are my "peers," when in fact only two of them are my peers and the other eight are work colleagues with a lot of time on their hands. I ask for input on the content.

What happens next? The same thing that happens a thousand times a day across America: From the reviewers who actually understand the topic, I get useful questions, comments, and intelligent insights on the content. The other reviewers, not wanting to appear as if they aren't contributing (i.e., not a "team player"), will spend 80 to 100 percent of their time looking for the only things they can find—spelling errors, word choice, punctuation, grammar, or formatting problems—and send me that input. In other words, a whole bunch of highly paid engineers or managers will spend time doing what one technical writer could do—only the tech writer would provide more accurate input and do so more efficiently.

Here's another example that I'm sure you'll recognize, but beware that the truth is often too painful to bear. A major telecommunications company spends several years and several million dollars implementing Six Sigma techniques to improve the quality of their cell phone software. The escaped (released) defect density is respectable (just below 1 percent), but the "culture of quality" police—the zealots that believe quality should be pursued for its own sake—have taken over headquarters. The underlying premise of the multimillion-dollar Six Sigma quality effort is that if the cell phone software defect density is reduced to almost zero, then more customers/consumers will buy the products and the company will expand its market share.

Several years and several million dollars later, the escaped defect density is reduced to near zero (100 percent or "total" quality), but there was no correlating increase in cell phone sales. Nice try, thanks for playing. So, it would seem that before the quality campaign, it took maybe 20 percent (plus or minus a sigma) to detect and capture most of the product defects before product release, but then another 80 percent (plus or minus a sigma) was spent to remove the last 1 percent of the defects. This sounds worthwhile until you realize that the last 1 percent of the product defects were things that the vast majority of consumers would never even notice before they tossed their cell phone and replaced it with a newer model. The high-cost defects captured via the Six Sigma program lived in features/functions that most consumers never even learned and hence wouldn't notice. Which executive (i.e., lamb) gets to go to the board and say, "I'm pleased to announce that we improved our quality by 1 percent while reducing your share value by 5 percent"?

In November 1990, the first widely distributed version of Microsoft Office was made available. Within a few years, the office productivity products within this product suite—Word, Excel, PowerPoint, and Outlook—and the extended products—Project and Visio—became omnipotent, the de facto productivity products for almost every information worker in the world.

With efficient and effective use of these tools, an information worker could dramatically increase his or her productivity. The line manager with a high proficiency in Excel could reduce the number of people needed in accounting. The engineer who was highly adept at Word could do her job and the job of the technical or specification writer. The division president who was also a virtuoso in PowerPoint could become a business capture manager and reduce marketing costs. Outlook could reduce the time spent communicating and yet communicate more effectively. Very little of this vision of productivity derived from these fantastic tools has been realized.

Why? Because people either can't or won't learn something new and then change. The following subsections provide just a glimpse into the 20–80 waste that I've seen; you've probably seen (or are guilty of) even more.

The Wrong Tool for the Work

Look at your latest PowerPoint presentation. Are there words covering the slides? Is it bereft of succinct, bulleted items and meaningful graphics? If you really wanted your audience to read a bunch of text, why didn't you create a document in Word? A presentation is supposed to make a few key points or summarize a significant message, not go into the subatomic level of detail of your technical paper. You spent 80 percent effort playing around with colors and type styles and sizes to make all those words "attention getting" and attractive, when you could have spent 20 percent effort just representing all those words in a Word document.

Did you use Excel just because you wanted to present information in tabular format, but with no requirement for formulas or calculations? It also limits formatting, which is something you don't want to take the time to learn about tables in Word. Go ahead: Pass the challenge in reading and digesting poorly formatted information to your audience...you got through it more quickly.

Or did you use a Word table to represent data or information that does require significant calculation? So, you work the formulas using a calculator and then manually represent the calculation results in the Word table. Not only did you spend 80 percent effort on this one table, you'll spend it again the next time you use those same external calculations. Why not just take the time to teach yourself a formula or two in Excel, especially if you know you're going to use them again in the future?

My favorite PowerPoint story comes from my days at Xerox. I was working in a product development group. One day I walked into Dan's office to get an updated project schedule. Dan said he was just updating it and would send a copy to the printer for me. I watched over his shoulder as he selected and dragged triangles to the right on what appeared to be time lines...all drawn in PowerPoint! I asked, "Dan, why don't you use MS Project for the project schedule? You could update the dates and the Gantt chart would automatically reflect the changes." Dan's response: "I spend all day updating this schedule, so I don't have time to learn Project." The tragic irony escaped him. An investment in learning would have made Dan more efficient in his work, enabling him to spend 20 percent on project schedules and leaving him time to spend performing other project manager duties that were being neglected.

Learning to Save

The MS Office products are replete with productivity-enhancing features; we just don't invest the time to learn them, so we don't become more productive and efficient.

If you're really quick, you can manually format a section heading in Word—font style, size, and other attributes—in about 30 seconds, and you'll spend 30 seconds every time you do it. You also then have to set the formatting for the text that follows the heading. Multiply this by the number of headings times the number of documents you'll produce in your lifetime and it adds up.

If you're really slow, you can teach yourself how to create Word styles in about 15 minutes and then take another 15 minutes to create them. By the way, the styles you create are not only available in the document you're currently working on, but also available in all of your documents.

Applying a style takes about 5 seconds, which is one-sixth the time required to format text manually. By the 60th heading, you've recovered your investment in learning Word styles, and from that point forward you are six times more efficient at creating Word documents than you were before. The small investment in learning a product's feature pays great dividends for as long as you are using MS Word.

Let's say you have a graphic or text that you want to appear at the top of every slide in a PowerPoint file. You couldn't be bothered to learn how to set up a master slide, so you copy the slide element from one slide to another, taking about

20 seconds each time you copy it and position it in the right place in the new slide. In a 30-slide presentation, you spend about 10 minutes doing this. It doesn't seem like enough time to worry about, but over the course of working professionally— let's say 30 years—you're likely to create 300 presentations, so your inefficient work habit will have a cost of 50 hours. It doesn't sound like a very high cost but, over time, these common behaviors incur a very high cost to the organization:

- People use the wrong tool for the work (PowerPoint instead of Word, Word instead of Excel, Excel instead of a database, PowerPoint instead of Project, Excel instead of Project, PowerPoint instead of Visio).
- People don't learn the features that enhance productivity.
- People don't learn or adopt work habits or practices that would dramatically improve their productivity.

The old saying that "perfection is the enemy of the good" illustrates a prevalent contributing factor to people spending 20 percent of the effort or money to get 80 percent of the value from their work, but then instead of moving on to other work, spending the remaining 80 percent of the effort/money to do the remaining 20 percent of the work that doesn't yield commensurate value. This happens frequently in product development and service delivery. A product development organization will spend 20 percent of the budget for a release to implement most or all of the high-priority customer requirements, and then spend 80 percent of the project budget and schedule on requirements that are not important to anyone.

Make Meetings Work

John Kenneth Galbraith said, "Meetings are indispensable when you don't want to do anything." Don't even pretend you aren't aware of this big, ugly, not-so-secret business truth! Whenever

I talk to clients about performance improvements, the topic inevitably includes a sentiment best summarized as "I could get something done if I didn't have to go to all these meetings."

The mistake that I and other consultants initially make is to recommend the ultimate and doomed-to-failure counterculture solution: have fewer meetings. That's an idea, but a bad one because it will never be implemented, so move on.

Here's an idea that does work: Make meetings work. By that I mean that, if you are going to have lots of meetings anyway (and you will), at least make them productive. Make meetings yield something more than an hour's worth of converting oxygen to carbon dioxide. Show me a meeting, and I'll show you waste.

What typically happens in meetings? A few really smart people, interspersed by meeting mongers who either have nothing else to do or don't really know their responsibilities, get together either physically or virtually. They talk for an hour plus. Some good—maybe even great—ideas are exchanged. Decisions are made, and people commit to action, and everyone adjourns saying "good meeting." Sometime between an hour and a few days later, all the good will, the good intentions, the good ideas and decisions, and all the actions that were temporarily held in the cache of our individual and collective synapses have evaporated into the ether, to be revisited in part or in full in the next meeting.

So in the next meeting, the first half of the hour is spent recalling the discussions, decisions, and actions (which have not been executed) from the prior meeting. Given this very common scenario and applying simple math, you would think that meetings are only 50 percent efficient, with half of each meeting spent revisiting the prior meeting. You would be wrong; such meetings are almost 0 percent efficient. If decisions and actions are never recorded, if they mostly evaporate until summoned like spirits with a Ouija board in the next meeting, and such summoning has to recur meeting after meeting, then your meetings are really adding up to a tragically monumental waste of time and money. Want to fix this? Table 4.1 identifies very

Table 4.1 Making Meetings Work

Meeting Element	Inefficiency/Inefficacy	How to Fix
Agenda	With no defined (written) agenda, there is no plan for the meeting and the topics. Meetings become a free-for-all, with every participant wanting to discuss his or her concern or issue du jour. Some people will leave the meeting satisfied that they were heard, but most people will leave knowing that not much of anything important was addressed.	Publish an agenda that specifies, at a minimum, prioritized topics to be discussed and expected outputs, such as expected resulting decisions or actions. An agenda published and distributed in advance of the meeting will have the ancillary positive effect in that people who really don't have any business going to the meeting will know it's obvious…and so will everyone else.
Participation	In almost every meeting, there are people who really don't need to be there. Their attendance has a triple negative effect on efficiency: (1) the cost of the time and lost opportunity of the irrelevant participants, (2) the cost of irrelevant participants derailing the meeting from achieving its intended purpose, and (3) the time lost by relevant participants wondering why the irrelevant participants are there.	Involve the right people for the right work at the right time. (Also see "Involve the Right People for the Right Work at the Right Time" in this chapter.) When the written agenda is developed, evaluate the topics and use that to determine the relevant participants. Send the agenda and the meeting invitation only to people who can and will contribute to the topics. Do not courtesy or FYI copy others; they might see it as an invitation.

Minutes	One of the reasons people resist recording meeting minutes is because they perceive that minutes have to reflect every word spoken in the meeting, much like a trial transcript recorded by a court stenographer.	The only really valuable elements of meeting records are the decisions that were made and the action items that were assigned or processed. See "Decisions" and "Actions" in this table.
Decisions	Waste is making the same decision multiple times.	Record decisions, who made them, the evaluation criteria, and decision methods involved. Establish a team rule or meeting policy that a decision will not be revisited just because someone wants it revisited, and that a challenger of a decision must present factual evidence that compels a decision to be revisited. Also see "Make Decisions Once and Make Good Decisions" in this chapter.
Actions	Unrecorded, unassigned actions or actions with no due date cause substantial waste. Subsequent meetings are spent with participants asking, "What was it we were going to do?" And since nothing was actually done since the last meeting, it's like the film *Groundhog Day*, reliving the same meeting over and over.	Record action items. Assign them to a person or a team to perform. Assign a due date. Track aging of each action item. Whenever possible, associate an action item with a parent WBS task or higher level project or work.

simple, easy-to-execute meeting management improvements that will yield performance results.

More Meeting Efficiency and Efficacy Tips

Another naturally occurring phenomenon that makes meetings wasteful is all the people in the room or virtual meeting space doing anything but contributing to the topics and discussions. Look around...they're reading e-mail, texting, checking their Facebook postings, or checking their tweets. They'll tell you they're listening and paying attention, which is easily disproven when you ask of someone, "What do you think about what I just said?" (Also read "The Multitasking Myth" in this chapter.)

I've learned the hard way that you're not going to stop this behavior, no matter how many times you point out to the multitaskers that their behavior is disrespectful and unprofessional; it is now the accepted norm. The best you can do to keep such behavior from making meetings a complete waste is to manage it.

One time, at the beginning of a meeting with a client, my wife and business partner, Jitka, came up with what turned out to be a simple and effective solution: She invented "e-breaks." Many adults are like me and need periodic biological breaks during long meetings to do things like visit the restroom or refill coffee cups. But just as I need to satisfy my caffeine addiction, many other meeting participants need to satisfy their digital communication addiction. We call them e-breaks, short for "electronic breaks," and they are set for 10 to 15 minutes and designated for people to turn on their cell phones or laptops to catch up on all their conversations with others. When we announce and describe the e-breaks at the beginning of a meeting, we ask that the participants reciprocate and leave their devices turned off between the e-breaks. We usually get no push-back; in fact, most people love the idea and willingly discipline themselves and stay engaged during the meeting. It's a wonderful and creative way to manage and limit the effects of distracting and wasteful behavior, and it works.

As a manager, you probably go to more meetings than people in other positions. Since it is unlikely that going to meetings is what got you promoted to manager (rather, it was doing real work), it is unlikely that going to more meetings will keep moving you up the ladder. Choose your meetings wisely. Go only to those in which—per the agenda—you have a real stake or can contribute to a discussion or decision. Otherwise, stay at your desk and work. In the long run, work is noticed and it is your work and your outputs that will enhance your career.

Ever notice that some people can't get enough meetings and that they would be happy to do nothing all day but go to meetings? There are two reasons for that: The first—for some small percentage of the work force—is that if they are in meetings all day, then they have a rock-solid alibi for not getting any work done. But the primary reason that some people really want meetings, and more of them if possible, is because they crave the social interaction with other people. They simply need to be around other people and talk.

Like the "multitaskers," you won't change this either, but you can use the e-breaks mentioned earlier to serve double duty as social breaks. Just make it clear at the beginning of each meeting that the e-breaks are for diving back into the digital existence or for catching up with others in person. If you want to make meetings work, especially long meetings, you have to give people designated time off from the meeting to do what they want to do. Otherwise, they'll do what they want to do for the entire meeting and not contribute to the work being performed.

The tyranny of numbers phenomenon can really amp up your productivity and efficiency gains if you make meetings work. Let's say that on any given day in your organization there are five meetings (conservatively low) and that each meeting involves an average of five people and lasts an average duration of 1 hour. If you implement the tips in this section, you could reasonably expect to gain 10 minutes of productivity per person per meeting. That's a savings of a little over 4 hours per day. The organization gained half of a person-year in productivity without hiring someone.

Involve the Right People for the Right Work at the Right Time

Have you ever wanted to turn to someone in a meeting and ask, "Why are you here?" I know I have wanted to do that many times but, of course, the culture of political correctness prevents us from ever doing any such thing and thus prevents us from finding and removing waste in our organizations. To be that blunt about recognizing waste in today's organizations is to reduce both your likability and your chances for advancement in the organization instantly and forever. As they say, it's career limiting.

If we were free to ferret out wasted time and money and could ask that question, conversation with the meeting monger (MM) would often go like this:

Me: Why are you here?
MM: I was invited.
Me: Well, are you presenting any information to us?

MM: No.

Me: Well, are you here to get information that you will use in your work or for some purpose?

MM: No.

Me: Well, then, why are you here?

MM: I was invited.

Have you ever been given both responsibility for a project and accountability for results but you didn't get to choose who would be on your team? It's like playing dodge-ball in school except that other managers have first pick of everyone they want on their teams, and your only choice of players is those not chosen by the other teams.

Sometimes, we do get to choose the people on our team, but we choose poorly because we select team members for all the wrong reasons. In 2011, my consulting firm was engaged by a national lab known for developing nuclear weapons. The project was to redesign and redevelop the organization's product realization processes, and my company was brought in for our experience and knowledge in process design and development.

The prevailing organizational culture, like so many others, was one of inclusion. The people managing the project really had no choice but to invite to the project meetings and events people from any department that claimed to be a "stakeholder" of the product realization process. By the second event, I knew we did not have the right people on the project team, and I also knew that the people we really needed—the people who develop product and would use the processes—were, for the most part, unavailable to the project.

Within months and after numerous project events, the project was "put on hold" indefinitely and, for all practical purposes, died. But it was a death that would have baffled even the most astute project management crime scene investigator. The requirements for the deliverable—a product realization process system—were well defined. The project plans were well defined and based on the requirements. Project monitoring and controls were established and were being performed, and active risk management was under way. But the project kept getting infusions of the wrong blood type; it needed O-positive and was getting AB-negative. It died underloved by people who really needed it to succeed and overloved by people whose jobs had little or nothing to do with the promised product and who didn't really have a stake in the project living and succeeding.

When Expertise Isn't Useful

Do you invite your plumber to come over and help you with your taxes? Do you ask your accountant to give you some tips on cooking a cassoulet? You don't and I don't, but in our place of business we regularly drag our "experts" into every meeting, every event, and every task and project regardless of whether the expert has any expertise in the topic being addressed. Why?

Maybe because the organization pays so much for the person that management needs to make it look like his salary is justified. Or maybe because the manager who hired the expert needs to have someone nearby who is so bright and shiny that no one notices the manager's dullness. Maybe because the manager—let's call him the expert's handler or pimp—wants everyone to see what a smart shopper he is: *Hey, everybody, look at this guy…he's the greatest info assurance person on the planet, and I got him for a great price!* (as if genius is acquired by association or osmosis).

But expertise, when inappropriately applied—that being for the wrong work or at the wrong time—is anti-improvement and negative ROP. In the now-dead process development project mentioned earlier, what we really needed were the people who would be users of the process— weapons designers, engineers, testers, and project managers.

What we got were people with expertise in areas the project was nowhere close to addressing. The problem is this: If you ask people for their opinion on a topic, you'll almost always get an opinion because people don't want to be seen as not making a contribution. But if it's an opinion posited at the wrong time or in work in which the opinion provider has no depth of understanding, it's an unqualified opinion. It should be accepted and thanked, but not necessarily pursued. When organizations pursue the unqualified opinion, there will be waste.

More Ideas Don't Produce Better Ideas

Another common cultural dimension in business today is the concept that more ideas is better—that, somehow, just having more thoughts and more inputs on a topic will advance the topic and create value. In process improvement, this belief can be detrimental to ROP.

In "Tip 3: Asking for Ideas Is a Bad Idea," in *Best Practices Are Stupid,* Stephen Shapiro cites multiple cases in which an organization's leadership sought ideas from large groups of people, such as all the employees. In many cases, he found that

> In an attempt to be more innovative, many companies start by asking employees for their ideas. This is a bad idea! The ideas that are submitted tend to be impractical and of low value and end up only creating an overwhelming amount of unproductive clutter in the system.

Many people will have difficulty reconciling this reality with their long-held beliefs that everyone has something to contribute. More ideas are good only if you believe that every idea is applicable, achievable, and valuable, which an analysis of the outputs of any corporate brainstorming session will easily disprove.

Aligning People with the Work

Most people would not consider changing the culture of an organization to be a "small change," and I agree. However, with almost any task or project we are assigned, we often have the initial opportunity to form our team, identify our stakeholders, and negotiate and define roles and responsibilities. In such situations, we are often offered people by other managers or departments, or we get "volunteers." Too often, we don't take the time to screen or evaluate the people being offered because we just want to get on with the work or because we worry that it might seem as if we're not a "team player" if we don't just blindly accept resources.

If the success of your task or project is important enough, you'll be forgiven for hiring the right people. Instead of accepting whoever volunteers or is offered to you for the work, act more like you're "hiring" by screening the "applicants." Here are a few questions you should ask your prospective team members and why you should ask.

Why do you want to be involved in this work? Maybe the prospective team member is genuinely interested in your project or task and thinks that he or she can contribute to the success. But maybe, the prospective team member doesn't have any other work (or codes to charge his effort), and your project is a way to continue looking busy. Maybe there's a reason none of the other current projects or teams in the organization will assign work to this person. If a person is on your team just to look busy, you're not getting a useful resource and it will cost you time and money to manage the person; it's a double negative.

How does your knowledge, skill, and experience relate to the work? This question is particularly important in process improvement projects. People think that the only skill you need for process definition work is technical writing, but what if the primary representation of the processes is graphical? What if what is needed are process

design skills and not writing skills? What if you need someone to analyze, develop, and manage the process system
requirements, and the resource you're offered only knows
how to perform quality assurance audits? The work should
define the skill needs, and those skill needs should define
the human knowledge, skill, and experience that you employ
on your project or task. Most projects don't have the luxury
of budget or time to invent work for the purpose of making
someone feel useful.

When will you contribute and how much? This is
more a question for the person who is selecting the team
members rather than the selectees. If the project is 9 months
long and the skill need is just for one of those months, what
would be the point of having a resource on the team not contributing for 8 months? In one process improvement project,
there were people from human factors showing up at every
meeting, but they weren't the skill that was needed since the
project was still defining an overall approach and architecture
for the product realization process system. Had the project
continued, the human factors skill might have been recruited
later in the project to provide input on the interfaces to the
system.

Learn One, Learn All

> By three methods we may learn wisdom: first by
> reflection, which is noblest; second, by imitation,
> which is easiest; and third, by experience, which is
> the bitterest.
>
> **—Confucius**

This is one of my favorite topics—one on which I've delivered
several conference presentations and webinars[2]—and it is one
of my favorite small changes that could yield big performance
improvement.

Every time someone in your organization learns something—learns to do something a better way or learns not to do something—there is potential for the organization to realize significant performance improvement in reducing the cost of learning and gaining knowledge. That performance improvement occurs when everyone learns from what one person learned; hence, learn one, learn all.

Sadly, in most organizations, it's learn one, learn one— many times over. Leaders in many organizations will proudly tell you they have lessons learned (LL) programs, but when you dig a little deeper, you'll find that it's just a lessons program sans the learning part. These organizations haven't established incentives, systems, or methods for capturing and reusing the lesson, and it must be relearned dozens or hundreds more times by other workers. When the organization does not learn (or learn how to learn), I call the syndrome "lessons not learned."

And what is ironic about lessons not learned is that the investment in this improvement is relatively low and inexpensive, and yet the potential payoff—the ROP—is significant. Let's say an individual or team learns something, and it takes 2 hours to analyze and record the lesson learned in a central repository or database. In the future, it takes others only 5 minutes to search the database for lessons learned that are relevant and applicable to the work they are about to perform. This simple improvement yields a 1:55 hour cost-of-learning savings every time the lesson is applied.

Lessons Learned Definitions

Before diving into why many lessons learned initiatives fail and how to fix that, let's start with a basic understanding of the terminology. You can find lots of definitions for the phrase "lessons learned," but the one I find useful in most situations and environments is "A lesson learned is a documented and shared experience concerning an action deemed worthy

of promoting for its benefits or to warn others of its pitfalls."
But be careful! The lesson really hasn't been "learned" if the
knowledge isn't reused or reapplied to similar circumstances
in the future. There isn't any ROP in amassing a huge database
of lessons if no one accesses or uses them.

Lessons Learned on Lessons Learned

I think that one of the reasons organizations fail to establish
lasting and effective lessons learned programs is because they
think they need to reinvent the concept of lessons learned;
they don't start out by learning the lessons about lessons
learned. In my consulting practice, I've witnessed several
initiatives to implement and institutionalize lessons learned,
and I've kept notes. The following subsections are my lessons
learned on lessons learned—what to do and what not to do.

How People Learn and the Relative Cost of Learning

There are essentially four ways people learn: (1) vicarious
learning (e.g., reading, watching others, benchmarking),
(2) simulation, (3) prototyping, and (4) on-line learning, which
is personally experiencing the lesson (not learning on the
Internet). Figure 4.2 illustrates the relative cost of each of these
methods of learning.[3]

When a lesson is learned the first time, it is on-line
learning, meaning the person or the team experienced the
lesson firsthand. This is the most expensive way to learn
because the experience and its subsequent analysis often
cause an interruption to the work being performed and
require some type of recovery activity. Lost productivity,
schedule impact, and increased risk are often the collateral
damage done by on-line or experiential learning.

An effective lessons learned program, one in which captured and recorded lessons are used to preclude having to
relearn the lesson experientially, is at the other end of the

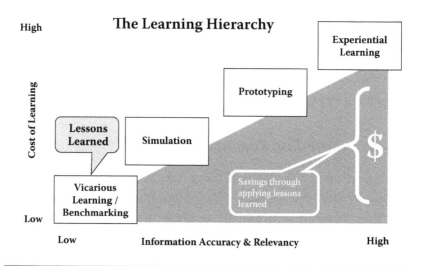

Figure 4.2 The learning hierarchy: four methods of learning and their relative costs.

cost spectrum—vicarious learning. Learning vicariously by reading and applying the experiential lessons learned by others is relatively inexpensive because it avoids the cost of work disruption and the analysis (hours of people gnashing their teeth trying to answer the question, "What the hell happened?"). The ROP of implementing an effective lessons learned program is calculated by determining the differential between the cost of experiential learning and vicarious learning. If people in an organization apply even 20 lessons learned each year, the ROP can be substantial. Effective lessons learned can provide other benefits that can also be valued in monetary terms:

■ Reduction of waste and rework
■ Improved process and work product quality by preventing the recurrence of errors
■ Greater job employee job satisfaction when learning is integrated with work, possibly causing greater skill retention and lower costs associated with employee turnover

Lessons Learned Challenges

With the relatively low entry cost and the high returns of establishing a lessons learned program, why do many organizations fail miserably at this? There are challenges to implementing and institutionalizing an effective lessons learned program, but they can be overcome…if you know about them. The primary challenges to lessons learned are the following:

1. Failure to establish incentives for participating in lessons learned ensures that participation will not become a priority activity for anyone.
2. Placing too much emphasis on negative lessons (what went wrong) and not enough emphasis on positive lessons (what went right) turns people off and creates anxiety about participating.
3. Having little or no criteria or structure for defining lessons learned leaves the quality of the lessons learned information to chance.
4. Failure to train people in lessons learned (their value, processes, and tools) will cause people to perceive that lessons learned are not important.
5. Failure to train people in how to create and use lessons learned also leaves the quality of the information to chance.
6. Inaccessible or difficult to find relevant lessons learned information discourages people from seeking and applying them.
7. There are cultural dynamics that are often counterproductive to a lessons learned program being established and institutionalized:
   a. Mistakes (learning opportunities) are punished; consequently, the admission of mistakes is repressed.
   b. Political correctness can stifle critical thinking and observations, thus diminishing the value and applicability of lessons learned.

    c. Failure to value or view learning as an essential component of work will not motivate people to participate.
8. Restricting collection of lessons learned to occur exclusively at the end of projects without regard to the project duration can cause the loss of lessons learned; they're forgotten.
9. Creating a dependency between lessons learned and the adoption/use of new technology can create resistance to establishing a lessons learned program.
10. Failure to address systemic or recurring issues or opportunities revealed by patterns in lessons learned can cause people to lose interest; they don't want to keep looking at the same lessons in perpetuity.

Tips for Establishing a Successful Lessons Learned Program

In the lessons learned efforts in which I have provided consulting, the successful programs shared some common traits that contributed to their success.

First, with almost all change initiatives, it is challenging to get people interested and involved in lessons learned. For people to care, lessons learned will need to be compelling, which these days means the initiative needs to be interesting, entertaining, relevant, useful, applicable, and functional. Relevant lessons learned need to be easy to access and easy to find, and lessons learned information needs to be perceived to be both adoptable and adaptable by users.

Institutionalizing lessons learned often involves having some supportive cultural dimensions in place. Consider the following:

◼ Facts, measures, and evidence are at least as importance as intuition and perception. Acquiring knowledge, sharing knowledge, and applying knowledge are rewarded more than merely possessing knowledge, which often requires redefining the word "expert."

- If software development is knowledge acquisition and storage, and if the most difficulty and risk are in acquiring unknowns, then the most valuable lessons learned are those that transform unknowns into knowns.

Recommended Approach

In this section, I outline an approach to implementing and institutionalizing lessons learned programs that are effective and lasting and that produce value and benefits to the organization. This approach entails the following tasks, which I then further elaborate upon in subsequent subsections:

1. Conduct lessons learned on lessons learned.
2. Present the business case for lessons learned to leadership; find out what it's worth to pursue.
3. Define a model and attributes for a lesson learned.
4. Adapt current technology to enable lessons learned creation, organization, and access.
5. Establish and implement incentives and motivation for lessons learned contributors and users.
6. Periodically measure and monitor the value of lessons learned and communicate results.

Conduct a Lessons Learned on Lessons Learned

Or just read this section ("Learn One, Learn All"). Before embarking on an effort to implement lessons learned in the organization, it seems reasonable to learn vicariously what has worked and not worked:

1. Conduct research or benchmarking on lessons learned programs in external but related businesses and organizations. Find out how well (or not) other organizations have fared in their attempts to establish lessons learned programs. Everyone—except maybe your competition—will be willing to help you avoid their mistakes.

2. Collect lessons learned on lessons learned from people within your organization. They won't hesitate to tell you what doesn't work, and they might have good ideas on what does work.

Learning from others about their experiences with lessons learned programs will require two things from your organization's leaders:

1. Suspension of the notion that your organization is so different from all other business organizations that the experiences of other entities can't possibly apply to your organization.
2. Suspension of the notion that only things created by your organization are good, and work done by other organizations isn't useful (the "not invented here" [NIH] syndrome).

Define and Promote the Lessons Learned Business Case

Those of you operating in the upper echelon of your organization already know this, so here's advice to the reader who isn't operating in a senior leadership position: Intrinsic value isn't, and no idea for change, innovation, or improvement has prima facie merit. If you walk into your boss's office and say, "Hey, Boss, I've got a great idea and I'd like your support," you're likely to be summarily dismissed as an "idea hamster." If an initiative such as implementing lessons learned intuitively has merit, then it's worthy of developing and promoting a business case. A business case for the lessons learned process improvement should be defined and should address these questions:

1. Why do we want to implement and institutionalize lessons learned? What do we believe will be the benefits of doing so?

2. What will be the cost of implementing and the total cost of ownership (TCO) of lessons learned?
   a. The cost of adopting and adapting a system and process to enable lessons learned
   b. The effort required for people to participate in lessons learned
   c. The cost of incentives or motivation to get people to participate
   d. The cost to maintain, monitor, and measure the improvement's performance and value to the organization

Develop a Model and Attributes for a Lesson Learned

As with many other forms of process improvement, a lessons learned system should be thoughtfully designed. If someone just throws together a spreadsheet or a SharePoint list without much thought, puts it somewhere on the intranet, and tells people to go use it, failure is imminent.

The quality of lessons contributed by people can be guided through the use of a model (i.e., a standard) and attributes for documenting lessons. Attributes of lessons could include:

1. Criteria to determine whether a lesson warrants being captured
2. A concise but accurate description of what was learned
3. Identification of whether the lesson arose from something that should be repeated or something that should not be repeated
4. Estimated value (e.g., cost savings) of the lesson if it were applied or used in the future
5. What should be done in the future to apply the lesson
6. Identification of the circumstances in which the lesson was learned:
   a. The type of project or work (e.g., project size, type of product being developed)

    b. The functional role (e.g., project manager, analyst, engineer, executive) to which the lesson best applies

    c. An estimation of the likelihood of or frequency at which the lesson circumstance is likely to occur or arise

Having defined attributes or standards for the information elements that comprise a lesson learned is particularly important if the lessons learned will be captured in tabular format (e.g., an Excel spreadsheet or SharePoint list) or in a database. If each of these information elements is a database field (or cell in the spreadsheet or list), then the organization has already enabled the "findability" aspect because people can use search, sort, or filter functions to locate the relevant lessons learned being sought.

Adapt Current Technology to Enable Lessons Learned

One interesting phenomenon that I've witnessed repeatedly in my consulting practice is the compunction of organizations to start shopping for a tool immediately when they are thinking about implementing something new like lessons learned. For some reason, the solution is always a new tool, even before the problem or challenge has been framed. This phenomenon is more likely to manifest when people start talking about enterprise-wide improvements such as lessons learned, measurement programs (e.g., balanced score card), or project portfolio management.

My observation is that people barely make use of the existing tools and systems that, in many situations, would more than adequately meet new needs and uses.

Define a simple process that describes how to contribute lessons learned and how to access them and use them. Try to use existing technology to manage lessons learned data and information. At a minimum, the technology used for lessons learned should:

1. Support the work practices of most of the LL contributors and users
2. Provide minimal database-like functionality such as sort and search capability
3. Require only typical office desktop products to access, read, update, and transform lessons learned (e.g., MS Office, Internet Explorer)
4. Enable and automate the generation, collection, analysis, and communication of measures and measurement data related to lessons learned
5. Date lessons learned or provide "most recent" functionality

Establish Incentives for Participation

If participating in lessons learned (contributing, accessing, using) becomes just *one more thing* people are asked to do, and they perceive it to be additional (not integral) to their work, the lessons learned initiative is likely to fail.

For success, organizational leadership and management must do the following:

1. Be explicit in articulating the new or changed behaviors expected for lessons learned to be successful.
2. Promote the business case (the "why") for lessons learned: how the organization will benefit and how individuals will benefit.
3. Establish and articulate the priority of lessons learned relative to other improvement efforts or initiatives (e.g., "collecting and using lessons learned is more important than reducing time-to-market").
4. Offer award and/or recognition for lessons learned participation. For example, recognition could be given to individuals or teams for

a. Most lessons contributed
b. Most lessons applied or implemented
c. Greatest benefit (cost or schedule savings, product quality) from applying a lesson learned
d. Highest rated lesson learned (if rating and review of lesson learned are implemented)

There may be nothing more valuable to the long-term success of your organization than learning, and there may be nothing more detrimental than not learning. Establishing a lessons learned program and structuring incentives for participation is one of the smallest investments you can make that will yield one of the greatest payoffs. Write into your subordinates' performance plans incentive and reward for capturing, contributing, and using or applying lessons learned.

Monitor, Measure, and Publicize Progress and Success

Improvement initiatives don't gain momentum on their own; they need care and feeding until inertia is achieved. The lessons learned initiative will require these things to get inertia:

1. The lessons learned initiative needs a sponsor or sponsors who care about and drive it to success; senior leadership needs to show interest and inquire about its progress and success periodically.

2. People need to be trained in the value and use of lessons learned using the organization's normal education methods.

3. The lessons learned sponsor(s) must monitor contributions and use of the lessons learned.

4. Sponsor(s) must measure progress and success and promote and publicize success of lessons learned to encourage increased contributions and use.

5. Projects should assign responsibility for lessons learned harvesting, plan and execute activities in the project life cycle to harvest and use lessons learned, and contribute to lessons learned *at least* at project close.

6. Organization leaders need to ensure that people feel safe contributing to lessons learned and that they are not used as a vehicle to evaluate people.

Do Only What Needs to Be Done (and No More)

Small changes that yield big performance results include small changes that we as individuals can make in our work habits and practices. If I improve me, if I change my behaviors and work more efficiently and effectively, it may not significantly contribute to the ROP or organizational performance. However, if my improved individual processes and practices are noticed and adopted by others in the organization, the tyranny of numbers principle says there will be positive change organizationally.

Two of the many ways that we as workers waste resources and time is that we often (1) don't do what really needs to be done, and (2) do way more than what really needs to be done.

Process improvement takes many forms and comes in many shapes and sizes. If we stop and think about how almost everything we do in our work day is a process (at least a performed process if not a defined one), then process improvement can involve changes to many activities, from our own personal work habits to our collective behaviors in a team environment. This section gives you guidance for finding ROP in areas of work not typically associated with process improvement initiatives.

The Useful–Interesting Paradigm for Managing E-mail

In most business endeavors, the pervasive form of communication between teams and individuals is electronic mail (e-mail). Initially, e-mail was viewed by many to be the solution to some communication problems, including the problem of communicating across time zones via telephone. If I'm on the East Coast, it's unreasonable for me to expect someone on the West Coast to pick up the phone if I call them at 8:00 a.m. in my time zone, so I can just send them an e-mail and they can respond after they arrive at work.

However, our heavy reliance on and use of e-mail has—in the opinion of many—caused more communication problems than it has solved. Among those problems is that the sheer volume of e-mail one receives on any day can be overwhelming, almost to the point of debilitating. Instead of being able to work more efficiently and effectively, I can easily spend the entire day doing nothing but frantically responding to e-mails or sending many of my own. On such days, I am doing nothing but responding/reacting to problems or questions posed by others; I am not creating and I am not working in an outcome orientation,* and I find such work days very unsatisfying. I have known professionals who receive very high volumes of e-mail so rapidly that they cannot process them at the rate at which they receive them. I've known some people who, upon finding themselves in this situation, simply shut down; they give up and stop responding to any correspondence.

---

* Womeldorff, David, "Primary Orientations," Leading Teams and Organizations, University of Notre Dame is one of the courses in the University's Executive Leadership program.

Even as a consultant, I have found myself in the dire situation just described. However, I knew that e-mail wasn't going to go extinct any time soon, at least not in the business world, and that I had to learn how to manage my e-mail efficiently and effectively if I was going to continue operating or thriving in the work place. This section describes a few simple work habits and thought processes I have developed and implemented that help me "get out from under the pile" so that I can spend time doing work that produces things more useful to others and more rewarding to me.

In the evolution of these e-mail management practices, I tried lots of things that failed. Among the practices that failed was my attempt mentally to parse and manage e-mail as it came into my in-box into the four Covey quadrants.[4] (See "Using the Covey Quadrants to Manage E-mail" in this chapter.)

Figure 4.3 defines at a high level the method for parsing and processing incoming e-mail that employs a practice of

	Useful	Not Useful
Interesting	**Responses/actions:** • Keep in in-box • Determine when useful • Determine response date and schedule task(s) or meeting requests for response • Analyze instantiation and abstract for systemic or long-term use • Record thoughts for interesting, abstracted, or systemic use • Respond to instantiation per scheduled task or meeting request • Delete from in-box • Follow up on developing interest or systemic use	**Responses/actions:** • Do not respond • Analyze whether interest is short-term or long-term • If interest is short-term, satisfy interest within 5 minutes • Delete note from in-box • If interest is long-term, save to interesting folder; delete note from in-box • Determine and schedule date for reevaluation; on that date, determine to keep or delete based on continued interest
Not Interesting	**Responses/actions:** • Keep in in-box briefly or until overcome by events or subsequent email • Determine when useful • Determine response date and schedule task(s) or meeting requests for response • Respond to instantiation per scheduled task or meeting request • Delete from in-box	**Responses/actions:** • Delete immediately … with prejudice • The sender doesn't know you, or s/he does not understand your work or your interests

Figure 4.3 The useful–interesting paradigm for managing e-mail.

mentally parsing e-mail in two dimensions concurrently: (1) interesting or not interesting, and (2) useful or not useful. Following is a more detailed explanation of how to apply this method using these two dimensions and examples of this method using actual e-mail. Note that in using this paradigm, all judgments about an e-mail note in your in-box ultimately result in the e-mail being deleted or moved from the in-box, which achieves the goal of not allowing an overwhelming quantity of e-mail to aggregate in your in-box.

Parsing E-mail Using the Interesting– Useful Dimensions

In order to manage e-mail effectively using this method, you must learn (through practice) the ability to make quick but confident mental judgments about incoming e-mail in terms of its being interesting (or not) and useful (or not). It is likely that people who score a higher preference in "perceiving" on the "judging–perceiving" scale of the Meyers–Briggs Type Indicator (MBTI⁵) will find it more challenging to implement this method than those whose MBTI scores indicate a judging preference. By their nature, people with an MBTI perceiving preference will find it difficult to draw sharp mental lines quickly between interesting or not interesting and useful or not useful; they will find the topic of many e-mails somewhat interesting and somewhat not interesting, partially useful and partially not useful.

Parsing E-mail Using the Useful–Not Useful Dimension

When I apply this method, the first mental parsing of incoming e-mail is in the useful–not useful dimension; secondarily, I decide my interest in the e-mail. This dimension is a spectrum bounded on either end by (1) useless and (2) very useful. Making a quick and confident decision about the utility of an e-mail requires you to have a constant and deep understanding of your work and your goals.

Determining the usefulness of an e-mail (or its attachments) can only be done within the context of that to which "useful" is being determined. If you don't understand your work, either current tasks or future tasks, then it's very difficult to know what information you need to perform your work. If you don't know what information you need to perform your work, or if you don't recognize information that applies to your work, you'll be challenged when trying to determine the usefulness of an e-mail in your in-box. Thus, although parsing e-mail using this dimension is subjective, it is less so than the parsing done in the interesting–not interesting dimension.

Here's a hypothetical (and oversimplified) example of parsing an e-mail using the useful–not useful dimension: Let's say I work as a consultant in software and systems engineering processes. I receive an e-mail from a colleague about a blog on water catchment systems. This note and the referenced blog might be interesting to me, but that's not my first judgment. Because I use the receiving e-mail address predominantly for business and because I am not a consultant in water catchment systems (or any system even remotely related), I judge the e-mail to be not useful. If I cannot satisfy my interest in less than 5 minutes and if I want to pursue my interest in the e-mail in the future, I save it to a collection (document folder) or I bookmark the URL to the referenced blog and then delete the note from my in-box. (See this hypothetical situation further processed in the next section.)

Parsing E-mail Using the Interesting– Not Interesting Dimension

Judgments about your interest or lack thereof in an e-mail are more subjective than the mental parsing done using the useful–not useful dimension because you may not realize your interest in a subject until you encounter it and because your interests may change from one point in time to another. The spectrum of this dimension is bounded by (1) not at all interesting, and (2) very interesting.

For some people, with whom "interesting" is everything with which they don't currently have familiarity or knowledge, parsing and managing e-mail using this dimension will be extremely difficult. If the amount of information or knowledge you possess is a grain of sand, then the total amount of knowledge is the Sahara Desert. For such people, everything that comes into their e-mail in-box is interesting, and they accumulate enough e-mail to choke mail servers or crash their workstation. Alternatively, this method probably won't be useful to people who have no interest in anything (but then such people are probably hermits and don't use e-mail very much.)

For many people, their interests are related to or generated by their work, hobbies, or preferences for entertainment. As such, an individual's interests are usually bounded and not infinite, thus enabling most people to determine their interest in an e-mail quickly and confidently. For example, let's say someone sends a mail note to Stephen Hawking and me; the mail note is about a subatomic collision event recorded in the CERN accelerator that supports the theory of warping the fabric of space and time. Hawking would probably find this mail note very interesting and pursue it with vigor, whereas I would delete it (a decision that I make immediately after determining its lack of usefulness). In a different scenario, let's say that someone sends a mail note to Hawking and me about the average price at which vintage first-growth house Bordeaux wines sold in recent New York cellar auctions. I imagine that Hawking would delete such a note out of lack of interest, whereas I would pursue it with vigor.

Now back to the hypothetical e-mail that I posed in the prior section—the one pointing to a blog about water catchment systems. On the useful–not useful dimension, I determined it to be not useful. However, since I plan to retire someday to the island of Hawaii and will then need to know more about water catchment, I am interested. Note that I cannot determine today that the information is useful; I can only determine that it might be useful someday.

Hence, according to the responses/actions in the table shown in Figure 4.3, I save the e-mail (or bookmark the blog), delete the e-mail from my in-box, and set a future date upon which I will reevaluate my continued interest in the topic.

Using the Covey Quadrants to Manage E-mail

Initially, I tried to manage my e-mail by parsing it as it came into my in-box into the four Covey quadrants: (1) urgent and important, (2) not urgent but important, (3) urgent but not important, or (4) not urgent and not important. I wanted to focus my time and attention on e-mail in quadrant 2. I realized that I could set up e-mail folders with the labels of the four quadrants and then drag and drop incoming e-mail into the appropriate folder. However, there are reasons this approach didn't work for me and probably wouldn't work for many others. The primary reason was that my criteria and definition for what constitutes "urgent" or "important" are, in most cases, different from the sender's criteria. When you have customers and you want to keep them, it is business suicide to treat correspondence from them as not urgent or unimportant, regardless of how irrational the customer's request, question, or complaint may seem to you.

Use of Covey's four quadrants to assign incoming mail generates more questions than it answers, primarily:

- For whom is the correspondence urgent—the sender or the receiver—and why?
- To whom is the correspondence important—the sender or the receiver—and why?

In using the useful–interesting paradigm to manage e-mail, these same questions exist, but are more readily answered:

- Question: For whom is the correspondence useful, and why? Answer: The usefulness of the e-mail or attachments is determined by me, the receiver, based on the relevance of the e-mail to my work and goals.

■ Question: To whom is the correspondence interesting, and why? Answer: Since I cannot usually determine the reasons for why the sender has an interest in the item he or she sent me, I have little choice but to default to ascertaining my interest in the correspondence; my interests are already known to me.

As a manager, it will become—if it hasn't already—your natural impulse to start perceiving the importance of e-mail based on the sender's position and power in your organization's hierarchy. Responding immediately to e-mail from the higher-ups and ignoring e-mail from those who report to you might initially get you accolades from (but not admittance into) the inner circle, but over the long run it will lead to your professional demise.

Why? There are two reasons: First, you're assuming that any e-mail from one of your bosses is urgent and important to the business, which is often not the case. But you're eager to please, and you want to compete with other managers trying to climb up the same ladder, so you want to be the first to respond. It's like watching a grade school classroom in which the teacher asks a question, and all the little Type A personalities-in-training shoot their hands up and say, "Me, me, me!" But, ultimately, the recognition of your contributions

from your bosses and your promotions are going
to be based on more than your record of having
beaten all your peers in responding to e-mail from
higher-ups.

Second, you don't have all the answers all the
time. It's likely that at least some of that e-mail from
your direct reports that you're ignoring contains
solutions or answers to the e-mail from your
higher-ups. How often have you asked one of your
subordinates, "Did you send me that report?" and
have the answer be, "Yes…3 weeks ago; it's in your
in-box."

Additional Approaches for Managing E-mail

The approach of parsing and managing e-mail using the
Covey quadrants and the useful–interesting paradigm both
involve making judgments and taking action on an e-mail
note based on assigning it to one of four quadrants based
on two attribute scales. However, it occurs to me that both
these approaches may be inadequate, and that more effective
e-mail management practices should involve a tiered decision
tree approach. For example, I can easily picture a set of decision criteria followed by if–then rules and resulting actions
for dispositioning e-mail similar to the following decision
hierarchy:

Valid or invalid?
  Useful or not useful?
    Urgent or not urgent?
      Important or not important?
       Interesting or not interesting?

Also, don't be your own worst enemy by encouraging or
inviting more e-mail (people often do this to themselves).
If you are one of many recipients on an e-mail and you are

not explicitly required or requested to respond, resist the temptation to provide your "two cents' worth." In many cases, the total cost of your thoughtful yet inconsequential reply and the cost of the e-mail chain via the multiple "reply to all" responses will be significantly higher than any possible "benefit" from your contribution.

Broader Applicability of the Useful–Interesting Paradigm

The useful–interesting paradigm can be applied to many aspects of work and life far beyond dispositioning e-mail. For example, I might want to relax in the evening and watch some television. As I scroll through the thousand or so cable channels, I can very quickly choose something to watch because I have so completely institutionalized the useful–interesting paradigm that it is part of my subconscious. Useful or not and interesting or not are determined almost instantaneously within the context of my life at the moment. I even use the useful–interesting paradigm to select television shows to watch and websites to visit.

The Right Amount of Analysis

A third aspect of doing what really needs to be done (and no more) is understanding and doing the right amount of analysis before executing. Individuals and teams often spend more time analyzing a situation or a problem than it takes just to do the work. Remember: Any amount of analysis in a process improvement increases the investment (the "P"), making it more difficult to get a high return (the "R") right from the start.

There are four paths to take when thinking about balancing analysis with execution:

1. Too little analysis and doing the wrong things
2. Too much analysis for the work or issue being addressed

3. Perpetual analysis and doing nothing
4. The right balance of analysis and doing

Too Little Analysis

Not spending enough energy and time analyzing a problem or a change such as a process improvement can cause people either to do the wrong things or to do the right things in an ineffectual way. In process improvement, this will likely yield a negative ROP, but the loss can be limited if people realize quickly that they are performing the wrong things (or performing the right things wrongly) and stop the effort or change course. If you're doing the wrong things, then the consumption of resources for both the analysis and the execution adds up to a negative ROP; doing the wrong things cannot yield a positive ROP.

Too Much Analysis

Too much analysis often occurs when the team or individuals engaged in the improvement effort don't have adequate decision-making processes or in situations in which the organizational culture doesn't support decisiveness. If a team spends 3 months analyzing a situation before executing an improvement when 1 month of analysis would have yielded the same execution, then the ROP can still be positive but not as valuable as it could have been.

Case Study

In 2011, a well-known organization in the defense sector contracted Natural Systems Process Improvement (Natural SPI) to help redesign and develop the organization's product realization processes. The current state was that the product realization process was represented in 150+ procedures (text-based narrative), and the organization had already collected over the years hundreds of inputs that indicated process users needed a different approach and representation of process; the 150+ procedures were just too difficult to perform.

We the consultants joined a cross-functional team to pursue a completely different approach, one that would create a mostly graphical representation of the process with easy task-contextual access to procedural detail and assets where needed by the process users. My company repeatedly demonstrated how this approach would overcome almost all the problems inherent in text-oriented process representation.

There were individuals on the team who, for whatever reason, just didn't want to believe all the information that supported moving the product realization process in a different direction (away from text). They insisted that it wasn't what the process users wanted, even though they were not themselves users of the process and even though some of them had been involved in collecting the user feedback on the legacy procedures. The design approach was simple and obvious to most people on the team...but not all. They wanted to go off and spend months designing and administering a survey of process users' wants, needs, and preferences before they would support the new approach.

In this case, the analysis of the problem and a solution approach were way more than what the situation warranted, and the value of the eventual ROP was diminished from the start.

Perpetual Analysis

You've all heard of this situation; It's often called "analysis paralysis." This condition exists when people have a decision to make, but perpetually analyze and reanalyze the decision factors and never arrive at a decision or move forward with the improvement effort. Without execution of a decision, there can never be a positive ROP because the process improvement never gets delivered. Perpetual analysis is usually caused by the following:

- Authority and responsibility for the decision are not overtly assigned or designated; the people responsible for the decision don't know they are responsible.
- The mix of people making the decision doesn't have the right mix of Myers–Briggs type indicators…there are no "Js" (judging) on the team.
- The people on the team are either handed or continually develop too many options or alternatives, or they don't have criteria for reducing the growing list of options.
- The organization doesn't have adequate decision-making processes and process assets.
- The people making the decision don't realize they are in analysis paralysis.

The Right Amount of Analysis

Obviously, the purpose of this small change to yield big improvements is to get people to invest the right amount of analysis consciously and overtly in decisions and changes related to process improvement. The "right amount" of analysis is an allocation of resources toward analysis that is proportionate to the allocation of resources in execution and proportionate to the expected value of the ROP.

Make Decisions Once and Make Good Decisions

In business, we make decisions every day—lots of them. Making decisions, whether it is done consciously or subconsciously, is integral to conducting work. So there is potential for a positive ROP by improving the decision processes used by individuals and teams. When made poorly, decisions can be a source of waste, error, and inefficacy as identified in Table 4.2.

Table 4.2   Diminished Performance from a Low Decision-Making Capability

Low Decision-making Capability Behavior	Resulting Diminished Performance
Inappropriate or wrong decision made and poorly implemented	This is the worst of all combinations of decision and implementation. The waste/loss is the effort expended on making the bad decision, followed by the effort expended implementing it.
Inappropriate or wrong decision made but valiant attempt to implement	A brilliant implementation can't save a bad decision, but it can hide it for a while. The waste/loss is effort expended in making the bad decision and the effort expended attempting to implement the decision.
Appropriate decision made but poorly implemented	If a decision is not executed, then the result is the same as if it hadn't been made at all. The biggest waste/loss in this situation is the multiple attempts to implement the decision.
Same decision made multiple times	The waste/loss is the effort expended on each iteration of the decision.
Decision made but not communicated to affected stakeholders	If the decision is not implemented because the right people didn't know it was made, then the waste/loss is the effort expended in making the decision.

A Brief History of Decision Making

Before the evolution of reason and logic, most decisions weren't really decisions at all; they were more reactions quickly and chemically formed in the limbic system. When we confronted the choice of fighting the lion with our bare hands or running, there would be a split-second choice to do one of the two, but it wasn't so much a decision. The performed decision processes had to be instinctive and quick in order to survive.

In the industrial and modern world, until relatively recently, most people didn't make their own decisions; rather, they were made for them by an authority figure such as an emperor, a king or some other royalty, a clergyman, or a conqueror. This decision can be characterized as patriarchal–autocratic and can be described in sum as "Father knows best."

In the postmodern world, especially in the work environment, many decisions are made collaboratively. Individual survival/success is often tied to group survival/success. Hence, decision making needs to be more inclusive to meet the needs of the group.

Today, business is all about making decisions…lots of them. Decisions are extremely complex, with lots of variables, options, and consequences. Individuals have choices and don't have to be "ruled" by the decisions of others. As it turns out, Father doesn't always know best.

The Importance of Structured Decisions

In business, we all make decisions every day, and many of our decisions are made ad hoc and intuitively. Whereas it is fine for some decisions to be made ad hoc, such as where to go for lunch, when we make all of our decisions without structure and rush headlong into action, only some subset of our decisions turns out to be good or right due to chance and luck. No one is always lucky; the universe randomly allocates each of us only a certain amount of luck, and we all eventually run out of it. In business, structuring some of our decisions can increase the chance for a desirable outcome, and it allows us to make our own luck and define our own fate.

Most successful work endeavors, and especially improvement or innovation initiatives, require the combination of appropriate decisions and effective implementation of those decisions. As Figure 4.4 shows, the combinations of decision and implementation other than appropriate decision and effective implementation have more probability of failure than success.

Think about the failed ventures—political, military, disaster recovery, business—in your lifetime. To every failed venture you can remember, you would probably find it easy to attribute the failure to either an inappropriate decision or ineffective implementation, or the combination of both. Essentially, successful ventures result from doing the right things for the right reasons.

There are benefits to structuring some types of business decisions, and improving the decision process should target these benefits as objectives to yield a positive ROP. The primary benefits of structured decisions are that they can

- Provide a way for people to repeat successful decisions and avoid unsuccessful decisions
- Enable people to improve their decision making capability continuously, making decisions both more efficient and effective

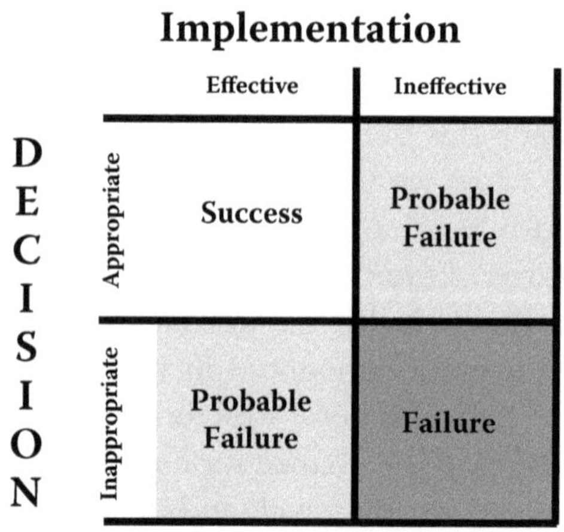

Figure 4.4 The decision–implementation paradigm.

- Enable an organization to perform an "autopsy" on decisions that have been made to find out what worked and what failed

The Decision-Driven Organization

According to a study published in the *Harvard Business Review*,[6] the defining characteristic of high-performing organizations is their ability to make good decisions and to make them happen quickly. The companies that succeed tend to follow a few clear principles:

- Some decisions matter more than others.
- Action is the goal.
- Ambiguity is the enemy.
- Speed and adaptability are crucial.
- Decision roles trump the organizational chart.
- A well-aligned organization reinforces roles.
- Practicing beats preaching...always.

Additionally, in organizations that make efficient and effective decisions, who makes which decisions is well known and usually defined. In organizations with low decision-making capability, the owners of decisions are not known, which causes confusion, waste, and often frustration and bad will between individuals and teams. For example, in the same study cited previously, the researchers found that at one automaker, marketers and product developers were confused about who was responsible for making decisions about new models. When asked, "Who has the right to decide which features will be standard?" 64 percent of product developers said, "We do," and 83 percent of marketers said, "We do." When asked, "Who has the right to decide which colors will be offered?" 77 percent of product developers said, "We do," and 61 percent of marketers said, "We do."

Often people who don't have "manager" or "lead" in their role or title think that it's not up to them to make decisions, and that decisions are for people higher up in the hierarchy to make. If you're in a process improvement role, you won't make much progress if you wait for someone else to make the decisions that need to be made. In fact, if you're in your process improvement role because of your knowledge, skills, and experience in this field, you are exactly the right person to make most of the decisions related to process and performance improvement.

Having a process and process assets can greatly improve decision making, but I have found this to be one of the most challenging areas to improve in organizations. In some organizations I've encountered, workers and leaders already believe they always make good decisions. They correlate the fact that nothing disastrous has happened yet, so they must be good decision makers. In other organizations, I find that there are powerful cultural dimensions that either enable or inhibit improving the decision-making capability. Table 4.3 identifies the major cultural enablers and inhibitors to improving decision making in organizations.

A Simple Decision Process

In the clients to whom I've provided consulting and that have succeeded in developing and implementing structured

Table 4.3   Cultural Inhibitors and Enablers to Improving Decision Making in Organizations

Enablers for Improving Decision Making	Inhibitors to Improving Decision Making
Management by fact	Management by emotion
Quantitative proof of performance	Unsubstantiated claims of performance
Data wins	Yelling wins
Process focus	Title/position focused
Work smarter	Work harder
Root cause analysis	Finger-pointing
People think and work proactively	People work in a reactive mode
Local decision making	Centralized, top-down decisions

decision processes, the process usually takes some form of performing these tasks:

1. Determine whether to use structured decision-making process, tools, and techniques. (Not all decisions require or are worthy of applying structure.)
2. Identify the type of decision to be made.
3. Plan the decision by allocating resources and schedule to perform the decision.
4. Identify the participants and relative stakeholders in the target decision(s).
5. Identify candidate solutions.
6. Select the evaluation method.
7. Define the evaluation criteria.
8. Select the decision method.
9. Collect data and perform the evaluation.
10. Make the decision.
11. Record the decision and decision data.
12. Evaluate and record the decision implementation results.

Of course, there's more to it than that. Tasks such as 6, "select the evaluation method," require guidelines that define the different types of evaluation methods, and which method is more appropriate for which types of decision. Successfully implementing 8, "select the decision method," requires the process performers to know the four decision methods, as well as which one to apply. Also, remember not only to give your process performers instructions, but also to give them templates, checklists, and other process assets that really help them perform the process. (Also see "Work Products That Work" in my 2004 book, *Real Process Improvement Using the CMMI*.)

In my consulting work, the useful process assets that I have developed and helped clients effectively implement to enable structured decision making include:

- A decision lexicon or dictionary
- Descriptions of classes or types of decisions
- Defined thresholds or guidelines for when to invoke structured decision making and for which types of decisions (e.g., a decision policy)
- Defined processes or methods used to collect information used in making structured decisions
- Defined information evaluation and analysis methods and tools
- A project decision plan template
- Defined decision process measures and measure collection and analysis methods
- Decision support templates
- Structured decision training materials

Increasing Decision Capability and ROP

As with other processes, organizations can evolve and increase their decision process capability by learning from past decisions, but only if the historical decision data are collected and structured in a way that enables their analysis. For each decision made, I recommend recording at least the decision information elements in Table 4.4.

Armed with the type of data in Table 4.4 from hundreds of historical decisions, your organization will be able to conduct analysis and start to understand the "ingredients" that go into an efficient and effective decision. With pattern (affinity or Pareto) analysis from hundreds or thousands of historical decisions, decision makers will learn answers to questions such as

- What is the optimum number of decision participants?
- How much effort is associated with good decisions versus bad decisions?
- Which type of decision do we make 80 percent of the time?
- Which evaluation methods appear to yield the best results?
- Which decision methods appear to yield the best results?
- What should we change in our decision processes and tools to get a better ROP on decisions?

Decision Making in the CMMI

I know many of you reading this book are looking for how to integrate these concepts with your use of the CMMI (Capability Maturity Model Integration). Table 4.5 defines the CMMI practices for which implementing an effective structured decision process will greatly help.

Do Less to Do More

Sometimes, the best improvement you can make is to do nothing. Really, I'm serious. Think about it...if your organization spends 3 years and $300,000 on a process improvement initiative that resulted in either no performance improvement

Table 4.4   Decision Data to Record for Learning and Increasing Decision Capability

Decision Record Information Element	Description and Examples
Name of decision	Record a brief name for the decision. Example: *Select a SCAMPI lead appraiser.*
Decision type	Record the decision type. Example: *Vendor selection*
Number of decision participants	Record the number of individuals and/or teams that participated in the decision, including the decision leader/facilitator. Example: *5*
Total effort hours expended on decision	Record the total number of effort hours expended on the decision by all participants. Example: *78*
Description of decision made	Record the decision that was made. Example: *We selected Appraisals-R-Us.*
Evaluation method(s) used	Record the method(s) used to evaluate the candidate solutions. Example: *We used industry benchmark reports to collect data about the candidate vendors. We then used comparative analysis of the options.*
Decision method(s) used	Record the decision method(s) used to make the decision. Example: *The decision team used consensus to select the preferred solution. This decision was then escalated to the VP of Engineering, who used the consultative method to make the final decision.*

Table 4.4 (*Continued*)   Decision Data to Record for Learning and Increasing Decision Capability

Decision Record Information Element	Description and Examples
Method by which decision was communicated to others	Record the method(s) used to communicate the decision to affected stakeholders. Example: *The decision was communicated to affected stakeholders via a teleconference.*
Decision effects and analysis	At a point in time following the implementation of the decision, analyze and determine if the decision was effective and achieved the intended or desired results. Record the results of this analysis and the effects of the decision. Example: *We will not use this vendor again. The lead appraiser's narrow experience in process implementation in the defense sector resulted in his constant inability to interpret CMMI practices within the context of our work. He also was disorganized and undisciplined, and the team suffered many very late nights working on the appraisal. These and several other decision lessons learned were contributed to the LL database.*

or far less than $300K worth of performance improvement, the ROP is negative. Wouldn't it have been better to have done nothing?

Don't get me wrong, I'm as much a capitalist as any other person, and I'm particularly fond of money being spent on consultants. However, I don't like to see capital wasted when good money is thrown after bad. I prefer results—provable, demonstrable ROP—and so do you.

Table 4.5   Decision Making in the CMMI

CMMI Process Area and Practice	*How a High-Capability Decision Process Helps*
DAR	Obviously, an organization using the decision analysis and resolution process area (a capability level 3 defined and managed process) will make good use of a defined and performed decision process that will yield information that can be used for continuous improvement.
SAM SP 1.1	A decision process, decision criteria, and an evaluation method can be implemented to determine a type of acquisition for a product or product component.
SAM SP 1.2	Suppliers should be selected using the organization's decision process and process assets.
TS SP 1.1	Alternative engineering solutions can be objectively selected by using a decision process, criteria, and evaluation methods.
TS SP 2.4	Make versus buy versus reuse is a type of decision that is typically made in many product development and service delivery organizations. A structured decision process can be implemented to consistently make these decisions efficiently and effectively.
OPM SP 1.3	With historical process performance measures and other data, a structured decision process can be used to evaluate multiple candidate areas for improvement and objectively (quantitatively) select one or more areas for improvement.
OPM SP 2.4	Selecting improvements for deployment "based on an evaluation of costs, benefits, and other factors" requires a stable and effective decision process and process assets.

Table 4.5 (*Continued*)   Decision Making in the CMMI

CMMI Process Area and Practice	How a High-Capability Decision Process Helps
OPP SP 1.2	An effective decision process can and should be used to select processes or subprocesses for process performance analysis.
QPM SP 1.3	An effective decision process can and should be used to select subprocesses and attributes (i.e., decision criteria) critical to evaluating performance.

Maybe it's just because I'm getting old, but I've really come to appreciate the concept of "conservation of motion" in that I'm always looking for ways to do more work with less energy. Efficiency, in its simplest form, is expending less effort while achieving greater results. Over the years, I have found many small changes that people can make to get big performance results, and this section describes a few of my favorites. Some of these changes are real changes in behaviors and work practices; others are really just a different way of thinking about work and process.

Activity Is Not Work

Well, it's not, but how many of us say we are "working" when we

- Go to meetings all day that produce nothing
- Travel to another site and watch TV on the airplane
- Dither with a cool new technology that neither we nor the organization has any intention of implementing
- Walk over to Starbucks across the street from the office and have a coffee
- Write a process that no one has ever used (or ever will)
- Engage (for hours or days) in an online opinion-fest in the Linked-In CMMI discussion group that was 100 percent

baseless in facts or actual instantiations and has no point
or resolution
- Check the postings on our Facebook page or Twitter
- Attend training that we don't need and will not apply to
our work
- Spend hours reading e-mail that has no relevance to our
task at hand

People will engage in some or all of these activities day
in and day out, and when you ask them why some task they
were supposed to perform isn't yet complete, they are sure
to tell you that they are "busy, busy, busy." The problem is
that in many organizations, we've come to accept activity
as work.

In 2010 and 2011, with the country still in a recession
and unemployment still high (for the United States), worker
productivity numbers took a slight uptick, but that was
primarily due to the fact that those people still lucky enough
to have full-time employment were working longer days and
weeks. The currently accepted productivity index isn't based
on results or output of work; it is based on hours worked.

Imagine if productivity were based on something real and
meaningful, like output to work ratio—in other words, based
on work instead of activity. Then imagine the productivity
spike if everyone actually worked while at work instead of
engaging in the many distractions mentioned previously. Of
course, the downside would be that business leaders would
pretty quickly realize that they only need some percentage of
their current workforce—the percentage that actually works
and produces outputs—and then national unemployment
would spike.

Getting everyone to stop engaging in distractions and
work is not a small change. However, applying the tyranny
of numbers principle, an organization can reap significant
productivity benefit even if a subset of workers individually
convert 1 hour each day from activity to work.

Leaders can also make this change by rewarding results instead of rewarding people showing up for 8 hours each day. Superficially, it may seem impossible to reward knowledge workers for output as you would pay someone for the number of buttons they sew on a garment in a day. However, all work, even knowledge work, can and should yield results. Let's say I task someone on my staff to research and compare enterprise customer relationship management (CRM) systems. Shouldn't I expect as a result a documented trade study, benchmark report, or at least a presentation that documents the findings of the research? Should I be satisfied and reward the employee if the only result of 120 hours of effort is that he happens to catch me in the hallway and says, "Oh, hi Boss…regarding CRM systems, we should go with product X"?

If my organization pays me for knowledge—knowledge that I acquire, elaborate upon, and contribute—and if I retire or leave the organization without codifying that knowledge such that it can be applied to ongoing and future work, then the organization has achieved a negative return on its investment in me as a human asset.

Assume It Already Exists and Don't Reinvent It

I have seen many things in process improvement, a few things truly original and clever, but most things just a variation on a theme; there is nothing wrong with playing a variation on a theme or even just replaying the same song as long as it provides value for the organization.

However, every day in organizations all over the world, people expend effort rediscovering that which has already been discovered, reinventing that which already exists, and redefining that which is already defined.

I once worked with an organization in which about eight people sat around for a full day trying to come to consensus on words like "lexicon" and "taxonomy"—words

284 ■ *Return On Process*

for which there were definitions to be had within seconds on Wiktionary and Wikipedia. Another organization coded a software application that had a tiny subset of the functionality of Microsoft Excel instead of just buying and using Excel. In process improvement, people with responsibility for the organization's standard processes will often start writing processes and procedures from scratch instead of buying or borrowing and then adapting existing process descriptions. Another team spent hundreds of hours doing their own trade study in a topic for which there already existed free literature online. These stories are a tiny fraction of the waste and loss incurred each day simply because people assume something or some information doesn't already exist.

My solution is that my basic assumption going into any line of thought or task is that everything I will need to know already exists, and chances are that it does. When I conserve motion and energy by Googling, my results-to-effort ratio goes way up!

Why do people and organizations reinvent, redefine, and rediscover? The reasons I've observed are the following:

- Our fragile egos can't reconcile our need to be seen as creative when the fact is that there really aren't many things left (in business, anyway) to create.
- Reusing, repurposing, and reapplying are not as glamorous or as much fun as reinventing.
- We're deluded to think that no one else has ever done what we're attempting to do. (Really? Are you sure no other organization in the world has ever tried to implement processes that are consistent with the CMMI?)
- We believe that our organization and what we do are so unique that information from other organizations or people couldn't possibly be applicable or useful.

It already exists. That piece of information you're looking for exists. That work you're about to perform has already been performed by someone else, somewhere else. That radical new approach you are thinking of attempting has very likely already been attempted. That "best practice" you're thinking of implementing may no longer be best. That lesson you're about to learn has already been learned by others many times before.

Think of the energy, time, and money that could be saved every day all over the world if we chose not to experience the *Groundhog Day* effect at work—if we could somehow not relive and redo everything that has already been done.

When I tried to collect case studies for this book, I had people say to me, "Well, Michael, organizations don't share that information because it's their trade secret." That's usually not exactly true, but what is usually true is that the organization doesn't want to reveal that its initiative wasn't all that innovative or successful.

Define Things Once

I belong to a Linked-In discussion group with a focus on the CMMI. In the almost 2 years since I joined this group, I have looked for but not witnessed a single inventive, innovative, or unique thought. The vast majority of the discussions are someone trying to get free online consulting, to which naïve (or desperate) consultants trolling for clients respond. (Here's a clue: Why would they pay for it after finding out that it's free?)

Other discussions are careless, thoughtless rants[7] that often contain myths or misconceptions about CMMI use. In such cases, I and a few other conscientious people try to intervene to set things straight; it's not in our collective best interest to allow misinformation to be perpetuated.

But the really interesting phenomenon that I've noticed in this discussion group is the lengthy and time-wasting and energy-sucking debates related to the definition and meaning

286 ■ *Return On Process*

or interpretation of words and phrases. One of the most ill-famed "digital stupid fests" was about the hypothetical situation of an organization "skipping" CMMI maturity levels, and to this day I'm embarrassed that I wasted 5 minutes posting to that discussion. At least two-thirds of the discussion was spent by real CMMI experts trying to prove to the novice that "skipping levels" doesn't exist, and that what he was really complaining about was organizations that skip CMMI appraisals (e.g., have a maturity level 5 appraisal sometime after their maturity level 2 or 3 appraisal—hence, skipping appraisals at each maturity level, which is not the same as skipping maturity levels).

The Multitasking Myth

With the advent and pervasiveness of laptops and mobile devices, workers have adopted a belief—almost a religion—that they can perform multiple tasks simultaneously. Knowledge workers believe that they can respond to e-mail or text messages while simultaneously receiving training or while engaged in a meeting with others, and they are therefore far more productive than if they were to focus on one task at a time. This belief is held with particular fervor among those with attention deficit or lack of attention, with or without technology.

The truth is that, yes, people *can* do more than one thing at a time—they just won't do any of them well—and that workers are less productive—not more—when they have fallen for the multitasking myth. The body of science that exists today proves that when you think you are multitasking, you are losing time, wasting effort, and introducing into your work errors and omissions that will require rework—by somebody—at a later point in time. Ah but, you say, I am the outlier to all of these studies and experiments…I am more productive when I'm multitasking. No, you are simply more delusional than most of us.

There are already a plethora of studies and statistics that prove that people can't drive well and text at the same time. Ultimately, the only real multitasking you can do in this situation is die or kill others while you're texting. But many people simply ignore these data when it comes to working, so here are some additional sources that indicate no one really multitasks:

- "The most common kind of multitasking doesn't boost productivity—it slows you down." (Dave Crenshaw, *The Myth of Multitasking: How "Doing It All" Gets Nothing Done*)
- "You and every other so-called multitasker are actually serial tasking. Rather than engaging in simultaneous tasks, you are in fact shifting from one task to another to another in rapid succession. For example, you switch from your phone conversation to a document on your computer screen to an e-mail and back again in the belief that you are doing them simultaneously. But you're not. A summary of research examining multitasking on the American Psychological Association's web site describes how so-called multitasking is neither effective nor efficient. These findings have demonstrated that when you shift focus from one task to another, that transition is neither fast nor smooth. Instead, there is a lag time during which your brain must yank itself from the initial task and then glom onto the new task. This shift, though it feels instantaneous, takes time. In fact, up to 40 percent more time than single tasking—especially for complex tasks."[8]
- "Technology has so many advantages, but some devices that were designed to make us more productive, are now creating a new set of productivity problems. When laptops, personal digital assistants (PDAs), and cell phones are close by, attendees at workplace meetings struggle to keep their focus on the speaker. It's just too compelling

and easy to check e-mail, text messages, and surf the web instead. Of course these workers think that they are multitasking. But, when it comes to the brain's ability to pay attention, the brain focuses on concepts sequentially and not on two things at once. In fact, the brain must disengage from one activity in order to engage in another. And it takes several tenths of a second for the brain to make this switch. As John Medina, author of *Brain Rules* says: 'To put it bluntly, research shows that we can't multitask. We are biologically incapable of processing attention-rich inputs simultaneously.'"[9]

■ "'People can't multitask very well, and when people say they can, they're deluding themselves,' said neuroscientist Earl Miller. And, he said, 'The brain is very good at deluding itself.' Miller, a Picower professor of neuroscience at MIT, says that for the most part, we simply can't focus on more than one thing at a time. What we can do, he said, is shift our focus from one thing to the next with astonishing speed. 'Switching from task to task, you think you're paying attention to everything around you at the same time. But you're actually not,' Miller says. 'You're not paying attention to one or two things simultaneously, but switching between them very rapidly.' Miller said there are several reasons the brain has to switch among tasks. One is that similar tasks compete to use the same part of the brain. 'Think about writing an e-mail and talking on the phone at the same time. Those things are nearly impossible to do at the same time,' he says. 'You cannot focus on one while doing the other. That's because of what's called interference between the two tasks. They both involve communicating via speech or the written word, and so there's a lot of conflict between the two of them.' Researchers say they can actually see the brain struggling. And now they're trying to figure out the details of what's going on."[10]

For most of us with normal brains (like me), when we switch mental tasks to one we were previously processing, we not only come to a full stop on the current task, but also don't resume the task we're switching to where we left off; we put our minds in reverse and have to back up before moving forward. This is because our mind needs context to regain mental inertia to make progress on the second or third task.

As I work on the manuscript for this book, I might end my writing day in the middle of a chapter or section. When I resume writing the next day, I can't resume work exactly where I left off the previous day because the new sentence I'm about to write won't make sense outside the context of the preceding sentences, paragraphs, and sections. So I must back up and read some of my own material before resuming the work of writing.

My wife and I enjoy renting from Netflix and watching broadcasted television series on DVD because we can then watch all the shows of the series in sequence at our convenience. One of our TV distractions at the time I was writing this book was the series "Downton Abbey." As we watch, we might be in the middle of a show but then pause for several hours to go do something else. When we return to the show, I usually need first to back up the DVD to some point before the point at which we paused. If I simply resume at the point of pause, the action and the dialog don't make any sense because I no longer have in my head the context of the scenes that came just before.

One of the most compelling studies I've seen on the productivity hit from context switching is shown in Figure 4.5. In this study, the more concurrent projects people were assigned to, the greater the loss in productivity, by orders of magnitude.

Still not convinced? Then you probably never will be because it serves your own purposes to continue believing the multitasking myth. If that's the case, you'll always need to work for bosses who also believe this myth.

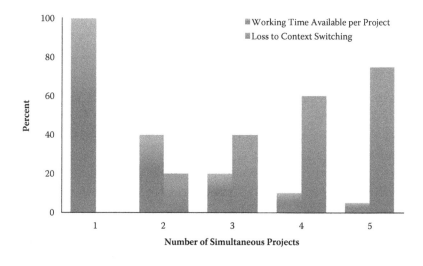

Figure 4.5   Productivity loss with concurrent projects due to context switching.

Endnotes

1. http://en.wikipedia.org/wiki/Pareto_principle: The Pareto principle (also known as the 80–20 rule, the law of the vital few, and the principle of factor sparsity) states that, for many events, roughly 80 percent of the effects come from 20 percent of the causes. Business-management consultant Joseph M. Juran suggested the principle and named it after Italian economist Vilfredo Pareto, who observed in 1906 that 80 percent of the land in Italy was owned by 20 percent of the population; he developed the principle by observing that 20 percent of the pea pods in his garden contained 80 percent of the peas. It is a common rule of thumb in business (e.g., "80 percent of your sales come from 20 percent of your clients"). Mathematically, where something is shared among a sufficiently large set of participants, there must be a number k between 50 and 100 such that "k percent is taken by $(100 - k)$ percent of the participants." The number k may vary from 50 (in the case of equal distribution, i.e., 100 percent of the population have equal shares) to nearly 100 (when a tiny number of participants account for almost all of the resource).

There is nothing special about the number 80 percent mathematically, but many real systems have k somewhere around this region of intermediate imbalance in distribution. The Pareto principle is only tangentially related to Pareto efficiency, which was also introduced by the same economist. Pareto developed both concepts in the context of the distribution of income and wealth among the population.

2. West, Michael, "Lessons Not Learned."

3. Bogan, Christopher E. and Michael J., English, *Benchmarking for Best Practices: Winning through Innovative Adaptation,* R. R. Donnelley & Sons, New York, 1994.

4. Covey, Stephen R., *The 7 Habits of Highly Effective People,* Simon & Schuster, New York, 1989.

5. Briggs Myers, Isabel, *Introduction to Type: A Guide to Understanding Your Results on the MBTI Instrument,* sixth edition, CPP, Inc., Mountain View, CA. 1998.

6. Rogers, Paul and Marcia Blenko, "Who Has the D? How Clear Decision Roles Enhance Organizational Performance," *Harvard Business Review,* January 2006.

7. The ill-famed "stupid fest" that I momentarily let myself get dragged into was started by a CMMI consultant named Orhan Kalayci. The initial subject was, "The dangerous side effects of skipping levels." The online debate evolved (degenerated?) into a digital war of words between Kalayci and several other very knowledgeable and very experienced CMMI consultants (lead appraisers and CMMI instructors). As it progressed, Kalayci made no attempt to hide his complete and utter lack of process development and implementation experience, which became more and more evident with each posting.

8. From *Psychology Today:* "Technology: Myth of Multitasking: Is Multitasking Really More Efficient?" Published on March 30, 2011, by Jim Taylor, PhD, in *The Power of Prime* (online).

9. Goman, Carol Kinsey, "The Myth of Multitasking," *Forbes,* April 2011.

10. Hamilton, Jon, "Think You're Multitasking? Think Again," Interview with Earl Miller, "NPR Morning Edition," October 2, 2008.

Chapter 5

Improving Process Improvement

We must become the change we want to see.

—Mahatma Gandhi

This chapter is written primarily for you, the person put in charge of your organization's process improvement initiative (even if you don't yet know what that means). I use the manager icon here because, whether or not "manager" is in your title, as someone responsible for delivering successful process or performance improvement, you will have to manage people, resources, cost/budget, schedule, and risks. Leading and managing a process improvement initiative that is successful and delivers results can make your career; doing otherwise can inhibit your aspirations. So, unless otherwise qualified, all my uses of "you" in this chapter mean those of you who are "on the hook," as they say, to lead a process and/or performance improvement initiative.

The content of this chapter in the process improvement life cycle can be the beginning of all things good or all things bad for you. Perhaps you've been selected to serve on some form of process team, or maybe you were hired to lead the process group because of your successes in other organizations (i.e., you've helped three organizations achieve Capability Maturity Model Integration [CMMI] maturity levels). Perhaps you are in a process role because of your skill, knowledge, or experience in process improvement. But, perhaps, you've been thinking, "There's got to be a better way." This is your chance to invent, to find a new path, to attain those "quick wins" your boss says she or he needs to see to continue funding process improvement. You, more than anyone else, can influence, change, and improve the work called "process improvement"...your work.

What Do You Think? What Do You Believe?

Take a minute and answer the questions in Figure 5.1. Then, once you've finished reading this chapter, complete the section at the end ("Reflect and Plan: What Did You Learn? What Will You Do?") to find out how much this information has helped you with your own process and performance improvement work.

1. True or false: People in process improvement work just need to know the CMMI.
   a. True
   b. False
2. True or false: It doesn't really matter what skills you have on the EPG or SEPG as long as they're willing to work.
   a. True
   b. False
3. A stakeholder in a process improvement project is:
   a. A senior manager or executive
   b. Someone who will work and contribute to the success of the process improvement project
   c. The sponsor
   d. Only the people to whom you have to provide status on the improvement work
   e. Everybody
   f. The CMMI lead appraiser
4. True or false: The best way to create defined processes is to get a bunch of tech writers together and write the procedures.
   a. True
   b. False

Figure 5.1   What do you think and what do you believe about improving process improvement?

Where It All Goes Right (or Wrong)

From the moment someone in an organization decides to initiate "process improvement," the initiative, in many cases, has little chance of actually improving anything or making improvements that yield a positive return on process (ROP). Why? Here's what usually happens…

An executive or manager has heard about or read about other organizations using a model such as the CMMI or a standard such as ISO to "improve" processes, or he came from an organization that had some flavor of process improvement. The manager does what every other organization does—he establishes a process group of some sort, often called a software engineering process group (SEPG) or engineering process group (EPG), and he asks his peer managers to nominate people to serve on this group. Those other managers aren't going to give up their best talent to serve on some process group, so who does the manager establishing the process group get?

That's right…the people who are currently underemployed or underskilled.* (See "Start with the Right Team" in this chapter.)

And then what does this group usually do? Some combination of the following:

- Decide that not having a CMMI maturity level, or International Standards Organization (ISO), Aerospace Standards (AS), or Telecommunications Standards (TL) registration is a "problem" and that the procedures need to be updated to be "compliant"
- Decide to "improve" their processes by documenting how everybody performs their work; form subgroups named after the process areas in the CMMI and start frantically writing stuff (because there's always a deadline)
- Initiate dozens or hundreds of kaizens to "Lean" the processes, often losing any Leaning results by fattening the process of process improvement
- Create (or copy from elsewhere) a quality management system (QMS), which is a big book of procedures that mimic the flavor of ISO the organization has adopted

After several months or years of writing or revising procedures, the process group conducts some form of assessment—CMMI appraisal or IS/AS/TL audit, or after several hundred kaizens, the organization claims victory…they have "improved their processes."

Often, they haven't improved anything. At best, they achieved or maintained an ISO registration or a CMMI maturity level that allows their organization to continue

---

* There are exceptions. In my consulting practice, I have had the great fortune to work with some exceptionally talented people who served in a process focus function. One group that comes to mind are the people who served on the Playbook team and as Playbook coaches in Deloitte Consulting. I also hold in high regard two process leads—Mike Rhinefield at DCS and Ed Dantes at ATK—who have always served as models of true professionals and leaders in their respective process improvement jobs.

bidding on government or Department of Defense (DoD) contracts. But all too often, the process improvement initiative has only consumed valuable time and resources and has achieved a negative return on process (ROP). Again, why?

Perhaps the one area of business that most needs improving is the one area of business people just don't think about improving: the business of process improvement itself. For more than 40 years, process improvement has taken the same worn paths, used the same old, tired "best practices," used the same old "benefits" data from the Software Engineering Institute (SEI) to sell process improvement, attended the same staid conferences to which the same people always go and whine about the same old problems.

In summary, many process improvement initiatives don't improve process performance and thus cannot improve business performance. Such initiatives are rife with the fatal combination of both inappropriate decisions and ineffective implementations. (See Figure 4.4 in Chapter 4, "Small Changes, Big Performance Improvement.")

The business and the work of "process improvement" are an area that needs improving perhaps more than any other area. We've improved project management, we've improved engineering, we've improved configuration management, quality assurance, and our measurement programs. Isn't it high time we improve ourselves and what we do for a living? Isn't it time to improve process improvement?

Start with the Right Team

Take a look around…who are your comrades in process improvement? What are their knowledge, skill, and experience (KSE)? What can they contribute to the process improvement effort and will those contributions add value? What skills do you need, and when in the process improvement project life cycle will you need them?

Why ask these questions, you ask? Why wouldn't you just go into process improvement with the people you have instead of trying to get the right people at the right time? Remember, every decision you make will reflect on you as a leader and a manager, so why not start right now, at the beginning?

Here's another reason: When you've seen enough process improvement projects fail—as I have—due to using the wrong people at the wrong time, you'll know why this is important. Here's what I've seen:

■ A senior leader in the organization assigns a bunch of underemployed technical writers to the process improvement project. This assumes a solution, even before the problem has been framed. The assumed solution is that the only work that needs to be done is to write a bunch of processes and procedures in text-based narrative representation. It turns out that wasn't the right solution because the problem wasn't with the defined processes; it was with process performance.

■ A VP forms an SEPG that is entirely composed of subject matter experts in different disciplines related to product development—requirements analysis, project managers, software developers, testers, etc. They are all very knowledgeable of the work they perform and how they perform it, but they are completely and utterly inarticulate when it comes to documenting and conveying their knowledge. The process improvement project dies on the vine.

■ A director staffs the EPG with department managers. They always have higher priorities than process work. The process improvement project never leaves the starting block.

Now that I've outlined for you what doesn't work, let me guide you toward what does work in terms of staffing the process improvement project. Table 5.1 identifies the key knowledge, skills, and experience that I have seen employed on process improvement projects that succeeded and delivered results.

Table 5.1 KSE Needed for a Successful Process Improvement Project

Project Role	KSE Descriptions	When Needed and Why
Process improvement project manager	Training and extensive experience managing all aspects of a product development and delivery project (the process system is the product), including requirements management, work estimation, risk management, communication, and project performance monitoring and measurement	The entire life cycle of the process improvement project, from inception to delivery of the process system
Process and performance analyst	Training and experience in analyzing business performance requirements and using those requirements to derive and develop process system requirements; also, knowledge and experience in evaluating/assessing both defined and performed processes against their requirements	Needed to derive and develop process system requirements, and needed at points in development to verify process designs against requirements
Process designer/developer[a]	Education and experience in developing process system designs based on requirements and performance expectations; skills include information mapping, process modeling, information representation techniques, systems thinking, database design, and human interface design. Experience should include having designed and developed business process systems in a variety of enterprises in various sectors of the economy.	Needed in process system requirements development to provide feedback on feasibility of requirements; needed to design and develop process system

(Continued)

Table 5.1 (Continued) KSE Needed for a Successful Process Improvement Project

Project Role	KSE Descriptions	When Needed and Why
Subject matter experts	Extensive knowledge and experience in the performance of specific aspects of the organization's processes, such as product engineering, service management, purchasing/acquisition, product testing, etc.	Needed for the development of the process system requirements (user needs); needed in process development to review and to provide feedback on process designs; needed at the end of process development to test or pilot new or changed defined processes
Sponsor/owner	Skills include leadership and management, communication and presentation, negotiation, risk management, decision making, and finance and accounting. The person in this role is accountable for the success and the results of the process improvement project.	The entire process improvement project life cycle

a Except in the fields of chemistry, petroleum, and manufacturing, process design—design of business processes—is not a subject that is widely taught in academic institutions. This is a burgeoning discipline in which much knowledge is acquired through hands-on experience.

In your first-round draft, find the process improvement project manager. You may have assumed that, as the person in charge of the process improvement initiative, that role should be yours. No one is born knowing how to manage a project. Watching an amateur try to manage a project is like watching someone play whack-a-mole—he fights to get the project back on schedule, only to see the quality slip, and then he jumps on the quality issue only to see the costs go out of control. When he whacks the costs back down, the schedule pops outward to the right. It's a sad scene to watch.

Believe me, if you don't have training or experience in project management (i.e., you're not a practicing Project Management Institute-certified project management professional), then you don't *want* this role. Find a really good project manager, preferably one who has experience in managing improvement projects.

Also be wary of volunteers; find out why someone is volunteering for the process improvement project. It might be because that person is altruistic and truly wants to apply his or her skills to the betterment of the organization. But it might also be because he or she doesn't have skills that are useful for any other purpose in the organization or because that individual has a personality no one else wants to deal with. Find out why someone is volunteering before you accept that person on the team.

Process Improvement Project Stakeholders

Ever notice how everybody wants to be a stakeholder right up to the minute when they realize they actually have to *do* something? "Stakeholder" seems to have become somewhat of a status or title, maybe because so many people treat stakeholders as if they are customers.

The "stake" means that a stakeholder has a stake in the success of the project. If someone has a stake in the success of a process improvement project, then that means that he or she should be willing to do work actively to ensure success, not just sit around and watch other people work and be catered to in project reviews and status reports.

Based on the prior chapters in this book that address real performance improvement, real process improvement, and realizing a positive ROP, the following subsections define the stakeholders in a process improvement project and their responsibilities as such.

Process Users

If stakeholders have rank, the intended users of the defined processes—those who will perform the processes—are more important than other stakeholders. Consider them the customers of the processes. (Also see "Build the Process for Its Users" in Chapter 2, "Real Process Improvement.")

Their responsibility to the process improvement project is to provide process system requirements and use cases or scenarios. They should also provide input on process designs and definition, as well as help test or pilot new or revised defined processes and provide feedback.

In process implementation, process users should be incented to contribute process lessons learned, best practices and example work products, and changes to the defined process based on performance and experiential data.

Executive Leadership and Senior Management

Executive leadership needs to be involved in the establishment of organizational business performance objectives and strategies. (Also see "Establishing Performance Objectives" in Chapter 1, "Real Performance Improvement.")

Executives need to be engaged in letting the process improvement project know what they expect—at a high level—in terms of improved process performance and how that improved performance should contribute to the achievement or the organization's performance objectives and strategy.

The process improvement project team should help executives and senior management integrate process improvement status and progress into their existing operational reporting.

Business Development

Whether your company is a telecom trying to achieve a TL 9000 registration or a defense contractor trying to achieve a CMMI maturity level, odds are that your business development organization is a stakeholder in the process improvement project. They are the people who will leverage every achievement—great and small—the organization makes to get new customers and enter new market space.

Because of their interest in the process improvement accomplishments, they are responsible for informing the process improvement project of upcoming proposals or bids so that the process improvement project can set realistic expectations for things like ISO registrations or CMMI appraisals.

Once a marketable accomplishment such as a CMMI maturity level is achieved, the process improvement professionals in the organization should offer business development help with accurately and correctly defining marketing collaterals such as press releases or announcements. When something like a press release about achieving a CMMI maturity level is so poorly and inaccurately written (as some I've seen have been) to the point that most recipients laugh at it, the organization that achieved the maturity level instantly loses all credibility, and the value of the accomplishment is significantly diminished.

Finance and Accounting (Cost Accounting)

Process improvement isn't free...never has been, never will be. A process improvement project, like most projects, will have a budget to which it is held accountable. This organization has a responsibility to help the process improvement project establish charge codes or objects for the process improvement work. It also has the responsibility to work with the process improvement project to help people understand and plan the work that can be legitimately charged to the process budget and that which cannot. Accounting people can look at the process improvement project work breakdown structure and the resources required to execute the project and then help the project plan budget allocations so that the project stays within budget. Finally, Finance and Accounting should help the process project track, monitor, and measure its actual expenditures against plans.

Human Resources

In many organizations, it is the Human Resources (HR) Department or team that plans, acquires, delivers, and coordinates training and education to the workforce. Regardless of whether the process improvement project is addressing the defined process, the performed process, or both, there will inevitably be some training that needs to be delivered for the new or revised processes.

The process improvement project has a responsibility to work with HR (or the organization's training team) early in the project's life cycle to identify training needs, costs/resources, and schedule. HR or the training team has a responsibility to ensure the success of the process improvement project by providing training services when they are needed by the project.

Defining Stakeholders

Here's one more useful practice when it comes to defining process improvement project stakeholders and their roles: Be very clear and overt about the responsibilities for each stakeholder. Typically, I see stakeholder involvement in a project defined using the old, worn-out RACI (responsible, accountable, consulted, informed) chart. The problem with RACI and the reason it doesn't work is because I can go ask any five people in any organization to tell me the difference between "responsible" and "accountable," and I'll get five different definitions. Or I can ask any five people what work is performed by someone who is "consulted," and I'll again get five different answers.

When I define stakeholder for any project—and especially for a process improvement project—stakeholder responsibility is defined by identifying the verb each stakeholder performs for each major task, event, or deliverable. Responsibility is defined using active verbs such as

- Create
- Review
- Approve
- Provide input
- Attend
- Audit

Don't leave a stakeholder's responsibilities open to his or her interpretation because then she or he can do almost nothing and still maintain stakeholder status.

Consultants

In the online discussion groups in which I sometimes partake, I often see a lot of discussion around the role and the value of consultants in process improvement. Having been both a purchaser and a purveyor of performance and process consulting, I can say with certainty that the right consultant can deliver significant value to your performance and process improvement effort, and the wrong consultant will just take your money. As with many other endeavors, it comes down to you first figuring out what you need that you don't already have, why you need it, and what is it worth.

In the CMMI and ISO worlds, every lead appraiser, every instructor, and every auditor will call himself or herself a "consultant," but that's a pretty loose application of the term. A CMMI lead appraiser or instructor can tell you how other organizations have used the CMMI to achieve maturity levels. However, unless he has walked in your shoes—used the model or standard in an organization to which he belonged to achieve process improvement and performance results—then he can't really help you apply the model or standard in your organization. He can guess or speculate, but how much is that worth to you?

Ask yourself this: How is having a CMMI appraisal process improvement? It's simply a measure of the organization's performed and defined processes consistency with practices in the CMMI. A measurement might codify improvement, but that doesn't mean the measurement itself is improvement. An introduction to CMMI class will teach some of your workers about the CMMI, but it won't teach them how to use the CMMI for the purposes of process and performance improvement. Learning is learning, but it's not *doing* until the learning is applied. Besides, anybody who can read can read and understand the CMMI for himself or herself, and there is no one right interpretation of a model or standard. An interpretation coming from a lead appraiser or auditor, or an instructor, doesn't make it any more valid than your interpretation.

The greatest value a process consultant can bring to your organization comes only from these deliverables:

■ Showing you how to avoid costly mistakes in process improvement that have been made by many other organizations, and how to apply lessons learned by other organizations

- Building or helping you build or implement processes and work products that, when performed, improve process performance
- Showing you how to achieve performance improvement through process improvement, and how to realize the ROP

What Does Your Organization Need and Why?

Before you go shopping for a process improvement consultant, just slow down and think about it as another resource for your organization, and treat it accordingly. Also, make sure your organization doesn't already have the skill set you're seeking in house, but you just don't know about it.

If you need a CMMI lead appraiser because you want to have an appraisal and there is no lead appraiser in your organization, then the answer is pretty clear: hire a lead appraiser. But if you need guidance on how to develop a set of standard processes that will, when performed, enable compliance with a model or standard, that need isn't necessarily filled by a lead appraiser or instructor.

If you need to develop and deploy processes for conducting research or experimentation, then a CMMI or ISO "expert" isn't going to be very useful since these models and standards don't address research, innovation, or experimentation processes. In this case, you're better off finding someone with a broad and deep base of experience in designing and developing process systems regardless of the specific environment or application.

Also, before you or your leadership decide to pay consulting rates, invest the time to be certain you don't already possess the sought-after knowledge, skill, and experience internally. I recall a situation when I worked for Xerox many years ago, back in the days of the software CMM. I and other members of the SEPG periodically met with the division executives and provided them with advice on advancing the enterprise-wide process improvement efforts. Most of our advice went unheeded. The execs then brought in Watts Humphrey and paid him a rate that was considerably higher than our fully burdened rate to give them the same advice we had already provided. Somehow, the advice is worth more when it comes from someone outside the organization. Even if your organization determines that it needs a particular skill or expertise that it doesn't already possess, that still shouldn't drive a hasty decision to outsource or subcontract. For example, your organization might have a near-term need for an "Introduction to CMMI" class—to staff an appraisal team—and your organization doesn't have a CMMI Institute-certified instructor. If you're not thinking long term, you'll come to the immediate conclusion that you need to contract an instructor, or send the people who need the training to a CMMI Institute class.

But what about the future? Maybe your organization is just one unit within a very large enterprise, and other units will also need people trained in the CMMI. You should try to determine the strategic training needs (OT SP 1.1) because a cost-benefit analysis might very well yield the result that, in the long run, it will be more cost effective to develop the capability in-house (get one or more employees certified to deliver the intro to a CMMI course) than contracting an instructor (at consulting rates) every time you need one.

As with all outsourcing or acquisition decisions, the decision to hire a consultant should be made using criteria and a structured evaluation process (think decision analysis and resolution (DAR)). Here are some criteria you can use to decide whether to outsource (hire a process consultant) or insource (develop the capability internally). Which choice—insource or outsource—

- Is most likely to meet our needs or requirements?
- Is cost effective or affordable?
- Can provide the service when it is needed?
- Has the right skills and knowledge required for the solution?

- Will provide the highest quality solution?
- Is more closely aligned with our core competencies?
- Is more closely aligned with our strategic direction and objectives?

Of course, as with all uses of decision criteria, those making the decision should weight the importance of each criterion.

Selecting a Consultant

In a process improvement role, you inevitably will get to go to some type of conference related to process or performance improvement. If you've never been to one, then you'll meet lots of nice, wonderful people dressed in nice clothing. You'll attend their presentations and learn a little, and you'll think all these people are so smart and that they can help you and your organization. Maybe they can; maybe they cannot. Learn to ask about the factual experiences and data that underlie the claims you see made in presentations. Realize that often marketing comes in the form of appearing to be free education from altruistic people. Few people in the general population—and no one at a conference—are altruistic.

If your decision process results in a decision to hire a process consultant, the next step is to find the right source. Again, this really goes back to the questions about what the organization really needs, which may not always be what it wants. Superficially, you might think that you just need a lead appraiser so that you can have a SCAMPI (standard CMMI appraisal method for process improvement) appraisal. But what if you can get a lead appraiser who can add greater value by not only leading the appraisal but also providing high-value post-appraisal improvement recommendations so that your organization can get a jump-start preparing for the subsequent appraisal?

In my consulting practice, I often provide the prospect with process guidance and decision assets for selecting a process consultant. I don't always get the work, but the prospect always gets a highly reusable asset for making vendor selection decisions and generates evidence for the DAR process area.

Some of the more useful selection criteria I have found for selecting a process consultant include:

- To what extent does the candidate vendor understand our organization's goals, requirements, and business sector?
- To what extent are other customers of the vendor satisfied with the vendor's services (i.e., referrals)?
- Compared with the same or similar service offerings from other candidate vendors, how cost effective is the candidate vendor?
- To what extent are the candidate vendor's services mature and stable?
- How mature and stable is the candidate vendor's business?
- How financially sound is the candidate vendor?
- To what extent does the candidate vendor meet our security requirements?
- To what extent is (or has been) the candidate vendor responsive to our requests for information?
- To what extent is the candidate vendor compliant with applicable standards, regulations, or laws?

Process Design and Development

As written in other parts of this book, a large focus for process improvement groups and teams has traditionally been on process definition. In "Improving the Defined Process" in Chapter 2, I introduced the concept of designing the process system before defining it. Although this topic is worthy of its own book (already in work), this section reveals some principles that underlie process design and development. My intent is simply to help you free your mind from the chains of conventional thought about process definition so that you can explore new and better ways of communicating process that will result in better process adoption and adaptation.

What Is Process?

Before diving into process design and development, it's worth spending the time with others responsible for process definition to discuss and achieve some level of consensus understanding of what is meant by the word "process." It's too easy for an individual to assume that process means the same thing to everyone else as it does to him or her, but the lack of an overt shared understanding will cause lots of problems later on.

At the subconscious level, process is a thought or concept that may not be easy to define or articulate, but can be and is easily lived every day. As I write this book, I can reflect and realize that I follow a process for writing. And even though I perform my writing process consistently no matter what the writing project, I have never documented that process. It's an undefined process that I live and perform. I live a process for backing my car out of my garage. I consistently perform a series of tasks and make several decisions, but all at the subconscious level. When we eat and drink, we perform a process, but not one that we have to define to perform consistently.

In business, there are many undefined processes— you might call them work habits—that are performed subconsciously, and there are many other processes that are performed consciously. Some of the consciously performed processes are defined; some are not. Regardless of whether process is conscious or subconscious, defined or undefined, people whose work is to improve process need an understanding of the meaning of process.

According to Wiktionary, the etymology of "process" is the old French word, *procés,* which means "journey." That fits because when you follow a process, you are moving from the state you are in right now to some other state. The changes in states can be you—your personality, your knowledge, your character—as you journey through the life process, or it can be changes in states of things you create, such as a product changing from nonexistence to existence via a product development process.

In terms of visualizing a process in advance of performing it and as you perform it, process is almost uniquely human. (There are studies that indicate chimpanzees and octopi might possess some level of conscious brain activity about a process they are performing.) Everything in our lives is a process: growing up, putting on your shoes, driving or taking the train to work, paying your bills, or enjoying dinner with friends. Process is organic to the human condition.

Pragmatically, what is really important in achieving and understanding of process is to address up front the questions that will come up over and over in a process improvement project. It is more efficient and effective to answer these questions at the beginning of the project and record the answers:

- What is the definition of "process" in our business and our environment?
- Which processes need to be defined, and which ones do not?
- How abstract or how specific should a process be? What level of detail does a defined process describe?

- What is the difference between "process" and other terms such as "procedure," "policy," "work flow," and "subprocess?"
- What are the basic information elements—the "building blocks"—that we will use to build a process? (Also see "Establish Process Design Standards" in Chapter 2.)
- Can each building block be ascribed to the specific process performance question it answers: What to perform? Who performs it? When is it performed? How is it performed? How much is performed? What is the result of performance?
- How do people and tools interact with process?
- What is our model for a process?

A Useful Model for Process

Over the years, through working with clients—especially those clients whom I've helped develop and implement advanced, state-of-the-practice process systems, I've had to evolve a useful mental model for process, which is illustrated in Figure 5.2.

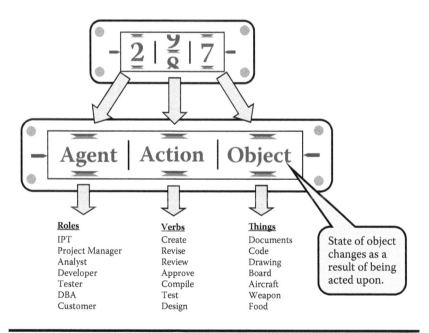

Figure 5.2   A mental model for "process."

In this figure, my mental model and meme for process is a combination lock with three drums that rotate to line up the right combination. The first drum gives me a selection of the element I call "agent," and there are lots of agents to choose from because this drum contains all the functional roles (not titles) in my organization. The second combination position comes from a drum containing the "action" element. This drum lets me select from all of the verbs that can be performed to change the state of something or someone. Finally, the third drum on the combination lock contains all the members of the element called "object," which are all the things or people that can be changed or transformed by performing the process.

From this deceptively simple model (shouldn't models be simple?), I can turn the drums on the lock to get combinations that define any process in my organization. Some combinations don't make any sense—customer + revise + food—but many combinations will make sense—designer + review + drawing.

Process Representation

Based on my experience, many of the defined processes in the world today consist of page after page, binder after binder, of text. Statistically speaking, this means that about half of the population of process users—the half that comprehend graphics more effectively than text—are not being considered by process developers. When you're building a product that you hope people will want, don't you build it with their preferences in mind, not yours?

The text people will posit all kind of bogus arguments for text, such as these that I have heard:

■ English is standard, but there is no standard for graphical diagrams.

- Everyone can understand words and sentences, but learning how to read graphics requires specialized training.
- The only way to describe procedural detail precisely is with words.
- It's easier and cheaper to write text-based processes because everyone can write.

On the other end of that spectrum, there are some people—unified modeling language zealots, for example—who would get rid of any and all words and make all processes look like this illustration—or the cuneiform illustration above.

In the nontext world, which is utopia for some, you can only adopt and perform the process if you're "in the club" or if you somehow acquire the secret decoder ring to deliver knowledge and enlightenment…"the precious!"

My caricature of the words-versus-pictures camps, polarized and locked in eternal conflict, is supported by firsthand observations and is not so far-fetched. The polarization and fractioning of language and technology are also consistent with and parallel to the same trends in world belief systems and politics.

But words to the exclusion of pictures or vice versa is a false choice; it is the either/or logic fallacy in classical philosophical thought. A process system that is adopted and performed by a diverse population of process users is one that provides the same content in a variety of ways so that each process performer can have it her or his way. This does not defy standardization because, in such a process system, the content remains standard while the representation is diverse for a diverse audience.

The Dynamic Process

In his 2004 book, *The Laws of Software Process,* Philip Armour wrote that the only process we can accurately define is the one we just performed. But all laws are temporal in nature and are true only within the context and the conditions within which they are written. Time, advancement in technology, and new thoughts that arise from experience and experimentation can change or negate previous laws.

Think about how you currently adjust or change a defined process so that it accurately reflects the performed process... there is always a delay between what was learned during process performance and the change to the defined process. In performing a process, I might find a better way to perform a procedure than the way it is described, or I might develop a more effective process asset such as a template, guide, or checklist. At the instant I make the process improvement, it is only an improvement for me or my team, but it doesn't really help any other users of the process. I must first complete some portion of process performance and then write up and submit a change request or lesson learned. Then there is time spent analyzing the change request or lesson by a group with responsibility for maintaining the defined process, followed by more delay due to changing and publishing the defined process or process asset. By the time the change is made to the defined process, other projects and teams have already worked through the part of the defined process I improved, but without the benefit of my improvement. What if you could shorten the delay between your (or others') improvement to the performed process and the consequential change to the defined process to near zero delay? What if process performers could change the defined process in real time, almost in the instant they make the performance improvements? What if the performed process and the defined process were always synchronized and reflective of each other?

Today's technology, if appropriately used, can enable that. What if the standard process were defined in a wiki, but process users could add to the defined process as they used it?

The Smart Process

There are already automated services and websites that "learn" and adapt to your preferences and the way you work. For example, voice recognition software can adapt its translation of your dialect and enunciation of words. Technologically, there's no real reason a process system couldn't do the same.

Imagine performing a digitally defined process that remembers the template you chose to use the last time you performed a step or a task and offers you that template (instead of a menu of others) the next time you perform the task. A smart process system could also remember if you preferred to perform steps in a sequence that is tailored from the standard sequence, or remember exactly where you left off in the process the day before and then remind you of your starting point the next day when you log in. You could tell a smart process system your functional role, and it could then regenerate the standard defined process to present just the process tasks or steps in which your role participates... MyProcess.com!

The Almost Perfect Process

OK, nothing is ever perfect and, moreover, in most endeavors the pursuit of perfection gets in the way of achieving the good and yields a negative ROP. However, the technology and the know-how exist today to build a process system that generates an almost perfect defined process every time with the click of a mouse.

You come into work one day to find that you've been assigned a project. You know—because it's policy—that you have to use the organization's standard processes, but you also know that a one-size-fits-all process is only theoretical, and that no project ever executes the standard process exactly as it is defined. In other jobs in the past, you had to spend multiple days trying to figure out how to tailor the process to suit your project or run the risk of being caught and ticketed by Quality Assurance for deviating from the process. But this organization you're working in now is much smarter than that...they have built an APP, an "almost perfect process."

You sit down at your workstation and log into APP. It brings up a web form that takes you about 20 minutes to complete. The form asks you a bunch of questions about the project, such as the following:

- Project type—development, service, production, maintenance, etc.
- Project duration
- Numbers and types of internal and external stakeholders
- Team size
- Size of work (via multiple submenus for selecting ranges of effort, ranges of deliverable sizes, etc.)
- Project deliverables (a list of check-boxes to select or not)
- The standard project roles you will staff and the level of experience of team members in those roles
- Compliance requirements—whether the project needs to maintain process compliance with any models, standards, regulations, or laws
- The project's relative ranked priority for cost, schedule, and quality
- Your level of expertise in using the organization's processes and assets

After you have completed the online form, you click the "Generate Project Process" button. Then, just as fast as your servers can work, APP reaches into and collects data from multiple repositories, multiple databases containing historical measures and measurement information, multiple asset libraries, and multiple experiential collections. It then performs some analysis and cross-checking against the data in your form and assembles the almost perfect defined process—including process assets such as prepopulated templates—for your project.

Fiction? To the best of my knowledge, the APP doesn't exist as of the writing of this book, but there is no technological reason why it can't; there are lots of business reasons why it should.

Process Improvement Project Management

In my first book, *Real Process Improvement Using the CMMI*, I addressed this topic in great detail that I won't repeat here. However, since that book in 2004, I have learned much and have evolved my thoughts and practices in process improvement project management, which I share with you in this section.

Process improvement projects are just like other types of projects in that they are constantly having to manage project scope, resources, priorities, schedule, and stakeholder expectations. And, as with other types of projects, the success or failure of the project depends almost entirely on balancing those dynamics.

It's hard to say which of those five project dynamics is the most frequent critical point of failure for process improvement projects; I've seen each of them become lethal when not managed. Having managed some successful process improvement projects and having brought some back from the brink of disaster, I think the following subsections reveal some insights and lessons learned about each dynamic in a process improvement project. These subsections will inform you of what is most likely to go wrong in each dynamic, and what you can do about it.

Scope

Managing project scope in a product development or service delivery project has become almost a science due to the now vast body of knowledge related to requirements management. But no similar body of knowledge exists for managing the scope of process improvement projects.

It is so seductive as to be almost insidious to be working toward an improvement objective and want to fix all kinds of other ancillary problems along the way. The problem with this natural human tendency is that it precludes ever actually completing *anything.* Here are my personal favorite scope-creep horror stories:

- In the middle of a CMMI appraisal (which I always plan and manage as a project), the customer asks if we can include an evaluation against the CMMI-DEV maturity level 4 practices, when the original CMMI scope was maturity level 3.
- Our initial contract and project for an Army organization is to help them build a CMMI-DEV-compliant process system. Near the end of that project, the government customer says that we were also supposed to conduct an appraisal to "certify" them at CMMI maturity level 2. (Also see "Managing Stakeholders and Their Expectations" in this chapter.)
- For another government organization, we have a very detailed and focused plan for achieving some targeted process improvement objectives. The project to improve document management and control is making very quick progress. Then, one of the stakeholders in the client organization goes to an "Introduction to CMMI" class. She then tells the improvement project that they have to

come up with a way to collect measures from document states and state transitions.

■ My company is 9 months into a 12-month process development and improvement project when we are told the process had to be compliant with Federal Aviation Administration standard DO-178.

The following subsections explain what you can and should do to manage process improvement scope and control or mitigate the effects of the inevitable scope expansion.

Learn to Say "No"

Learn to say "no" as sweetly and as politely and with as much humility as possible, but say "no." We've all come to fear saying "no. We think if we say "no," it will cost us our job, or our next promotion, or our current or future contract. So even before you learn to say "no," learn to ask yourself, "What would I do if I weren't afraid?" "No" is often the very best answer, not only for you but also for your boss or your client. "Yes" often feels really good, but only for a few minutes or for a day, and then the negative consequences of "yes" are felt for the remainder of the project.

Learning to say "no" is one of the greatest challenges you will face in your career. You've worked in cultures in which someone who says "no" is considered to not be a "team player," and he or she then gets marginalized. On the other hand, the compunction always to say "yes" when the right answer was really

"no" has often come back to cause you grief. As
with all work habits, this takes courage and practice.

Remember that, if all you ever do is say "yes"
to your boss, then one of you is redundant; guess
which one?

Learn to Say "Yes, and…"

Like many of you, I used to say "yes, but" or "yes, if"; now
I say, "yes, and…." The reason is that the conjunctions "but"
and "if" change the dynamic of "yes"; they stall or stop the
forward momentum gained by the "yes." How do you think
the conversation phenomenon has evolved in which one
person says "Yes" and pauses, and then another person in the
conversation says, "But?"

Using "and" after the "yes" maintains the forward
momentum of the "yes." Table 5.2 provides some practical
implementations of the "yes, and…" concept in a process
improvement project.

Resources

Process improvement project death arising from resource
complications comes from one or both of these two causes:
(1) insufficient resources for the work and the schedule, and/
or (2) the wrong resources.

Insufficient Resources

It's math, simple math. If your process improvement project
has resources to complete its work in 3 years, but the project
is requested to complete in 1 year, does anyone besides me
see a problem? If one of your process improvement project
team members is resource loaded at 234 percent, does anyone
besides me see a problem?

Table 5.2   Examples of Using "Yes, and…" in a Process Improvement Project

Your boss or your client	You and/or your team
I need you and your team to include process implementation support after you've released the new processes.	Yes ma'am, and I'll get with you later to estimate the cost for that support so that you can plus-up the purchase order.
While your team is addressing the requirements management process, I want you also to help us select a requirements management tool.	Understood. When can you and I get together to estimate the cost and schedule impact of performing that additional work?
In addition to implementing the lessons learned program, we also need your team to develop a project management measurement repository.	Yes, and I'll help you open a change request for that work so that we can give it the attention it deserves.
We're going to bid on a major contract. Can you and your team move up the schedule for the appraisal by 3 months?	Yes, and we'll need your help updating and managing the risk associated with a shortened schedule.
We need the process improvement project to address AS9100 in addition to the CMMI.	Yes, and I'll take that as your commitment to drop one or more of the other improvement objectives that we were originally going to achieve.

The most insidious form of insufficient resource allocation to a process improvement project (or any project) is what I call "death by crumbs." If you lock me in a cell and don't feed me anything and give me no water, I'll die in about 6 to 10 days. If you give me water, but no food, I'll die in 20 to 35 days. But if you give me water and a few crumbs of bread, I'll hang onto the very edge of life for a really long time.

So too is there a life–death threshold for projects. If you give a project just 10 percent of 10 people when what it really needs is 50 percent of 2 people, the project will cling to life for a really long time, but the status reports will indicate that 100 percent of the resources were spent in this period compiling the status report that reports that nothing was done. It turns out that math isn't always real life. Ten percent of 10 people is mathematically the same resource as 50 percent of 2 people. However, when we prioritize our daily work, there is a threshold below which we say, "It's just not worth it," and we always find something else to do other than that 10 percent work. If the project you're sponsoring or leading is facing a death by crumbs, you and it are both better off shooting it and putting it out of its misery. But don't miss; kill the project properly. As Larry the Cable Guy says, "I had a horse with a broken leg, so I shot it...now I got a horse with a broken leg and a gunshot wound."

And don't try to address the resource insufficiency problem as a cost problem by replacing your resources with lower cost labor, because that will simply transfer the insufficiency problem to a different problem known as...

The Wrong Resources

Do you hire an accountant to fix your plumbing? Do you hire a lawyer to mow your lawn? Do you hire a Java developer to design and develop processes? It doesn't matter how many letters-after-name (LAN) someone has, if he or she can't perform the specified work to deliver the specified products to achieve the specified objectives, then he or she should not be on the project team.

The resources you need for the successful execution of a process improvement project are defined in Table 5.1 and don't need to be repeated here.

What can you do if you don't get the right resources? Negotiate any or all of the following with the project sponsor:

■ Trade the resources you were given for the resources you really need. Perhaps you were allocated the under-employed and overpaid PhD with advanced degrees in mathematics and astrophysics…not skills really needed for a mainstream process improvement effort. So advertise him and his value; find him a home where he's really needed and wanted and then trade him for that young project manager who's really organized, has her act together, and is a great communicator.

■ Accept the resources you were allocated, but negotiate for more time and money because more of both is what you'll need to convert the low-use resources into high-use resources. You'll need money and time to get them trained in process improvement and in the specific skills you'll need them to apply to the project. This approach amounts to replanning the project.

■ Negotiate for lower quality project output and deliverables. If the resources you were allocated won't achieve the process and performance improvement objectives, then identify which lesser objectives they will achieve, redefine those targets, and be overt about it.

Priorities

Unfortunately, in many organizations, there is a big gap between the stated or published priorities and the *real* priorities. Discovering such a schism is as easy as observing the work people focus on every day and then comparing and contrasting that with the stated or published priorities. For example, let's say my customer service organization has a published priority for an improvement to shorten call-to-close durations by 50 percent. But all of the meetings and all of the work every day are spent working individual call issues and no one is measuring call management performance or implementing any improvements; then I know the real priority is something other than improvement. Follow the money, follow the effort, observe the behaviors, and listen to the conversations, and you'll learn the organization's real priorities.

Once you have reconciled the stated priorities and the real priorities, there are two dimensions to process and performance improvement priorities:

- The priority of a specific improvement relative to the priority for accomplishing other improvements
- The priority of improvement work relative to all other work in the organization

Both of these two priority dimensions are determined by attributes of the priorities themselves, with the primary attributes being (1) a priority's dependency on the accomplishment of other priority work, and (2) a priority's constraints.

Determining a priority's dependencies is relatively easy and in many cases obvious. If I look at an improvement initiative to improve a business process, I know of at least one major improvement dependency, and that is to be able to measure or quantitatively characterize the phenomenon's current performance. As with all strategic initiatives, including process and performance improvement, there is the dependency that the organization must stay in business to implement the improvements. That means that no commercially viable or for-profit organization can spend 100 percent of its effort only on improvement (unless it has private equity angels who don't care about their money.) Hence, it is to the benefit of the organization and the people in charge of improvement initiatives constantly to demonstrate how the improvements are helping the organization stay in business. (Also see "From the Strategy to the Performance Objective to the Process Performance Objective" in Chapter 2.)

Constraints also affect the relative priority of an improvement, and saying that something is "our highest priority" has a psychological exclusionary effect on other priorities in the minds of workers. When an exec or a leader says, "This is our highest priority," then everything with a priority of two or lower may as well have a priority of zero or not even exist.

Other constraints on priorities are the usual suspects: money and schedule. The budgetary constraint comes in two forms: (1) the value of the resources allocated or budgeted to the priority work, and (2) the individual or team incentives for accomplishing the priority. In the first case, the amount of resources an organization allocates to an improvement initiative in many ways indicates the real priority, which may differ from the stated priority. For an exaggerated but illustrative example, if the process lead is told that the highest priority is to get the organization to CMMI maturity level 3 but is then given no resources (the constraint) to do so, the effective priority for accomplishing the maturity level is zero.

As individuals, we all do what we are motivated to do and rewarded for doing. Imagine that you're the operations director, and your annual bonus is based on specified progress or accomplishments in these areas and percentages:

- Customer satisfaction: 60 percent
- Employee satisfaction: 20 percent
- Intellectual asset development: 15 percent
- Process improvement: 5 percent

On a daily basis, which type of work will have your primary focus, and which work will you tend to make a low priority or constantly put off until "later"? At some threshold, which differs for each individual, a person will simply ignore the work and priorities for which he or she has the least incentive to pursue. In the preceding example, if I have only one more task to accomplish toward customer satisfaction before the end of the year, and if accomplishing that task means the difference between the full 60 percent bonus or only 50 percent, and if I don't have time to do anything else, my customer satisfaction objective will trump the process improvement objective.

Schedule

One of my favorite managers at Xerox—Joe Larossa—liked to say, "Software is never late; plans are bad." Another one of my project manager role models, when asked how long it would take to deliver a release, would say, "As long as it takes." Both were everlastingly right.

Can you accelerate a process improvement project? Can you take some shortcuts? Can you shorten the schedule? Sure, you can, but there will always be a trade-off, whether or not you are aware of it and its consequences.

For many projects, especially those in subtier contractor organization, there is a specified burn rate, which is the rate at which the budget can be spent. There is also, of course, a specified amount of work that must be accomplished— deliverables—within budget spent. Such expectations often also exist for process improvement projects. So, if you shorten the schedule—pull it in to the left, as they say— the project will obviously spend its budget faster. Will that be OK with those who control the purse strings? And will shortening the budget enable enough time to accomplish the work that must be performed within that time period? What if the project's resources are not the right resources... remember how that requires more budget and longer sched-ule? Maybe you can shorten the schedule and still produce the required outputs even with limited or less than optimal resources, but will the quality of the output be diminished as a result?

Executives hate it when you say: Good, fast, or cheap; pick any two. But true leaders understand this paradigm, and true leaders will, with consultation from their talent, choose two of the three.

Balancing the performance dimensions of a process
improvement project—scope, quality of deliverables, resources/cost, and schedule—requires some
degree of systems thinking. You need to know that
you cannot make an adjustment to one of the performance dimensions without affecting the others;
to do so is simply tampering, and it will create the
right conditions for the "whack-a-mole" syndrome
to afflict your project. Also see "Context-Based
Performance Measures" (Chapter 1) and "Start with
the Right Team" (this chapter).

Managing Stakeholders and Their Expectations

Again, this is a topic worthy of a book unto itself. Here's what
I've learned and what is true to me: When I effectively manage
stakeholders' expectations in a process improvement project,
the project is always *perceived* as a success.

But even before you can manage stakeholders or their
expectations, you have first to establish clearly who the stakeholders are and their expectations of what and how they contribute to the process improvement work. (Also see "Process
Improvement Project Stakeholders" in this chapter.)

Here are experience-based tips that have proven effective
in managing stakeholders and their expectations:

■ Choose your battles. Yes, it is important for a stakeholder
to know how his or her participation—or lack thereof—is
affecting the process improvement project, but it is not all

that important for you to argue with him or her that there is no "certification" of CMMI maturity levels. If stakeholders want to use words that are convenient for them, don't irritate them over what, in the end, amounts to trivia.

■ When a stakeholder states an objective or expectation that is not within the scope of the process improvement project—that is, not defined in the plans—then make the time to have a discussion (one on one) with the stakeholder to explain the difference between his expectation and what the project will really deliver. If he thinks the scope should be changed, then negotiate for the commensurate increments to the budget and schedule.

■ Constantly remind stakeholders of how important their participation and contributions are. When your stakeholder involvement monitoring measures start to indicate someone is not involved per the plan, have an honest discussion with that person. Let her know how her lack of involvement is negatively affecting the project and ask if she can either reenergize her involvement or assign another person to fill her stakeholder role.

Reflect and Plan: What Did You Learn? What Will You Do?

Now review the following postchapter guide and think about what you've learned and how some of your views toward process and performance improvement have changed. Think about what you will do with the information you've learned (and how it makes you feel).

What Are You Doing or about to Do? Why?

Perhaps you're new to the process group in your organization, or perhaps the process group was just formed. Perhaps you and the others in the process group just come in every day and do more of the same that your predecessors did, and no one questions it.

Here are questions you and your colleagues should ask of yourselves—not just once, but every day or every week:

1. We're supposedly in the business of process improvement, but what are we improving, and why are we improving it?
2. What do we (or someone) estimate to be the ROP yielded by the improvement? If we can't determine that there will be a positive ROP, will we have the courage to stop doing what we're doing and do something else?
3. Do we have a shared understanding or mental model of the word "process"? What does it mean and have we written down that meaning?
4. Do we really understand what it means to "improve process"?

Who Is Involved?

It takes a pilot to fly a plane and keep it in the middle of the air successfully—the edge of the air is hard and can't be flown through! It takes a nuclear physicist to design nuclear energy systems. It takes a farmer to farm successfully. And guess what…it takes someone with both broad and deep skills and experience in process theory, process development, process implementation, and process institutionalization to effect process improvement. Before you and perhaps a whole gaggle of other well-meaning people, all of you with your hearts in the right place, go off and waste a lot of resources to accomplish little or nothing, please ask and honestly answer these questions:

1. Besides personal interest, what are your qualifications— knowledge, skills, and experience—that will enable you to effect real process and performance improvement?
2. Ask the preceding question for the others on your process improvement team.

3. Who are the process or performance improvement project's stakeholders? What are their qualifications to be stakeholders?

4. Besides watch and ingest status, what will the stakeholders actually *do?*

5. Does the improvement initiative have sufficient resources, or, given its objectives and schedules, will it simply die of starvation by crumbs?

6. Knowing the amount or sufficiency of resources, what is the adequacy of resources? Are they—the improvement team and the stakeholders—the right resources, with the needed knowledge, skills, and experience to fulfill their roles?

Balance

In balance, there is abundance. In imbalance, there is waste, devastation, and loss; this never more true and never more painfully obvious than in process and performance improvement projects. So what's in your balance?

1. What are the articulated or published priorities for the improvement effort in which you're involved? How does that priority differ from what you see people doing every day? What are you going to do to reconcile the difference between the stated priorities and the *real* priorities?

2. What are your measures, thresholds, or indicators of the scope of the improvement effort expanding or contracting? in other words, how will you know? What are your tactics, methods, or processes for accommodating scope change or mitigating its negative effects?

3. What is your plan to monitor and manage stakeholder involvement?

4. Have you thought about and, better yet, scripted, the possible conversations you will need to have with stakeholders to manage their expectations of the improvement project?

Chapter 6

Process and Performance Myths

So...so you think you can tell
heaven from hell,
blue skies from pain.
Can you tell a green field,
from a cold steel rail?
A smile from a veil?
Do you think you can tell?

—Pink Floyd, "Wish You Were Here"

Myth: Achieving Model or Standards Compliance Indicates Performance

Really? You've read all of this book to this point and you still believe that?

What's wrong with models, methods, and standards? Nothing. Can the use of the CMMI, Lean or Six Sigma, Agile methods, or ISO-based standards improve process and performance? Of course, it *can*. Does the use of any of these bodies of work by an organization necessarily improve anything? No, not necessarily.

Sometimes, the pursuit of achieving compliance with a standard not only does not yield performance improvement, but also provably causes performance degradation:

- A telecom company is young, vibrant, well capitalized, and growing its customer base through market penetrations and acquisition of competition. But the volume of product defects released to the field is exacting a heavy toll on customer satisfaction and is making it tough on the sales force to get existing customers to trust product upgrades. Meanwhile, the company wants to move up from being a tier 3 supplier to a tier 2 and knows that it needs to be TL 9000 compliant to play in that league. An external consultant defines a very clear path for improving product quality—one that is based on proven concepts—but implementing that plan will take a lot of hard work and time and will likely elongate release schedules in the near term. What does the company's management do? Well, since TL 9000 provides guidelines for a "quality management system" and "quality" sounds just like the word used in "product quality," the obvious choice is to bypass the more difficult improvement plan and hire contractors to write processes that address the content in the TL 9000 standard.

- A large defense contractor needs to maintain both its AS9100 registration and its CMMI maturity level rating. Between the AS9100 audits and CMMI appraisals, the management either terminates or drives out the people with process skills, and their process systems are not maintained. So, when it comes time to renew the AS registration or maturity level, the organization incurs extremely high costs by bringing in consultants and personnel from other organizations to do triage on the processes and help get the organization ready for the audit or the SCAMPI.

■ A manager in an online testing division of a large
education company decides that his organization
should achieve a CMMI maturity level by a certain date.
A consultant initiates improvement efforts that yield
measurable positive performance results, but a realistic
date for achieving a maturity level is beyond the date
arbitrarily set by the manager. People soon stop doing
things that really achieve better performance and start
doing things that align with CMMI practices. As the pressure from the manager increases, employee cynicism
increases and morale decreases. Finally, the consultant
(a CMMI Institute-certified lead appraiser) and one of the
true leaders in the organization tell the manager that the
pursuit of the maturity level is hurting the organization,
not helping. The pursuit is abandoned.

Myth: If We Develop Good Procedures, We'll Improve

Perhaps, but not likely. An organization can develop the greatest, most robust defined processes and procedures the world
has ever known, but what good is it if no one in the organization adopts and uses the processes?

The subsequent but non sequitur argument is, "Well, we'll
just make our people follow the processes." You can try, but
process—if we're not talking about chemical or mechanical
process—is a human endeavor, and humans are those recal-
citrant creatures who want to do what they want to do. And
when they don't want to do what you want them to do, they'll
simply present to you the story that you want to hear, while
they go about doing what they want to do. You'll not only
believe the story, but also repeat it to your boss.

Read "Understanding Defined Process versus Performed
Process" in Chapter 2 and you'll understand that you cannot
improve performance simply by improving process definition.

Myth: If We Hire the Right People, We Don't Need Processes

Even if this were true, you won't always hire the right people. And when the right people leave your organization and you still have no processes, you've increased your operational costs because you've increased the cost of retelling the process story to the new people.

Think about it...Let's say you have a very experienced system engineer making $180/hour in your telecom company who is 3 months away from retiring. To replace her, you hire "the right person," a younger but very bright system engineer from another company who has experience in enterprise resource planning (ERP) systems; the new system engineer is a bargain at $120/hour.

The processes that the retiring system engineer performs are her personal processes that she evolved over many years at the company, and none of them are written or defined in any way; they are in her head. Management realizes that in order to bring the new-hire up to speed, he will need to spend most of his days shadowing the retiring expert for mentoring and knowledge transfer. So for 3 months, the cost of learning for the new-hire is $300 per hour ($180 + $120).

Imagine if the expert could have spent some small portion of her time over the years documenting routine processes, checks, thoughts, and lessons learned. With that, the new-hire could do some of his learning just by reading, and the cost of succession would be kept closer to $120/hour than $300/hour.

In many cases, the organization doesn't get 3 months notice from someone who possesses a great amount of organizational and process knowledge. If much of your organization's knowledge assets walk out the door in someone's head tomorrow, then all of the organization's and its shareholders' investment in building that knowledge over the years is completely lost. You can amortize equipment (and even really expensive software), but how do you get the write-down on knowledge assets when they remain wet-ware?

Myth: If We Just Implement the Right Tools, We Can Automate Things and Accelerate Our Business

Yep, you sure can…you can accelerate it right into the ground. Finish the sentence: A fool with a tool is…. This myth is so easily proven to be not true, it's hardly worth the effort.

If you hear some version of this myth, ask these questions of the one(s) perpetuating the myth:

- Which tool will resolve the problem we're having with employee morale?
- Which tool will turn around our diminishing revenue and market share?
- Which product will address the poor relationships we have with our customers and our vendors?
- What is the automation that will help our leaders make better decisions and be better leaders?

Moreover, when you accelerate a flawed process, then you're likely just to create errors and defects at a faster rate. If your automation perpetuated or accelerated defect creation, then the corrective actions and rework are likely to require more human processing, which probably will turn your investment in the tool into a negative ROI.

Myth: We Need to Hire a Lead Appraiser to Improve Our Processes

This is only true if the person you hire or contract with is much more than just a lead appraiser and much more than someone knowledgeable in the CMMI. If his or her only experience and knowledge is the CMMI and CMMI appraisals, then she or he might be able to guide your organization in achieving a CMMI maturity level, but that's not the same as achieving real process and performance improvement. I know a person who is a CMMI instructor and lead appraiser. He prides himself on being able to recite verbatim the practices in the model. It's a mildly entertaining parlor trick, but it doesn't do much for clients in terms of helping them achieve an ROP. (Also see "Selecting a Consultant" in Chapter 5.)

Index

A

"Activity" as work, 3, 106–107,
    109–110, 281–283
Airline flight connections, 103–105
Airspeed program, 98, 187
Almost perfect process, 317–319
Analysis, using right amount of,
    266–269
Analysis paralysis, 268–269
Apple iPhone and iPad, 119
Armour, Philip, 99, 316
AS9100, 20, 93, 98, 334
Asset-level tailoring, 140–141
Automation and business
    acceleration, 337

B

Balance, 332
Balanced score card (BSC), 85, 86
Baseline performance measure,
    64–65, 177, 202
Benchmarking, lessons learned
    programs, 251
Best practices, 94, 157–158
  business failures and, xxi–xxii
  CMMI and, 94, 157, 167
  innovation targeting matrix,
    19–20

place for in performance
    improvement, 19, 20*t*
ways to think about, 167–168
Best Practices Are Stupid (Shapiro),
    19, 22, 94, 167–168,
    193, 243
Brainstorming, 22, 243
Budget, *See* Resource allocation
Business development
    stakeholders, 303

C

Capability Maturity Model
    Integration (CMMI), 19, 93
  appraisal process as process
    improvement, 306
  appraisal scope creep, 320
  "best practices," 94, 157, 167
  CMMI-DEV, 21, 70, 71–73, 112,
    218, 320
  cost-benefit analysis for
    improving, 71–72
  decision making in, 277,
    280–281*t*
  lead appraiser role, 306, 307, 310,
    337–338
  process group issues and ROP
    outcomes, 295–297

Milton Keynes UK
Ingram Content Group UK Ltd.
UKHW031126141024
449569UK00006B/412